Betty McLellan is a feminist psychotherapist who established her own practice in Townsville in 1984. She returned from study in the United States in 1977 and has been active in Australian feminist politics since, being a frequent speaker at political demonstrations and conferences throughout the country. She is a consultant to the Aboriginal and Torres Strait Islander Mental Health programme in Townsville and is responsible for establishing the annual Winter Institute for Women held in North Queensland. She is also the author of *Overcoming Anxiety: A positive approach to dealing with severe anxiety in your life* (Allen & Unwin, 1992).

For Cog

BEYOND PSYCHOPPRESSION

A Feminist Alternative Therapy

Betty McLellan

Spinifex Press Pty Ltd
504 Queensberry Street
North Melbourne, Vic. 3051
Australia

First published by Spinifex Press, 1995

Edited by Janet Mackenzie
Typeset in 11/14 pt Times by
    Claire Warren, Melbourne
Indexed by Trischa Baker
Made and printed in Australia by
    Australian Print Group
Cover design by Lin Tobias

National Library of Australia
Cataloguing-in-Publication entry:
CIP
McLellan, Betty, 1938–
    Beyond psychoppression: a feminist
    alternative therapy.

    Bibliography.
    Includes index.
    ISBN 1 875559 33 7

    1. Feminist therapy. I. Title.

616.8914

Contents

Acknowledgements

A book like this is a long time in the making. Its genesis can probably be found as far back as 1970 when I flew out of Australia for the adventure of my life—to study in the United States. Little did I know, then, what an adventure that would be, for it was during those years that this earnest, 31-year-old deaconess from the Methodist Church in Australia turned into a feisty, furious feminist!

At last, through the philosophy and passions of the feminist movement, I was able to make sense of the puzzle that was women's lives. I was able to realise that the pain of women would not be alleviated by anything a male-dominated church or male-dominated therapy had to offer, but only by the liberation of women collectively from the oppression inherent in the structures of patriarchy.

Thinking back on all the influences that have made this book possible, I want to acknowledge my indebtedness, first, to the courageous authors of the early feminist texts which had such an impact on my life and attitudes during those early years, in particular, to Mary Daly, Phyllis Chesler, Robin Morgan, Simone de Beauvoir, Betty Friedan, Germaine Greer, Shulamith Firestone and Kate Millett.

I am indebted, too, to the small group of feminist friends with whom I shared many important moments during my years of study at the School of Theology at Claremont in California. Calling ourselves Sister Circle, we met regularly to discuss the latest books and papers on feminist issues. Now, more than twenty years later, I still have fond memories of stimulating discussions and warm friendships.

I am particularly indebted to the late Nelle Morton, who came to live in Claremont in her retirement, and who was one of the early members of our group. In her feminism, Nelle was radically political, while at the same time expressing the need for women to care for each other, to "hear one another to speech". Nelle Morton's attention to both the personal and the political had a profound impact on my development as a feminist and, subsequently, on the development of my theory of feminist therapy presented in the pages of this book.

Another member of Sister Circle who also had a powerful influence on my development as a feminist and a therapist was Charlotte Ellen. It was from Charlotte's example that I learned how crucial were the principles of loyalty and mutual support amongst women (as amongst members of any disempowered group). In addition to being a good friend, Charlotte was also a member of my doctoral dissertation faculty committee, and I am indebted to her for challenging, inspiring and supporting me through those difficult days of doctoral study.

In recent years, back in Australia, I am sustained and stimulated by my involvement with the Townsville Feminist Collective, a group of about fifteen women who meet monthly to discuss the latest feminist research and writing. My thanks to all of you for your friendship and vision and unrelenting determination to build a better world.

Two members of that collective are my long-time friends, Jan Woodley and Coralie McLean, who happily and willingly made time in their busy lives to read and reread my manuscript as it developed, helped me struggle with ideas, made valuable comments and suggestions, and encouraged and supported me all the way. Thanks to both of you. To Jan for your careful attention to detail which enabled you to pick up on important points that might otherwise have gone unchallenged, and for your special brand of humour that helps us all keep our sanity in a world intent on driving women crazy. And to Coralie for your absolute commitment to radical feminism and for the ways in which you have challenged and expanded my thinking over many years. Your revolutionary vision combined with your clarity of thought and expression have been invaluable to me in our discussions of this present work.

Finally, to the wonderful women of Spinifex Press, Sue Hawthorne and Renate Klein, thank you for your faith in this project, for your wise comments and suggestions which enabled me to broaden my thinking in crucial areas, and for your encouragement and support throughout.

Betty McLellan

Introduction

Psychotherapy, as it has been practised for the past one hundred years, has a lot to answer for in terms of the oppression of women. Feminists like myself who believe there is still a role for therapy in society must urgently develop a therapy that offers a radical alternative for women, both feminists and non-feminists. This book is an attempt to respond to that imperative.

Since the radical push of the 1960s when psychotherapy was exposed as one of patriarchy's most effective mechanisms of social control, feminists have made three clearly identifiable responses to the suggestion that some kind of therapy is still needed to help women deal with their personal emotional pain.

The first response, and the one chosen by the majority of feminists who are therapists, has been to continue their involvement with mainstream therapy. The idea is that, regardless of the kind of therapy they practise (psychoanalysis, client-centred, gestalt, family therapy, etc.), their practice will be informed and influenced by their feminist philosophy. They will be always careful, ever vigilant, to ensure they are not oppressing women.

While many are genuine in their attempts to ensure therapy is liberating for women and men who seek their help, what Part Three of this book points out is that, regardless of the good intentions of many feminists who are therapists, it is the institution of therapy itself which is oppressive when practised according to the rules of mainstream psychology. Whether or not it is even realistic to take part of an oppressive regime, mix it with a feminist philosophy and expect the result to be liberating is open to question.

A second response made by many feminists has been to become involved in all manner of alternative therapies. Everywhere, including feminist newsletters, magazines and journals, lists of opportunities are advertised for women to enter into rebirthing, reiki, meditation, yoga, relaxation, massage, tarot reading, spiritual journeys, spiritual healing, attitudinal healing, discovering the goddess within, and the list goes on and on. The search for personal, individual meaning seems to have taken on such importance for many who still call themselves feminists that the political nature of the feminist movement seems to be lost to them. In the 1980s and 1990s, the individual search for inner peace appears to have replaced the need many women felt in the 1960s and 1970s to be involved in collective feminist action.

This personal emphasis, of course, comes out of the genuine belief that an individual woman needs to get her own act together before she can work effectively with other women to bring about our collective goal, but the problem is that the emphasis on personal development is seductive. Once involved in the search for personal improvement, positive affirmation and inner peace, it is often difficult to remember there is a war going on. To speak of the war being waged every day in society against women somehow seems too negative to those who spend their time in the pursuit of the positive. To suggest that women need to speak out and express our anger about the continuing oppression of women by men seems almost foreign to those whose minds are on supposedly higher endeavours.

A third response, made mainly by radical or revolutionary feminists, has been to denounce therapy altogether. Some speak strongly against the oppressive nature of the theory and practice of psychotherapy as we know it, but leave the door open on the possibility that an alternative therapy for women could be developed—an alternative which is radicalised and politicised (and which, in turn, radicalises and politicises). Others insist that it is the very idea of therapy that is oppressive, no matter how it is practised, and that there is no point in feminists attempting to develop a therapy that is not oppressive. The oppression, they say, is inherent in the very idea that one woman be set aside for the special purpose of hearing and responding to the pain of her sisters. If what we are involved in is collective political action, then the idea of individual women going off to individual therapists will only serve to fragment the community and undermine the feminist cause. The ideal, they say, is that feminists be able to share all their pain with their sisters in community.[1]

This response is a very important one and must not be dismissed lightly. It is true that a community of women working together to bring about a new order, free from the oppressive patriarchal structures of present-day society—women reflecting together, analysing, talking, writing, loving, inspiring each other—has tremendous therapeutic potential. The problem is, however, that such a sense of feminist community is not the experience of most women today.

It is in acknowledgement of that fact that this book begins. Realising that most women do not have access to a group which operates as a therapeutic community when the need arises, and that it is neither possible nor desirable to manufacture such communities where they do not exist naturally, there are two things the feminist movement must do. First, we must take the personal needs of individual women seriously, and second, we must respond to those needs by providing a therapy that is a feminist alternative to mainstream and New Age therapies, and that is seen as a necessary and integral part of the revolution.

---

1. This point is made very powerfully by Celia Kitzinger and Rachel Perkins in *Changing our Minds: Lesbian Feminism and Psychology* (1993). In particular, see Chapters Three and Four.

When the principle "the personal is political" emerged in the 1960s and women were encouraged to view their personal experiences of pain and isolation as political, it was never intended that the personal needs of women be ignored in favour of the political. The personal was to be interpreted politically, it is true, but there was no suggestion that women's personal pain would cease to be an important concern or would magically disappear once oppression was understood to be its major cause.

For an individual feminist therapist, the requirement that feminism take the personal needs of individual women seriously and respond appropriately to those needs means that she must deliberately expand her vision beyond her own particular experience of the world. It is too easy, particularly for those of us who are white and middle-class, to act as if *all* women experience oppression equally. While it is true that all women suffer daily oppression for no other reason than that we are women, it is also true that many suffer multiple oppressions due to the existence of racism, heterosexism, ableism, etc.[2] A woman's personal pain and the potential for her to suffer severe emotional and psychological distress are magnified with every oppression she experiences.

While the intent of this book is to focus mainly on the devastating psychological effects on women of the oppression we experience because of our sex, the magnifying effect of more than one oppression is always acknowledged.

The reality is that the collective oppression of women creates a tremendous amount of pain and isolation at a personal level for individual women. Even after almost three decades of Second Wave feminist activism, the role expectations of women in Western societies remain virtually unchanged. Those areas where most pressure is brought to bear, where the expectation on women to conform is greatest—marriage, motherhood, heterosexuality, thinness, "happiness"—represent the major areas of women's oppression and, consequently, the areas where women experience the kinds of emotional distress that lead them to seek the help of a therapist.

The first of the expectations mentioned above is that of marriage. This particular expectation puts pressure on women throughout their entire lives. A single woman is under pressure to choose marriage even when there is no man she particularly wants to be with; a woman who is married or living with a man is under pressure to stay that way regardless of the quality of the relationship; and a woman who is divorced or widowed is often under pressure to marry again. The strength of society's expectation that women will be married means that many women are living in unsatisfactory, often abusive, relationships that cause them to experience low self-esteem, frustration, resentment, depression, anxiety and other forms of emotional distress.

The expectation of motherhood, too, causes problems for many women. Those who choose not to have children live with the knowledge that many in society are

---

2. In a paper, "Feminism and Racism: What Is at Stake?", presented in December 1994 at the Women's Studies Conference, Deakin University, Geelong, Denise Thompson described *all* of the inequalities and oppressions inherent in patriarchal societies as "a function of the invidious hierarchical divisions among categories of people which are required for the maintenance and continuation of male supremacy" (p. 2).

critical of their "selfishness". Those who choose to have an abortion cannot escape the clear and often aggressive messages from some sectors of the community to the effect that they have no right to exercise such control over their own bodies.

Those women who are unable to conceive feel the pressure to try every available avenue to achieve motherhood. More and more women are entering IVF programmes only to find that the very process causes them to become obsessed with the imperative to give birth to their own biological child. Everything else they ever wanted to do with their lives is swallowed up by this one overwhelming desire—to become a mother, whatever the price. Those who consider withdrawing from the programme when the weight of the many disappointments, wasted years, monetary problems, feelings of frustration, depression, low self-esteem, all become too much for them are often spurred on by guilt to try yet again for the precious prize of motherhood.

Another expectation is that of heterosexuality. The sanctions against any other choice cause many women who would choose a lesbian relationship or a celibate lifestyle to give in under the pressure to be "normal". To gain the approval of society, they seek relationships with men and go on to suffer the consequences of having "chosen" a lifestyle they did not want. Those who resist the strength of the compulsoriness of heterosexuality and pursue their desire for lesbian relationships also suffer. No matter how certain they are of their choices, they are never free of the sense of society's disapproval and pressure to change.

The expectation of thinness has also created tremendous problems. This expectation is responsible for the fact that so many women in Western countries have become absolutely obsessed with the need to be thin. While dieting and exercise are burgeoning multimillion-dollar industries, eating disorders are increasing at an alarming rate. Anorexia nervosa is killing young women in large numbers, (Wolf, 1990, pp. 147–50) and bulimia nervosa is drastically affecting the lives of women of all ages.

Then there is the expectation of "happiness". Women are not supposed to show they are unhappy, not supposed to complain about anything. Whether they are, in fact, happy or not is of no consequence. The important requirement is that they give the illusion of happiness so that life can run smoothly for everyone around them. Such suppression of women's true feelings usually leads to problems for which many seek therapy, problems such as depression, anxiety, alcoholism, drug addiction, eating disorders and insomnia.

While women who try to conform in these areas are likely to suffer emotionally as a consequence of their oppression, those who refuse to conform also suffer at the hands of the patriarchy. As feminists throughout the ages have discovered, patriarchy has an endless array of punishments for those who choose not to conform, and though the suffering of feminists might sometimes be different from that of other women (by virtue of the fact that it often comes as a result of their own awareness, defiance and anger), the fact remains that all women are oppressed, and many suffer personal, emotional distress because of that oppression.

It is usually when a woman feels she can no longer cope, when she feels she is being crushed under the weight of her many oppressions, that she seeks the help of a therapist.

If there is no feminist therapist available, she will be exposed in her vulnerable state to a therapist who works to legitimise her oppression, to mystify her into believing she ought to accept her lot in life, and to help her find ways of feeling better about fulfilling society's expectations.

The personal needs of women do exist and, while feminists continue to fight the all-important *political* battles needed to effect real change in society, the movement must also take the *personal* needs of individual women seriously. Victory in the political battles will be much more difficult to achieve while individual women—those who have not embraced feminism and those who have—continue to be paralysed at a personal level by their own emotional pain and despair. The feminist movement must have an active concern for both the personal and the political. How feminism can respond adequately to the personal distress of individual women is the subject of this book.

While it is my hope that this work will contribute in a significant way to the debate amongst feminists about the value or otherwise of feminist therapy, my main aim here is to begin the process of developing a therapy that will be a radical feminist alternative to mainstream and New Age therapies, and an important tool for the revolution.[3]

The book is organised in four parts. Part One comprises one chapter which is historical in nature, and which begins by reviewing the work of important figures from the early days of this Second Wave of feminism, women like Naomi Weisstein and Phyllis Chesler. Their work in the early 1970s represented a radical critique of traditional therapy, and called for psychology to offer something less oppressive and more liberating for women.

Following that early phase when, for a brief time, feminist psychologists and therapists were intent on developing a more radical, socio-political philosophy, the radical focus seems to have been lost. Almost as a backlash against the radical, the humanistic emphasis with its open-minded, anything-goes philosophy took over, and

---

3. I have deliberately chosen to use the word "revolution" throughout these pages to illustrate my belief that feminism is still a political movement whose aim continues to be that of changing the structures of society in a radical way. It is only when sexism, racism, ableism and other such oppressive structures are eliminated, that feminists will be able to move, at last, into post-revolutionary mode.

In 1988, Andrea Dworkin challenged feminists with a question that is even more relevant today, given the strength of the debate sparked by Naomi Wolf's *Fire with Fire* (1993). Dworkin asked: "Will feminism continue the difficult and costly politics of confrontation—rebellion against the power of men in public and in private, resistance to a status quo that takes the civil inferiority of women to be natural, sexy, and a piece of political trivia; or will an élite of women, anointed to influence (not power) by the media, keep demonstrating (so that the rest of us will learn) how to talk nice and pretty to men, how to ask them politely and in a feminine tone to stop exploiting us?" (1988, pp. 325–6).

There is no doubt in my mind that we must "continue the difficult and costly politics of confrontation". Phyllis Chesler expresses these same sentiments in her latest book, *Patriarchy: Notes of an Expert Witness* (1994). Disagreeing with the thesis that "women have won the gender war" and that the only problem facing women now is that of learning how to use the power we have gained (Wolf, 1993), Chesler makes her own position clear when she says: "Women have not won the war against women; we have only begun to fight. The heat of battle is intense. Many women are running scared, smiling as fast as they can. Clearly, it's too hot in the kitchen for Naomi Wolf and she's made her exit" (p. 56).

feminists who were therapists began putting energy into improving existing mainstream therapies rather than rejecting them and developing something new. This journey from the radical phase, through the liberal humanist phase and on to the present day where effective, politicised feminist therapy is almost non-existent, is traced in Part One.

Part Two is concerned with the philosophy or assumptions on which a politicised feminist therapy is based. Therapy based on the medical model begins with the assumption that any woman who is a "patient" of therapy is sick, and humanist therapy begins with the assumption that any woman who is a "client" of therapy has a problem with personal empowerment. In contrast, a feminist therapy is based on a socio-political philosophy that refuses to begin with the blaming of women. Every woman who seeks the help of a feminist therapist is seen in the context of her whole life. It is believed that she is a victim of oppression, and that the therapist's task is one of assisting her in her struggle for liberation. The issues dealt with in Part Two are: oppression as the cause of women's distress, access, honesty, passion and justice.

Part Three is concerned with presenting a strong case against those therapies that blame the victim in order to get results. One of the frustrations for therapists of all persuasions is the knowledge that a person's circumstances will change only if it is within that person's power to decide to make some changes, and that when the cause of her unhappiness lies with someone else, it is almost impossible to help her feel better. Rather than admitting that the task is impossible, mainstream therapies simply change the focus of the blame. When the victim is blamed, it serves to make the task of the therapist so much easier but, for the victim, such a change of focus amounts to psychoppression—that is, oppression within the context of therapy.

If a woman is very depressed, for example, because her husband's only communication with her over several years has been to curse and swear about how "stupid" she is, she does not have the power to change her mood of depression because she does not have the power to change her husband's behaviour. The feminist approach is to help her to understand how her husband's attitude and behaviour are affecting her, to admit that his attitude toward her is totally unacceptable and the cause of her depression, to release some of the anger and resentment built up inside her over the years, and to make a decision to withdraw from the situation that is oppressing her, thereby taking back her power. If she cannot bring herself to leave the marriage, then the aim of therapy ought to be to help her withdraw emotionally so that his oppressive behaviour no longer has the power to depress her.

When such a woman is determined to continue trying to "make the marriage work" and is, therefore, unwilling to withdraw emotionally, the fact is—and this is hard for most therapists to admit—there is nothing more that can be done.

Most mainstream and New Age therapies, refusing to admit "failure", employ an elaborate confidence trick at this stage which, as I just mentioned, involves changing the focus of the blame. Instead of allowing the woman in our example to discuss her husband's behaviour and place the blame for her depression squarely on his shoulders, the therapist works to help her see how she could be to blame for her husband's attitude which, in turn, means she is to blame for her own depression. The theory is that if I can be made to see that I am responsible for my own feelings, I will then see that I have it within my power to change myself. My happiness does not depend on the other person's behaviour at all. If I feel depressed, I have it in my power to change the way I feel.

While such a tactic on the part of a therapist is dishonest in the extreme, it nevertheless allows the woman to believe that therapy has achieved something for her. The therapist feels good, and the recipient of therapy feels good—at least in the short term. The woman feels good until her husband, who has the real power in the relationship, begins to exercise that power again. Once again, she experiences utter powerlessness and her depression returns. This time, however, her suffering is doubled. Whereas before, she only *wondered* if she might be to blame for her husband's behaviour, now, after having been deceived by the therapist into believing she is to blame for her own unhappiness, she is *convinced* her husband's behaviour is her fault. Regardless of her utter powerlessness, she now believes she ought to be able to empower herself and rise above her depression.

The therapies that are critically analysed for their oppressive effects on women include Freudian psychoanalysis (Chapter Five), the humanistic therapies (Chapter Six), New Age and popular psychologies (Chapter Seven), and lesbian sex therapy (Chapter Eight).

Part Four is concerned with the actual practice of a feminist alternative therapy based on the philosophical and theoretical issues discussed in Part Two. Chapter Nine suggests that any radical feminist therapy comprises two major elements: support and demystification. The skills required by a feminist therapist to ensure an adequate response to each of these elements are also discussed. Chapter Ten is concerned with process. How will a feminist alternative therapy actually proceed?

I want to stress at the outset that the development of this particular feminist alternative is not an attempt to find a middle road between the personal and the political. It is not a call for feminists to indulge in a bit of political activism and a bit of self-indulgent personal focusing, so that there is some sort of balance in their lives. The radical view is that the call for a "balanced" attitude to one's politics and one's life is a call to mediocrity, and indicates a reluctance to take a definite stand on anything.

Far from attempting to promote a middle-of-the-road approach, the feminist alternative presented here calls for total commitment to feminist action in the world. There is no question about that. A feminist's political commitment to changing the oppressive structures of the patriarchy and working collectively with other women toward that end is given top priority. Coupled with that, however, is the recognition that feminist activists and other women get bruised and battered, sometimes physically, but most often emotionally. Integral to our radical political action, therefore, must be the provision of constant and reliable support for all women whenever they need it.

In a broad sense, this book is offered in the hope that it will provide inspiration and stimulation to all women interested in the issue of therapy for women, whether from the perspective of a recipient, a provider, or simply an interested observer. More specifically, it is an attempt to encourage feminists to consider the need for a therapy that retains its political base; that explodes the myths about women's mental and emotional "illness"; that demystifies women's oppression enabling them to understand why they feel as badly as they do at times; and that dares to offer women support, affirmation, strength and hope. Because the personal experiences of individual women are tied so closely to society's attitude toward and exploitation of women collectively, a therapy that recognises the political nature of our relationships must pay attention to both the individual and the collective needs of women.

PART ONE

FEMINIST VOICES,
PAST AND PRESENT

1

PSYCHOTHERAPY AND FEMINISM:

A HISTORY

During the 1960s and early 1970s, when consciousness-raising (CR) groups made it possible for women in Western cultures to speak out about their various oppressions, many women—and some men—were appalled to learn of the high incidence of what are now called the "private" oppressions of women. As women took courage and spoke about their own experiences over many years, the gruesome picture slowly unfolded of women and children in great numbers suffering physical, emotional and sexual abuse in their own homes, at the hands of the very men society said should be their protectors.

Another of the "private" oppressions of women that began to come to light at that time was the oppression that took place in therapy, almost always by a male therapist. Women told of years of hospitalisation, shock therapy, excessive use of tranquillisers and anti-depressants. They told of the crazy mind-games that therapists played with them until they were so confused that they began to believe they must, in fact, be mad. They told horrific stories of sexual exploitation by male therapists. They told of mystification, intimidation, manipulation, lies—all in the name of therapy.

They told of the conspiracy between husbands and therapists which kept them incarcerated in psychiatric hospitals for months and years, or drugged so heavily that they could be nothing but dependent and submissive. They gave examples of therapist after therapist not believing them, not even listening to them.

They told of their feelings of guilt and helplessness and hopelessness as blame was heaped on them by therapists, regardless of what they went to talk to the therapists about. If a woman talked about her husband's violence, she was encouraged to try to be more understanding of the stresses her husband might be experiencing or, worse still, she was encouraged to look at what she was doing to "provoke" his violence. If she talked about her lack of interest in sex, she was reminded that men needed sex, and warned that if her marriage broke up and her children were fatherless, it would be her fault. If she ventured to speak about having been sexually abused in childhood, she was led to believe that perhaps it was all in her imagination, because men simply did not behave in this way. There was very little support forthcoming from therapists: only blame. The victim was to blame.

Women who had previously remained silent about their experiences in therapy were now, in CR groups, finding the courage to share their stories with each other. The more they talked, the more they understood what had really happened, and the angrier they became.

Barbara Findlay's account of her experiences appears in a book edited by Dorothy Smith and Sara David, called *Women Look at Psychiatry*. Published in 1975 by the Press Gang collective in Vancouver, Canada, this anthology contains several powerful accounts of women's experiences and is compulsory reading for any feminist with an interest in therapy.[1]

In her first year of university, feeling lonely and isolated and unable to find anyone to talk to, Barbara Findlay decided to make an appointment to see a psychiatrist. She was just seventeen years old. As she recalls, she had "absolute confidence in psychiatrists and their ability to help" (p. 61), and consequently had no idea that this was to be the beginning of several years of hell on earth. The following are excerpts from her account of her experiences:

> I have been mentally ill . . . I have credentials as long as my arm certifying that I am an abnormal female, desperately in need of help to adjust to society and function in it "normally" . . .
>
> I have done the whole trip—psychoanalysis, tranquilizers, suicide attempts, mental institutions. And the only surprising thing about it is that I emerged from it all still sane (p. 59).

Referring to her numerous experiences of interrogation by psychiatrists, she said:

> It was a double bind . . . If I refused to answer their questions I was resistant; if I told them it didn't matter I was denying. There was no way to convince them otherwise. Because they are the sane, normal, healers, and I was the insane, abnormal, sick patient. *They* got to decide what was true and real for me. And their job was to convince, persuade, seduce or threaten me to accept that reality as my own (p. 63).

She gives a frightening description of the total lack of privacy accorded to her during her first experience as a patient in a psychiatric ward.

> My first incarceration coincided with my first-year university exams, which terrified me, and were largely responsible, in retrospect, for my panic . . .
>
> However it never occurred to me at the time that the exams were worrying me; I was just psychotic. And so I ended up in the psychiatric ward of the general hospital. The hospital was hideous. Since I was suicidal they put me on "constant observation" which meant that I was watched 24 hours a day by a ward aide who sat at the foot of my bed . . . Every move that I made was "symptomatic"—a feature of my disease. They searched my belongings . . . They read my poetry anthology while I was asleep, and the fact that many of the poems were "morbid" was a bad sign. They sifted through my garbage and picked up all the bits I'd written. I was naked and there was nowhere to go to escape their eyes (pp. 68–9).

---

1. The titles of some of the articles give a clear indication of the radical nature of the book: "It was an eighteenth century horror show" as told to Marsha Enomoto; "Struggling to be born" by Judi Chamberlin; "Shrink! Shrank! Shriek!" by Barbara Findlay; and "I'm not crazy after all" by Barbara Joyce.

At the end of her story, Barbara Findlay describes how she came to realise she was not insane and did not actually need to depend on psychiatrists.

> In my last years at that university I had three very fine women friends, who were very important in making me see that at least I was not alone. Friendships with women were discounted by the shrinks as trivial. It never occurred to them that women had anything to say to each other or to learn from each other. I couldn't put together what I heard the women saying with what I heard the shrinks saying. But when I moved away at the end of the four years, and set myself up away from the shrinks' insidious influence, the credibility gap got greater and greater. I read *Sisterhood is Powerful*, and I was on my way to understanding what the psychiatric trip had been all about.
>
> As a woman I am now much more at home in the world, because I see that the "fault", which I saw as my moral fault, was only the "fault" of having been born female. My guilt and fear of competence have dropped away (p. 71).

Many women around that time also revealed that they had been victims of sexual advances by male therapists. Phyllis Chesler devotes a whole chapter in *Women and Madness* to the issue of sex between patient and therapist. "Such a transaction between patient and therapist, euphemistically termed 'seduction' or 'part of the treatment process'," she says, "is legally a form of rape and psychologically a form of incest" (1972, p. 138). An excerpt from Chesler's interview with a patient called Joyce describes how sex with her male therapist started, and gives an indication of the mind-games he used to play with her:

> The week before he'd made me put my head on his lap just like I used to do with my father when I had a bad headache, and he'd stroked my hair. It was very warm; I was a little girl and he was my father. Then his hand slipped . . . The next session he helped me on with my coat, turned me around to him, and kissed me quite passionately. And I was quite shocked . . . and then I burst into tears. I'm melodramatic anyway, but I was really upset. Because I didn't know what to make of it. And I said, "Why did you do that?" It was a stupid question to ask, really, and he said, "What? Do what? What are you talking about?" And I said, "Kiss me." "I don't know what you mean," he said . . . he was really playing into my hangup. Because my parents would do that to me. Whenever my mother did something or said something and I said: "Why did you do that?" she'd go "What? I didn't do anything" (p. 152).

Another very common theme in the stories women shared with each other was that of the role of therapists in maintaining the status quo. An excerpt from Barbara Joyce's story, in *Women Look at Psychiatry*, presents a good example of women being urged to keep their proper place, which was always subordinate to their husbands:

> My two-year struggle to keep my marriage together had just ended in failure . . . In addition, I was just starting to pull out of the worst stages of a "nervous breakdown" which began, rather ironically, only weeks after the wedding. And it was now apparent that because of financial difficulties I would also be a failure in my attempt to educate myself. I had married at 24 . . . it had soon become obvious to me that there were more thorns than roses surrounding my marital cottage, and I had sought help in the only way available to working-class women: my general practitioner had referred me to one and then the other of . . . two psychiatrists . . . who . . . told me to quit competing with my husband (I, too, had wanted to

go to school), and to wash out the toilet when I was depressed. When I rejected this, I then resorted to paying a Catholic marriage counsellor who told me to stay home and be a good wife (Smith and David, 1975, pp. 183–4).

The above accounts are representative of the flood of stories that began to be told at that time by women whose eyes were finally opened to the ways in which therapy and therapists had oppressed them. In addition to the powerful voices of recipients of therapy, there were also practitioners and academics who began exposing the oppression inherent in therapy, particularly when the one receiving the therapy was a woman. The following history of feminist attitudes towards therapy, since the early 1970s, reveals the radical nature of those early voices compared with the more accommodating libertarian influences that followed.

Radical beginnings

Influenced by the consciousness-raising that was occurring at all levels, feminists who had some involvement with psychology or psychiatry, either as academics or practitioners, began writing about the institution of therapy and exposing it as an oppressive tool in the hands of the patriarchy.

They began pointing out that therapy, which had always been seen as concerned with the personal and not the political, was indeed a very political activity. It was about power. It was being used deliberately as a vehicle of social control. One of its main functions was to ensure that those who tried to deviate from the roles and attitudes expected of them were brought back into line. In particular, because women were more discontented with their allotted roles and were, therefore, clients of therapy in far greater numbers than men, it was used to keep women in their proper place in relation to men.

Naomi Weisstein

One of the earliest feminist critiques of psychotherapy was that by Naomi Weisstein in a paper she delivered at a meeting of the American Studies Association in 1968, called "'Kinder, Kuche, Kirche' as Scientific Law: Psychology Constructs the Female".[2] In this paper, she exposed psychology as a field of study and research that already had its mind made up about women. Women's anatomy and biological functioning determined that they would be happy and fulfilled only if they were immersed in the roles of wife and mother. Psychologists believed that, because women were "made" for those roles, they were not fit for anything else, and it was only when women became dissatisfied and tried to move out of those roles that they began to have problems.

Weisstein voiced her strong objection to such stereotyping of women and charged that psychology had been "strangled and deflected" by the "common prejudice" against

---

2. This paper was given wide exposure in feminist and other radical anthologies, and can be found in the following: Robin Morgan (ed.) (1970), *Sisterhood is Powerful*; Joanne Cooke, Charlotte Bunch-Weeks and Robin Morgan (eds) (1970), *The New Women*; Vivian Gornick and Barbara K. Moran (eds) (1971), *Woman in Sexist Society*; Hendrik M. Ruitenbeek (ed.) (1972), *Going Crazy*.

women (Weisstein, in Morgan, 1970, p. 207). To illustrate her point, she quoted two well-known and very influential psychologists of the day. The first was Bruno Bettelheim of the University of Chicago, who said:

> We must start with the realization that, as much as women want to be good scientists or engineers, they want first and foremost to be womanly companions of men and to be mothers (Weisstein, p. 206).

The other was Erik Erikson of Harvard University, noted for his work on the struggle for identity in adolescence, who said, when asked about identity development in women:

> Much of a young woman's identity is already defined in her kind of attractiveness and in the selectivity of her search for the man (or men) by whom she wishes to be sought . . .

According to Erikson, fulfilment for women rests on the fact that their

> somatic design harbors an "inner space" destined to bear the offspring of chosen men, and with it, a biological, psychological, and ethical commitment to take care of human infancy (Weisstein, p. 206).

In other words, a woman's biology is her destiny and she will not be happy or fulfilled unless she does what her body is designed for—to mate with a man of her choice, and produce and care for "his" babies.

Weisstein went on to say that because psychology is bound by such prejudices against women, "it is relatively useless in describing, explaining or predicting humans and their behavior" (p. 208). She continues:

> It then goes without saying that present psychology is less than worthless in contributing to a vision which could truly liberate—men as well as women.
>
> My central argument . . . is this. Psychology has nothing to say about what women are really like, what they need and what they want, essentially, because psychology does not know (p. 208).

Then she addresses the question of the causes of psychology's failure which, she says, are "obvious and appalling":

> the first reason for psychology's failure to understand what people are and how they act, is that clinicians and psychiatrists, who are generally the theoreticians on these matters, have essentially made up myths without any evidence to support these myths; the second reason for psychology's failure is that personality theory has looked for inner traits when it should have been looking at social context (p. 209).

In discussing the first reason, the use of *theory without evidence*, Weisstein points to Freud as the one who started this tradition which has been so destructive of women. Freud based his theories on the "insights" he gained through "years of clinical experience", and his example has been followed by clinicians and psychiatrists ever since

(p. 209). "The problem with insight, sensitivity, and intuition", she warns, "is that it can confirm for all time the biases that one started out with" (p. 210).

The second cause of psychology's failure discussed by Weisstein is that which she calls *inner traits*. She urges psychologists to "turn away from the theory of the causal nature of the inner dynamic and look to the social context within which individuals live" (p. 213). To understand human behaviour, one must understand the context in which people live, the expectations that are put on them, and the pressure they experience to conform (p. 218). In response to the "uselessness of present psychology with regard to women", she insisted that "one must understand social expectations about women if one is going to characterize the behavior of women" (p. 219).

Phyllis Chesler

Phyllis Chesler's now classic text, *Women and Madness*, was the next major feminist assault on traditional psychotherapy. Published in 1972, it examined women's socially defined "madness" and presented serious criticisms of those who had the power to pronounce women sick or mad, and of the society that gave psychotherapists such power.

An important theme in the early years of this wave of feminism was the oppressive nature of "sex-role stereotyping", and Chesler's criticisms of psychology and psychiatry were based on that theme. Women were expected to be dependent, passive, compliant, lacking in confidence, indecisive, emotional and so on, while men were expected to be independent, assertive, individual, confident, decisive and rational. Chesler made the point that those expectations which accompanied the female sex-role were all representative of behaviour that had no value in Western societies, and that was often associated with mental illness. Women are rendered powerless by society's expectations and then, because of their powerlessness, they are proclaimed "mad".

> Most twentieth-century women who are psychiatrically labelled, privately treated, and publicly hospitalized are not mad . . . they may be deeply unhappy, self-destructive, economically powerless, and sexually impotent—but as women they're supposed to be (p. 25).

Chesler's central criticism of psychology's definition of "madness" as it related to women was that it made it very difficult for any woman to escape being labelled mentally ill. On the one hand, a woman who immersed herself fully in the female role was vulnerable to being labelled sick or mad while, on the other hand, a woman who refused to take on the female role could just as easily be labelled sick or mad.

> *What we consider "madness" . . . is either the acting out of the devalued female role or the total or partial rejection of one's sex-role stereotype.* Women who fully act out the conditioned female role are clinically viewed as "neurotic" or "psychotic". When and if they are hospitalized, it is for predominantly female behaviors, such as "depression", "suicide attempts", "anxiety neurosis", "paranoia", or "promiscuity". Women who reject or are ambivalent about the female role frighten themselves and society so much so that their ostracism and self-destructiveness probably begin very early (p. 56).

It is not only women in psychiatric institutions who are labelled mad. Such an accusation is a common occurrence for women in Western countries. As a matter of fact, all a woman has to do to attract the label of madness, at times, is give her opinion, or stand up for what she believes, or disagree with a man.

Many women who seek the help of a therapist do so because they have been told for years, usually by their spouse, that they are mad. Given that it is difficult to maintain perspective after years of having one's sanity called into question, it is understandable that they seek out an "expert" to have their madness confirmed or denied. The problem is, though, that those therapists who focus only on the inner dynamics of the person before them, and ignore the social factors involved in that person's fear or anxiety or depression, will probably confirm the woman's worst fears. Yes, there is something wrong with her, and yes, she will need some therapy to help her deal with her "problem".

On the other hand, a therapist who acknowledges the effect social factors have on one's self-definition and emotional stability will help put her fears to rest immediately. This is done, first, by encouraging her to talk about the pressures being brought to bear on her and the resultant powerlessness she feels and, second, by explaining that one's emotional distress is often caused by social and interpersonal factors, and that such distress will be relieved when changes are brought about to those external factors.

Chesler's criticisms of the institution of psychotherapy were many:

> for treating unhappiness as a disease . . . ; for behaving as if the psychotherapeutic philosophy or method can cure ethical and political problems; for teaching people that their unhappiness (or neurosis) can be alleviated through individual rather than collective efforts . . . : [for its use] as a form of social and political control that offers those who can pay for it temporary relief, the illusion of freedom, and a self-indulgent form of self-knowledge (p. 107).

Another of her criticisms was that therapists are trained to see pathology everywhere. The problem with that, she said, is that such readiness to label any and all behaviour as "sick" allows us to "banish the concepts of good and evil from the arena of human responsibility" (p. 66n). A person can indulge in all forms of morally reprehensible behaviour and be excused because he or she is simply "sick".

Another important insight offered by Chesler was the similarity, for women, between the psychotherapeutic relationship and marriage.

> For most women (the middle-class-oriented) psychotherapeutic encounter is just one more instance of an unequal relationship, just one more opportunity to be rewarded for expressing distress and to be "helped" by being (expertly) dominated. Both psychotherapy and white or middle-class marriage isolate women from each other; both emphasize individual rather than collective solutions to woman's unhappiness; both are based on a woman's helplessness and dependence on a stronger male authority figure; . . . both control and oppress women similarly (p. 108).

Finally, Chesler criticised psychotherapy for its dishonesty in dealing with women. When therapists insisted on focusing on inner dynamics and ignoring the reality of female oppression and the effects of such oppression on women's mental and emotional health, they set up a situation where women were never able to have "real" conversations with their therapists, because what was real to those women was not judged to be appropriate material for the therapy session (p. 110).

The work of Weisstein and Chesler is representative of the courageous stand taken against therapy by a small number of women at that time but, as will be seen in our discussion of the "libertarian influence" later in this chapter, the early radical voices were quickly silenced by those who preferred a softer approach.

Other feminist voices

Alongside the radical voices, there were other feminists who were also speaking out against the oppressiveness of psychiatry and psychotherapy, but in a way that was less angry and less radical than that of Weisstein and Chesler. It was as if the feminist therapy movement began to be coopted by mainstream therapies almost as soon as the movement was born.

The strength of the initial work of Weisstein and Chesler lay in the fact that they did not attempt to locate their radical feminist theory within the confines of any of the mainstream therapies as did other feminists writing at the time. Weisstein does not give an opinion about how or if the practice of psychotherapy should proceed, because her emphasis was on psychological research, psychology as a scientific endeavour. Chesler, on the other hand, does seem to favour the continuation of psychotherapy, but only if it is drastically reformed and politicised, and even then, she has some reservations.[3] She was obviously influenced by the radical therapy movement of the 1960s but, while giving credit to the radical insights of men like Ronald Laing and Thomas Szasz, she also made it clear that she was not completely won over by their theories. As she put it, "The ideas and alternative structures of a 'radical' or feminist psychotherapy both excite and disturb me" (p. 113).

Juliet Mitchell

Among the early feminists who acknowledged the oppressive nature of therapy for women, but who continued to work within mainstream therapy, was Juliet Mitchell, a psychoanalyst and outspoken supporter of Freud. When feminists like Simone de Beauvoir, Betty Friedan, Eva Figes, Germaine Greer, Shulamith Firestone and Kate Millett raised their criticisms of Freud and it became fashionable in feminist circles to talk about how destructive Freud and his psychoanalytic theories had been to women, Juliet Mitchell stood firm in her defence of him. Her influential book *Psychoanalysis and Feminism*, in which she addressed the criticisms made by feminists, was published in 1974.

While acknowledging that psychotherapy had been used against women, she insisted that Freud and psychoanalysis as he developed it (before it was "perverted") were not guilty. In her criticism of psychotherapy, she said:

> I think there seems overwhelming justification for the charge that the many different psycho-
> therapeutic practices, including those that by formal definition are within psychoanalysis,

---

3. For a discussion of her reservations, see Chesler (1972), pp. 112–13.

have done much to re-adapt discontented women to a conservative feminine status quo, to an inferiorized psychology and to a contentment with serving and servicing men and children . . . Furthermore, the tendency to judge men and women in terms of conventionalized psychologies and punish them accordingly is on the increase: imprisonment for aggressive criminal men and mental hospital incarceration for passive "disturbed" women (p. 299).

Her criticism continues: "With the greater popularity of mental treatment— lobotomy, leucotomy, electric shock, drugs, adaptive therapy—women are the main victims" (p. 299).

But, having made these strong criticisms, she then went on to absolve Freud altogether by saying, "on the whole this has nothing to do with Freud or psychoanalysis, only with its grotesque perversion for punitive or ideological purposes" (p. 300). Her response to feminist criticisms of Freud was that "the Freud the feminists have inherited is often a long way off-centre". What they were doing, she said, was "rejecting a Freud who was not Freud" (p. 301).

In a later book, *Feminine Sexuality: Jacques Lacan and the école freudienne* (1982), edited jointly with Jacqueline Rose, Mitchell continues her criticism of the way Freud's work was abused by analysts who came after him. Because of the contradictions in Freud's writings, she said, "subsequent analysts have developed one aspect and rejected another, thereby using one theme as a jumping off point for a new theory" (p. 1). The belief that it is "legitimate for everyone to take their pick and develop [Freud's work] as they wish" has resulted in a situation where Freud's essential theory has been lost (p. 1). Mitchell identifies French psychoanalyst Jacques Lacan as the one who "went back to Freud's basic concepts" (p. 2), and for this, he has her support. He "dedicated himself to the task of refinding and reformulating the work of Sigmund Freud" (p. 1).

The majority of feminists rejected the theories that were central to the work of Freud and Lacan on the basis that they were phallocentric and, as such, presented men as fully human and women as less than human. Juliet Mitchell, however, continued to argue that such a view simply revealed a lack of understanding of the basic concepts of psychoanalysis. The concepts of the phallic phase and the castration complex, developed by Freud and underlined and reformulated by Lacan, presented Mitchell with no problem. In psychoanalysis, she says, the "castration complex is *the* instance of the humanisation of the child in its sexual difference" (p. 19).

Questions raised by feminists and others about the blatant subjugation of female to male, about social justice, biology, anatomy and development, are simply passed off as being "outside the field of psychoanalytic enquiry" (p. 20).

Anne Kent Rush and Anica Vesel Mander

Anne Kent Rush was a feminist with a completely different focus from that of Juliet Mitchell but she, too, continued her involvement in mainstream therapies. Her book, *Getting Clear: Body Work for Women* (1973) was enormously popular. Rush called herself a "feminist body therapist", and worked with women (and men) in the San Francisco Bay area of California. Her interest in body therapy began with her involvement in yoga and massage. She then received some training in Polarity Therapy which is "an Oriental pressure point system (based on Chinese acupuncture) for releasing deep body tension". Also she "trained with a Reichian therapist in Wilhelm Reich's breathing techniques" and with the "Gestalt Institute of San Francisco learning Gestalt verbal techniques to use with the body work" (p. 6).

In 1974, she teamed up with Anica Vesel Mander to write *Feminism as Therapy*, in which they spelled out more clearly the connection they saw between therapy and feminism. Their central argument, as the title of the book suggests, is that feminism *is* therapy. Through their involvement with other women, with consciousness-raising groups, with feminism, they believed that feminism was fulfilling a very important therapeutic function for many women.

> Through feminism women are becoming active, adult, responsible members of our twentieth century society and so it is clear that feminism has been functioning as a healing mechanism for women (p. 4).

They were not suggesting that that was all there was to feminism, or that CR groups were nothing more than therapy groups where women talked about their personal problems in order to make themselves feel better. On the contrary, it was the political nature of CR groups, the awareness of oppression, the anger, the determination to work together for change, that lifted women out of their self-indulgent, individualistic pursuits and gave them a more global vision. It was this that was therapeutic.

In their criticism of traditional psychotherapy, they objected to "the traditional *therapeutic mystique* that there is something sacred and holy and inviolable about the philosophies our culture calls 'therapeutic'" (p. 3). Pointing to its role as a mechanism of social control, they described traditional therapy as "synonymous with socialization, that is, adjustment to the current cultural mode" (p. 37). They called for all people to be freed from "the restrictions of their culturally defined sexual roles" (p. 39), and insisted that one of the important tasks of feminist therapy was to "point out to women the social roots of their oppressions and sicknesses" (p. 50).

Regardless of their radical-sounding theory, however, Mander and Rush were careful to show support for much of the work of Freud, Jung, Reich and Gestalt and, in terms of practice, continued to be locked in to Body Therapy as their preferred option.

Miriam Greenspan

Ten years later, another important feminist voice speaking out against the oppressive nature of psychotherapy was that of Miriam Greenspan, a therapist in private practice in Boston. In her book *A New Approach to Women and Therapy* (1983), she pointed out the ways in which both traditional and humanist therapies had failed women.

In her section on traditional therapy, she acknowledged the great influence Phyllis Chesler's work had had on her and other feminists who were therapists, but lamented the fact that "the problems of Woman as Patient in traditional therapy are not a thing of the past" (p. 91). Her criticism of what she called the "Father Knows Best model of therapy" (p. 88), echo those of Chesler ten years earlier:

the traditional therapy relationship is one in which a powerful, impersonal (culturally masculine) Expert acts upon a vulnerable, emotional (culturally feminine) supplicant. The therapist is the authoritative father. The patient is the ignorant, helpless child (p. 87).

Describing the situation of women in Western societies, she concludes a list of women's "symptoms" by saying: "We feel empty and lost and panicked and worthless. We hate our bodies. We are depressed. We feel powerless" (p. 97).

While traditional psychotherapists see these as the personal problems of individual women who present for therapy, Greenspan says:

These are the problems of femininity. Most women have experienced one or several of them, or know women who have. The symptoms are systematically socially produced. Yet they are experienced as, appear to be, and are diagnosed as wholly individual and personal. Thus the "cure" that traditional therapy peddles for the relief of these symptoms is part of the problem. Traditional therapy confirms the man-made woman in her most deeply internalized conviction of personal failure (p. 97).

Humanist therapy, characterised by the growth therapies of Carl Rogers, Gestalt, Transactional Analysis and others, was a vast improvement on traditional therapy, but there were still problems. As Greenspan pointed out, humanist therapy perpetuated the myth that if you have a problem "it's all in your head". While traditional therapy focused on a person's inner instincts and impulses as the cause of her emotional problems, humanist therapy encouraged people to "blame themselves for lacking total control over their lives" (p. 124). All of us can be whatever and whoever we want to be, and if we do not succeed, it must be our own fault.

The idea here is the simple proposition that you are responsible for your own reality—not society, not the environment, not the past, but you as a person right now. Personal problems are not seen as products of pathology, as in the traditional system. But they are still seen exclusively as products of your own mind (p. 124).

Greenspan says that for women and other oppressed groups "the myth of individual freedom sold by the new growth therapies is yet another betrayal". The suggestion that people ought to "reject any forms of collective responsibility for one another's pain and to embrace instead absolute individual responsibility for one's own life" means that "the humanist orientation is ultimately useless to the oppressed" (p. 129).

In developing a new approach to therapy, a feminist approach, Greenspan emphasised the need for therapist and client together to focus on "social reality" rather than inner dynamics. This means that a feminist therapist will "listen" in a different way.

The traditional therapist listens for pathology. The humanist therapist listens for self-awareness. The feminist therapist listens for the connections between the personal and political in women's stories (p. 233).

While Greenspan's "new approach to therapy" was a very important development in terms of emphasising the need for therapy to be grounded in a radical, socio-political philosophy, she was, nevertheless, still not willing to let go of the old altogether in order to create something new. "In my own work," she said, "I have tried to combine the strengths of the traditional and humanist approach with the strengths of a political approach to women in therapy" (p. 233).

Libertarian influence

The radical movement influenced by the early works of feminists like Weisstein and Chesler seemed to disappear as a movement almost as soon as it started. Individual women, like Greenspan, continued to speak out, but socialist or radical opinions were not popular.

On the increase in popularity amongst feminists was the more palatable, libertarian emphasis as found in the therapies of the human potential movement, notably, in Transactional Analysis and Gestalt. Such therapies were less angry, less radical, and less divisive and, while emphasising the need for women to seize every opportunity to develop to their full potential, they were always careful to take into account the needs of men.

Transactional Analysis

Transactional Analysis became very popular amongst feminists and non-feminists alike in the mid to late 1970s. Developed by men, notably Eric Berne and Claude Steiner, it was welcomed by women as a therapy that was practical, positive and progressive—and affirming of women. The book *Women as Winners* (1976), written by Dorothy Jongeward and Dru Scott, was seen by many feminists as an important one for women, yet, in all of its 318 pages, there is not one mention of the word "feminist". As a matter of fact, it was unashamedly dismissive of consciousness-raising groups and the anger women felt about their oppression, as illustrated in the first lines of the foreword written by Mary Edwards Goulding:

> I am delighted with *Women as Winners*. It is a happy, useful book for women and men who want women to be all they can be.
> Women do not have to be inferior or feel inferior. They do not have to sit around in groups playing "Ain't It Awful" about men or society or parents (p. vii).

The book was happy. It was useful. It was positive. It was sugary-sweet. And it was painstakingly supportive of men. One wonders why Transactional Analysis (TA) was embraced so wholeheartedly by feminists, until one remembers that this was the period immediately after the very public discussion of women's discontent, the period when so many women were bending over backwards trying to find ways to make sure men did not feel threatened as women sought to improve their lot. Both TA and Gestalt were seen to be very useful tools in removing the blame from men and placing the focus on women. The onus was on women to stop blaming men and take responsibility for their own happiness.

Gestalt

While the popularity of TA lasted for several years, it was only a "fad" in comparison with the long life of Gestalt. Of all the humanistic therapies, Gestalt has been the most influential, and while there are relatively few feminists today who would claim to be exclusively Gestalt therapists, there are still many whose style of therapy includes Gestalt attitudes and techniques.

Frederick Perls, the founder of Gestalt, while emphasising the need for increased personal awareness and the empowerment of men and women through the actualising of human potential, at the same time exercised amazing power over those who participated in his group therapy sessions. Without a doubt, it was *he* who had the power. He saw himself as a guru, a role which seemed to allow him to be extremely rude towards and destructive of those who sought his help. His group "techniques" included ignoring people when they spoke; calling them "phony" and "stupid"; harping on how stupid they were till they broke down and cried, and then taunting them for trying to "manipulate" the group with their tears; being physically violent when he decided it was appropriate; and encouraging group members to turn on and verbally attack one member when he thought it would teach them something—all this in the name of therapy.[4]

Many feminists saw the Gestalt philosophy—that all people must take responsibility for their own feelings and life circumstances—as an important message for women, and so they embraced the philosophy and found many of the techniques helpful also.

Again, one can see how feminists at that time, not wanting to appear too radical in their feminism and seeing the need for women to become more responsible for their own happiness, would have seized on Gestalt as a useful tool, but one wonders how such a destructive system, grounded as it was in its founder's need for power and dominance over others, could have appealed to so many for so long.

The Esalen Institute in California, established by Perls, was a very popular place in the 1960s and 1970s. Women and men from all over the United States and, indeed, the world, flocked there to be a part of the powerful "growth" movement that was said to be overtaking the Western world. In a book called *The Aquarian Conspiracy: Personal and Social Transformation in the 1980s* (1980), Marilyn Ferguson wrote:

> A leaderless but powerful network is working to bring about radical change in the United States . . .
>
> Broader than reform, deeper than revolution, this benign conspiracy for a new human agenda has triggered the most rapid cultural realignment in history. The great shuddering, irrevocable shift overtaking us is not a new political, religious, or philosophical system. It is a new mind (p. 23).

Despite such high hopes for the growth therapies that exploded on to the market promising personal and social transformation, what actually developed was a rapidly

---

4. This information comes from Perls' autobiography *In and Out the Garbage Pail* (1969), which he chose to write with no page numbers.

expanding *industry*. More and more people were enticed into more and more growth experiences by those who were living comfortably off the profits. One growth experience would leave a person hungering for more, and pursuing one's own personal "growth" became an end in itself.

There were seminars, courses and group experiences springing up everywhere. Erhard Seminars Training (est) was very popular, as were, among others, Silva Mind Control, Lifespring, A Course in Miracles, and Alpha Dynamic. The result was not personal and social transformation but an exaggerated emphasis on inward-looking, self-seeking individualism.

A relic from the 1970s and 1980s which continues to attract crowds in Australia is the Alpha Dynamic Training Seminar where, for a large amount of money, one is promised improved performance, improved confidence, improved self-discipline, and improved goal achievement through improved mind-control.

Even now, in the 1990s, the libertarian philosophy continues to be the favourite of many feminists who still believe individual growth and personal empowerment will eventually lead to liberation for all women.

Self-help emphasis

During the height of the libertarian era, some feminists, in an attempt to reject traditional and humanistic therapies, began to emphasise the need for self-help groups, and developed ways whereby women could help and support each other. While this seemed at first to be a positive move, it was not long before serious problems were apparent.

A central feature of the self-help movement was an arrangement called co-counselling. Each woman was encouraged to seek out another woman with whom she felt she could be compatible and discuss with her the possibility of setting up a co-counselling arrangement. It was stressed that one's co-counsellor should not be one's lover, mother, daughter or sister, so that a degree of objectivity could be maintained. The strategy was to get together once a week for a couple of hours to talk about problems and offer each other support. Both women were to have equal time and both were to invest equal energy in terms of speaking and listening, so that it would be truly mutually supportive.

Some of the problems that caused the breakdown of this system were: one woman consistently dominating the session with her own concerns and leaving no time for her co-counsellor to do any talking; one or both women talking about traumatic childhood experiences, bringing up deep and long-repressed feelings from the past that neither of them knew how to deal with; both women enjoying the experience of sharing their intimate secrets so much that their meetings became more and more frequent until their whole lives became centred on the inward-looking, self-indulgent sharing of personal feelings and they had little interest in anything else; and the intimacy of the co-counselling experience turning into sexual intimacy, thereby causing feelings of hurt, betrayal and anger in their ex-lovers which reverberated throughout their particular feminist or lesbian feminist community.

New Age

Many feminists who began by experimenting with co-counselling as an alternative to mainstream therapies drifted into New Age therapies when co-counselling proved more of a hassle than it was worth. Others embraced such therapies because they seemed to offer something positive to replace the emptiness and meaninglessness women felt in the 1980s.

Most of us involved in the feminist revolution of the 1960s and 1970s really did believe that men would change as soon as they understood what we were saying about the oppression of women, that society would change and that life would be better for all of us as a result, but we were wrong (McLellan, 1992, pp. 71–2). It was disappointing and depressing to discover that most men treated women as they did, not because they were ignorant of the effect it had on women, but because they were aware of the considerable advantage such a situation gave to men. Still today, it is obvious that most men resist with amazing vigour the kinds of changes women are fighting for, and there is no evidence that that will change in the foreseeable future. While many of us responded to that profound disappointment by realising that we must maintain our anger and be prepared to see our involvement in the feminist revolution as a life-long involvement, others responded by becoming increasingly disillusioned and lost, till the New Age movement with its focus on "feeling good" (through yoga, meditation, relaxation, massage and spirituality) came along and filled the void.

The New Age preoccupation with the self, which demanded that more and more energy be taken up with new and different ways of looking inward, however, left many women socially and politically destitute.

It was this indulgent preoccupation with the self, encouraged first by the liberal humanist therapies, then by the co-counselling emphasis and finally by the New Age therapies, that provoked a new wave of radical feminist voices to speak out against therapy as it had developed.

Radical feminist critiques

Any attempt at developing a radical feminist alternative to therapy must take seriously the comments of radical feminists whose opinions and writing have offered such important insights in so many areas of feminist scholarship throughout the years.

As will be seen, some (notably Mary Daly and Janice Raymond) speak out strongly against therapy in general and feminist therapy in particular, but do not close the door entirely on the possibility of some form of therapy as an activity of the feminist movement. Others (namely Celia Kitzinger and Rachel Perkins) reject the very idea of therapy and see absolutely no place for it in a feminist context. A third group (represented here by Louise Armstrong and Renate Klein) speak about therapy as it relates to specific areas of women's pain. While speaking out against the oppressive nature of therapy for women, they also acknowledge the deep wounds individual women suffer at the hands of the patriarchy (as victims/survivors of incest, rape and reproductive technology), and call for a new and radically politicised form of therapy. A fourth group (represented here by Kate Millett) courageously tell of their personal journey into "madness" and back again, describing the horrors of a system that sedates and incarcerates those who are different, thereby destroying every vestige of their human dignity.

Mary Daly

In *Gyn/ecology*, Mary Daly is uncompromising in her criticism of much that passes for feminist therapy, but a careful reading of her work reveals that she does not totally reject the need for some kind of therapy for women, even if she does reject the use of the word "therapy" to describe it (1978, p. 282).

> I am *not* saying that genuinely woman-identified counseling cannot and does not take place, nor am I denying that, given the state of alienating structures in which we live, there is an urgent need for drop-in centers and other places for women to go *in crisis situations* (p. 280).

Then she goes on to say:

> My criticism concerns therapy as a way of life, as an institutionalized system of creating and perpetuating false needs, of masking and maintaining depression, of focusing/draining women's energy through fixation upon periodic psychological "fixes". My criticism concerns the emotional, economic, and intellectual hooking of women into a perpetual procession of cyclic re-turning, which provides false security and prevents independent risking/questing. It concerns the woman-crippling triumph of the therapeutic over transcendence (pp. 280–1).

After exposing Freud's "violation" of his women patients (which will be dealt with in more detail in Chapter Five), Daly warns against the development of feminist therapy because, she says, some Women's Centres have been turned into Taming Centres.

> In the Name of Feminist Therapy, and of Radical Feminist Therapy and of Wholly Lesbian Therapy, Women's Centers, originally the products of creative/wild woman-identified energy, are sometimes converted into Taming Centers, where independent gynergetic being is treated as a source of disease (p. 281n).

Also, she warns feminists who are therapists that this "Thoroughly Therapeutic Society" will "craftily con" women "into the role of unwitting token victimizers, in the name of Feminist Therapy" (p. 280).

While it is obvious that Daly is extremely wary of feminists being involved as therapists, her much-quoted statement that "the very concept of 'feminist therapy' is inherently a contradiction" (p. 282), is often taken out of context and misquoted by those who want to claim her support in their total rejection of therapy (see for example Masson, 1988, p. 262n).

This statement is made in the context of her criticism of the "addictive" nature of therapy. She speaks of those "who fixate defensively on 'feminist therapy' rather than expanding their vision to comprehend a long and complex analysis of androcratic atrocities and tactics" (pp. 281–2). It is this limited focus, this focus on the personal and therapeutic to the exclusion of the broader political analysis of what is actually going on in society in terms of male atrocities against women, that "suggests that the very concept of 'feminist therapy' is inherently a contradiction" (p. 282). The kind of therapy that does not include a broader political analysis cannot be called "feminist". Daly then says:

> I hasten to add that gynergizing, en-couraging, healing communication among Hags/Crones is not a contradiction. Therefore, when this is taking place it should *not* be called "therapy" (p. 282).

Among her many criticisms of therapy are the following:

> therapy . . . tends to replace transcendence, assuming/consuming all process, draining creative energy, eliminating Originality, mislabeling leaps of imagination, shielding the Self against Self-strengthening Aloneness. The Self becomes a spectator of her own frozen, caricatured history. She is filed away, mis-filed, in file-cabinets with inaccurate categories. Thus filed, she joins the Processions of those who choose downward mobility of mind and imagination (p. 283).

In summary, while Daly's criticisms are strong, she is clearly not saying there is no room for therapy as an activity of the feminist movement. She recognises the need, "given the state of alienating structures in which we live", for safe places "for women to go *in crisis situations*" (p. 280).

Janice Raymond

In *A Passion for Friends*, Janice Raymond writes about therapy in the same vein as Mary Daly. Her criticisms are of "therapism" or "therapy as a way of life", which includes:

> not only going into therapy and often staying there for years but making of one's relation-ships with women a therapeutic context. Therapism is an overvaluation of feeling. In a real sense, it is a tyranny of feelings where women have come to believe that what really counts in their life is their "psychology" (1986, p. 155).

She asks women to consider the fact that (in the United States) "feminist therapy is a booming business", while many other feminist ventures such as "restaurants, book-stores, health centers and credit unions have gone out of business" (p. 156). The reason, she says, is the high value placed on "disclosure of self".

> the women's movement, like society at large, has fast become a therapeutic society where self-exposure ranks as one of the highest virtues. Women must show and tell all. Little about body and mind can be mysterious. Thus women engage in massive psychological strip-teases that fragment and exploit the inner life (p. 156).

Raymond laments the fact that, with the strong emphasis placed on self-disclosure, "true and deep subjectivity is hard to find". Therapism reduces the inner life "to an exercise in therapeutics". It "reifies subjectivity, that is, it thingifies it, by externalizing and wrenching the inner life out of its depths" (p. 157).

In a therapeutised society, "friendship becomes reduced to . . . a context for constant self-disclosure" (p. 158). Talking about emotions becomes more important than the emotions themselves (p. 157). Pointing to Mary Daly's contrasting of real passions and plastic passions (Daly, 1984, pp. 200–1), Raymond says: "In therapism, what is missing is passionate exchange. The sharing of feelings predominates over the revelation of passionate truth (p. 158)." Continuing this theme, she says:

> Therapy as a way of life filters out the passion and lets the feeling through . . . The "therapeutizing" of friendship is based on a particular loss of Self, the loss of the passionate Self, and the loss of the original Self who was one's original friend (p. 159).

Janice Raymond's criticisms of therapism are strong and clear, but she takes time to assure her readers that she is not criticising those women who genuinely seek the help of therapists. She says:

> There are, of course, instances in which women justifiably seek help in a therapeutic setting. I am not criticizing this genuine need . . . Certainly people must be able to free themselves of torturous feelings, pent-up emotions, and troublesome trials. There may be times when women will seek out therapists for help . . . Genuine self-revelation should not be confused with perpetual therapeutic manifestations (p. 156).

Celia Kitzinger and Rachel Perkins

In contrast to Daly's and Raymond's stand against "therapy as a way of life" while at the same time allowing for the possibility of some kind of short-term therapy within a feminist context, British feminists Celia Kitzinger and Rachel Perkins take an absolute stand against therapy. In their work on lesbian/feminist psychology and therapy, they argue that feminism and therapy are "*not* ethically or politically compatible" (1993, p. 198) and, consequently, call for "an end to therapy altogether" (p. 27).

In a discussion of the role of psychology and therapy for lesbians, conducted by *The Spoken Word* (Hall *et al.*, 1992, pp. 7–25), Kitzinger says in her opening statement:

> Psychology has nothing to offer feminism. It's destroying our politics by translating the political into the personal, by offering individualized language which focuses on the private inner life instead of the public external world of oppression (p. 9).

Perkins, in the same discussion, points out that the terms of psychotherapy are provided by patriarchy, "to individualize, to privatize, to personalize". Feminism is destroyed, she says, unless we address "those areas that we call 'personal', our desires, our sexuality, our 'private lives', in political terms" (p. 12).

Kitzinger takes up that point and elaborates on it and, in so doing, gives a clear indication of her belief that the lesbian/feminist community could and ought to be a substitute for therapy for members of that community:

> one of the things that happens with psychology and psychotherapy is that individual women disappear with their "private" problems into their therapist's office. I mind very much when my friends go off to their therapists to talk about their mother's death, or their break-up with their lover or their miserable sex-life. It seems to me that those are issues which we all of

us own, as a community, and that we all of us ought to be able to deal with, *as a community of lesbians*, there for each other (p. 12).

While their arguments are strong and convincing, they still struggle with the practical issue of what to do about women's personal pain, or "social disability", as they prefer to call it (Kitzinger and Perkins, 1993, pp. 165f). The suggestion that individual problems be dealt with in the context of one's lesbian/feminist community is somewhat idealistic, but nevertheless an important aim of any such community.

Another suggestion they make as a substitute for psychotherapy, however, reveals a glaring inconsistency in their argument. It concerns their support of the use of prescription drugs. Following their important discussion about the need for the lesbian community to provide help and shelter to individual lesbians in need of "a place where they can gain relief from the stresses and strains of everyday life", they go on to suggest that when lesbians are in need of relief from "distressing thoughts and feelings . . . sometimes additional assistance in the form of drugs may be valuable" (p. 180).

While acknowledging the potential for abuse in the use of drugs (pp. 181–2), they insist that some people need drugs to enhance their functioning and coping. They say: "For some lesbians and women, drugs are quite literally a life-saver when distress becomes too great to tolerate" (p. 182).

My disagreement with them in this context is not a disagreement about the rights and wrongs of drugs. In fact, I agree that there is a place for drugs in the treatment of some emotional and psychological conditions. My position on the use of drugs for those suffering from anxiety and/or depression, for example, remains the same as that expressed in an earlier publication: that drugs can, in some circumstances, be useful on a short-term basis (McLellan, 1992, p. 171). For those suffering from schizophrenia or other psychotic conditions, the use of drugs on a long-term basis can be crucial to their very survival. For this reason, it would be nothing short of irresponsible to suggest that drugs are never needed. Sandy Jeffs, an Australian poet who has had a long struggle with schizophrenia, reveals some of her own experiences in *Poems from the Madhouse* (1993). In one of her poems (p. 37) she makes it clear that getting through some nights was only made possible, for her, by drugs.

Whatever Gets You Through the Night

Prothiaden
Ativan
Serenace
Modecate
Cogentin
Dreams
Sleep
More Dreams
Thoughts
Animals
Hope
A Miracle.

My concern about the stand taken by Kitzinger and Perkins in relation to drugs is not with the question of drugs per se, but with the inconsistency such a stand brings to an argument which purports to be absolute in its renunciation of therapy. First, it is inconsistent in terms of who prescribes the drugs. Mind-altering and mood-altering drugs do not just come out of the air. They are prescribed by someone, usually a psychiatrist or medical practitioner. In most cases, drugs are not prescribed without the prescriber (doctor) first getting the patient to talk about her distress and personal pain, so that the doctor is able to make an assessment as to the kinds of drugs that are appropriate. Such a procedure, surely, constitutes a form of psychotherapy.

Also, it is inconsistent to argue, on the one hand, that therapy is "*not* ethically or politically compatible" (p. 198) with feminism and, on the other hand, that the taking of mind-altering and mood-altering drugs *is*. The prescribing of drugs for emotional and psychological distress has just as much potential (I would argue, *more* potential) for oppressing and controlling women as psychotherapy itself.[5]

Louise Armstrong

Among those radical feminists who express an opinion about therapy in the context of their writing on specific areas of women's oppression is Louise Armstrong. Author of *Kiss Daddy Goodnight* (1978) and *Kiss Daddy Goodnight: Ten Years Later* (1987), she wrote and spoke about her own childhood incestual assault and encouraged other women to do the same in the hope that such courageous action would bring about real change.

In 1990, looking back on more than a decade, she wrote:

In speaking out, we hoped to raise hell. Instead, we have raised for the issue a certain normalcy. We hoped to raise a passion for change. Instead, what we raised was discourse— and a sizeable problem-management industry (Armstrong, in Leidholdt and Raymond, 1990, p. 43).

Continuing in the same vein, she said:

Our speaking out, as adult survivors, about our childhood incestual assault, did not threaten the status quo. It challenged nothing in the present; cost those in power nothing in the present—economically or politically. In fact, our coming forward opened a new frontier for therapeutic specialization (p. 45).

Armstrong is highly critical of the role psychotherapy has played in having the emphasis taken off the criminality of childhood sexual abuse and replaced with a therapeutic explanation, thereby releasing perpetrators from blame and accountability. When women spoke out about their childhood experiences and called for justice under

5. For a courageous account of one woman's experience of becoming hooked on benzodiazepines, see Beatrice Faust (1993) *Benzo Junkie: More Than a Case History*. Also, Renate Klein's review, "Survival is a Privilege which Entails Obligations", in *Australian Women's Book Review*, June 1994, 6 (2), pp. 34–5.

the law, mental health professionals intervened and called the assaults "sick", thus providing a therapeutic explanation or excuse for criminal behaviour. "We called it criminal, they called it sick", she said.

> "Sick" became so thoroughly ingrained as the correct way to "understand" that even the appearance, in 1980, of a group of perfectly respectable doctors and professors under the banner of the "pro-incest lobby" could not shake the public's need to disbelieve the obvious (p. 50).

What followed was even worse. Because the labelling of these crimes against children as a sickness would mean admitting that there were an awful lot of "sick" men in our society living otherwise normal, productive lives, the mental health professionals came to the rescue again. They invented terms like "incest family", and encouraged us to look at the crime of incest as "a 'family disease', a 'symptom of family dysfunction'" (p. 51). Also, they introduced the term "incest mother".

> It was this "incest mother" who provided the very foundation on which the experts built their "disease model," their treatment intervention schemes, their decriminalization defense. It was she around whom intervention was structured, toward whom counseling was aimed. She, who was the justification for the proliferation of treatment programs designed to "keep the family intact." The fact was she seldom existed. But by now facts didn't have much power to bother anybody. The state had its new mythology. The "experts" had their problem-management industry. The paternal child molesters of America were once again safe (p. 51).

Lamenting the fact that "Incest in the present has not been a priority issue for feminists" (p. 53), Armstrong points out that feminists in significant numbers simply accepted the judgment that childhood sexual abuse is "an individual emotional problem, and they—with the help of the new therapeutic experts—lost sight of the political/power issue at hand" (p. 53).

Then, in a statement supporting the development of a therapy that is radicalised and politicised, she says:

> That is not to say, of course, that there is no place for individual counseling, individual help, individual support. It's just to say that when you are looking at a systematic, system-endorsed power abuse, individualized solutions—exclusively individualized solutions—are antithetical to change (p. 53).

In her latest book, *Rocking the Cradle of Sexual Politics* (1994), Louise Armstrong reiterates and expands the themes expressed in her 1990 paper. That which began as a powerful political act, she says, was defused by the therapeutic ideology, much of which "was deemed to be *feminist* therapy" (p. 209). This ideology that has taken over the issue of sexual assault of children is more aptly described as "a comforting blend of feminist language and mental health credo" (p. 208). Armstrong explains that it is "the therapeutic ideology, in apposition to the feminist worldview" that she is taking issue with (pp. 208–9).

Feminist understanding (in my understanding) opens the personal to the political and to a comprehension of the larger issue. The therapeutic ideology—whatever its language—raises the personal to the paramount, placing the individual as the hub of her own claustrophobic universe; putting her "in recovery", as though that were a geographic location . . .

The distinction I'm making is not between seeking, or not seeking, emotional help as a private enterprise, but between "the personal is political" and the "personal is all" (p. 209).

Renate Klein

Another radical feminist voice expressing the need for a therapy for women in the context of her work in a specific area of women's oppression is that of Renate Klein. An outspoken critic of the way women are oppressed and destroyed by reproductive technology, Klein agrees with Armstrong that, while exclusively individualised solutions do little to effect real change, there is a need for a therapy that addresses both the individual predicament of women and the political necessity for change.

The kind of therapy/counselling offered by in-vitro fertilisation (IVF) programmes, Klein says, is "clearly a misnomer", and she calls for "independent counselling" (1989a, p. 20), that is, counselling that is offered independently of IVF and its promoters. One of the women interviewed in her survey described her experience of IVF counselling like this:

I felt everyone was pushing me into it . . . gently but steadily . . . my husband, my mother, my best friend, even a girl at work whom I had told about it. I felt really caught . . . When we went to the initial counselling there was no space to say any of this. We were given the impression that it was a big privilege to be accepted—and we were—so we had to be grateful. I shut up and began three years of utter misery (p. 21).

In an article written for the *Feminist Therapy Newsletter* in 1989, Klein expresses the need for feminist action to occur at two levels. First, feminists need to be involved in continuous political action to expose "the f(ph)allacies of the 'technodocs'", the lies told to women to exploit their desire for their own biological child and thus lure them into IVF programmes where they surrender their bodies to be used as "test-sites" (1989b, p. 12). At another level, feminists need to be involved in the support of individual women desperate for help in finding themselves again, in having their sense of dignity and worth restored, after the experimenters have finished with them and cast them out. She says:

elaborating on the bad and truly sinister motives behind IVF, isn't enough to help you cope with the woman sitting in front of you in sheer and utter misery: sad, devoid of life-energy, suicidal, and often with just one wish: a biological child. I believe that feminist therapists have an increasingly important role to play in supporting these women; in fact, with very few exceptions most of the women in my survey who "survived" their IVF experience and have found new joy in their lives have achieved this with the help of a feminist therapist or counsellor (p. 13).

Klein goes on to suggest various options for feminist therapy and draws attention to an article by Traute Schönenberg and Ute Winkler in which they discuss their work at the

Feminist Health Centre in Frankfurt, Germany (Klein, 1989c, pp. 207–24). The work of the Frankfurt centre will be discussed further when other therapeutic alternatives are examined in Chapter Ten.

Kate Millett

Kate Millett entered the world stage in 1970 with the publication of her first book, *Sexual Politics*. As a result of that courageous book, she became one of the pioneers, and also one of the heroes, of Second Wave feminism. Now she has written a book which is even more courageous than the first, because in it she describes her own personal journey into the nightmare state called "madness".

In the beginning of the book, entitled *The Loony Bin Trip* (1991), she tells of how, in 1973, she found herself incarcerated in a psychiatric institution at the instigation of friends and family members who thought it would help her. Whilst in there, she worked with civil rights lawyers who succeeded in securing her release but, as she explains, it was after that devastating experience that she became profoundly depressed.

> Following my release I became profoundly depressed, my confidence broken by confinement; despite the fact that I had won my freedom through the intercession of civil rights lawyers and a trial—unusual in itself—it was accepted by those around me that I was "crazy", so I might just as well be. Moreover, there was the ominous diagnosis of manic depression, a professional scientific verdict of insanity. I began to crumble in fear and loneliness (p. 12).

At this time, she began taking lithium because she believed she needed "help". She took it for seven years, during which time she "lived with a hand tremor, diarrhea, the possibility of kidney damage and all the other 'side effects'" (p. 12). Then, in 1980, she decided to take herself off it, and to her surprise was met with an incredible amount of disapproval from friends and family. Reflecting on their response, she says:

> Mystical state, madness, how it frightens people. How utterly crazy *they* become, remote, rude, peculiar, cruel, taunting, farouche as wild beasts who have smelled danger, the unthinkable. One must maintain one's reason now in this, yet how difficult not to give way to rage. And after hours of patience I blow up, full Irish steam, a stream of words, abuse matching theirs. Mine counts against me, theirs does not (p. 67).

She continues:

> How crazy craziness makes everyone, how irrationally afraid. The madness hidden in each of us, called to, identified, aroused like a lust. And against that the jaw sets. The more I fear my own insanity the more I must punish yours . . . (p. 68).

Of lithium, she says:

> The psychiatrists don't seem to know, or profess not quite to understand, just how the lithium ion, once in the bloodstream, affects the brain . . .
> So everybody is dutifully swallowing an unknown. Not just an experimental bunch now but tens, maybe hundreds of thousands. And they are swallowing on the say-so of a

profession that cannot understand the workings of this stuff on the brain and admits it but still goes ahead and swears to its efficacy. And insists you take it (pp. 54–5).

At the insistence of her friends and relatives, Millett agreed to go back on lithium:

I could not pit my truth against so many, against the power of science, nor could I live without other people. I surrendered my understanding, lost myself trying to survive and accommodate. And I went on taking lithium. It seemed a condition of parole: if I stopped taking it and were found out I might be confined again (p. 309).

Years later, after attending a conference where she met members of the anti-psychiatry movement, she decided to withdraw from lithium again but, this time, resolved not to tell any of her friends. In 1988, on her birthday, she reduced her intake and began weaning herself off the drug which, she said "had created a stifled fury in me for years" (p. 310). Once off it, absolutely nothing happened. She just gathered the threads of her life together and got on with it. Looking back on it all, she wrote:

The psychiatric diagnosis imposed upon me is that I am constitutionally psychotic, a manic-depressive bound to suffer recurrent attacks of "affective illness" unless I am maintained on prophylactic medication, specifically lithium. For a total of thirteen years I deadened my mind and obscured my consciousness with a drug whose prescription was based on a fallacy. Even discounting the possible harm of the drug's "side effects", it may seem little consolation to discover that one was sane all along. But to me it is everything (pp. 310–11).

In the concluding paragraphs of her book, Millett suggests that "insanity" does not exist, but that maybe "madness" does:

Madness? Perhaps. A certain speed of thought, certain wonderful flights of ideas. Certain altered states of perception. Why not hear voices? So what? . . . But surely it is the law of Thought Crime to forbid, punish, or incarcerate different thoughts. Mental activity at the margin. Or over the line (p. 315).

Then, in a powerful affirmation of the human mind, she makes it clear what she thinks of incarceration in psychiatric institutions. She says:

Bring down the madhouse, build theaters with its bricks, or playgrounds. Let us leave each other "alone." No longer meddled with, we can muddle through without interfering relatives or state psychiatry. The human condition is helped best by being respected.
   Let us stop being afraid. Of our own thoughts, our own minds. Of madness, our own or others'. Stop being afraid of the mind itself (pp. 315–16).

Sandy Jeffs reiterates Millett's angry, exultant theme, at the conclusion of her poem "The Madwoman in the Attic":

> madwoman that I am,
> who scorns our history of abuse and misunderstanding,
> I wish to declare us the curators of our own psyches
> (1993, p. 39).

This historical overview of feminist attitudes toward psychotherapy places us in a better position to make decisions about the role, if any, we want therapy to play in the feminist revolution in the present and into the future. The radical feminist consensus from Naomi Weisstein and Phyllis Chesler to Mary Daly, Janice Raymond, Celia Kitzinger, Rachel Perkins, Louise Armstrong, Renate Klein, Kate Millett and many others, is that the institution and practice of psychotherapy approved of in Western countries is oppressive and demeaning of women.

There is also agreement about society's ongoing oppression of women, described variously as "the state of alienating structures in which we live" (Daly, 1978, p. 280); as "systematic, system-endorsed power abuse" (Armstrong, 1990, p. 53); as having "bad and truly sinister motives", causing women to experience "sheer and utter misery" (Klein, 1989b, p.13) and "torturous feelings, pent-up emotions, and troublesome trials" (Raymond, 1986, p. 156).

Many radical feminists, but not all, also agree that there is a need for some kind of therapy (even if it is not called "therapy") to provide an avenue of support and care for women crushed by patriarchy, and that such therapy be made available as an integral part of the work we are doing to end women's oppression and develop visions for a better world.

On the question of therapy, then, it seems that the feminist movement has three options. The first is to ignore the personal, individual pain of women today and place all our energies into social and political action with the aim of changing society, so that at least future generations of women will not be subjected to the kinds of pain and distress women presently experience. This option is not suggested or supported by any of the radical voices quoted above, but it is a suggestion one hears from time to time.

A second option is to reject the idea of therapy altogether and encourage women to look to their friends, mothers, sisters, daughters, and lesbian lovers for help in times of social and emotional distress. This option is problematic because it fails to take into account the fact that most women who decide to seek the help of a psychotherapist do so only after every other avenue has been tried. Women usually talk about their sadness and distress to family members or friends first, and it is only when such talking fails to ease the pain, or when they find themselves getting more distressed as they talk, or when they feel their friend/listener is losing interest, or getting impatient, or does not have the time, or expresses a feeling of helplessness because of lack of skills, that they decide to turn to a psychotherapist for help.

If the feminist movement turns its back on therapy altogether, then, we would be simply delivering women, at the height of their vulnerability, into the hands of main-stream, non-feminist therapists whose attitudes to women most often match those that exist in society at large.

A third option is to work at developing an alternative therapy that is radicalised and politicised and that is an integral part of the revolutionary work feminists are involved in. Parts Two and Four, to follow, represent an attempt to do that, and while this work is not offered as the definitive word on therapy for feminists, it is offered in the hope that it will spark serious and productive debate.

I am sure of two things: first, that we need to develop an alternative therapy capable of caring for all of us "mad" women during those times when the constant day-to-day battle with patriarchy overwhelms us; and second, that the therapy we develop must be worthy of us.

PART TWO

THEORETICAL ISSUES
FOR A FEMINIST THERAPY

2

OPPRESSION:

CAUSE OF WOMEN'S DISTRESS

Oppression is the first of five socio-political issues I will discuss in this part. Before moving into the specific focus of this chapter, however, which is to examine in detail the role oppression plays in much of the emotional pain and distress experienced by women, it is important to begin by taking a look at the broader picture in relation to the feminist alternative therapy to be presented in the following pages.

Any attempt at developing an alternative therapy must pay attention to both theory and practice. While the practical application of a feminist therapy is examined in Part Four, the discussion of issues in the next three chapters contains the theory or philosophy on which any feminist therapy must be built. Since the feminist movement is a socio-political movement, the issues that inform the development of a feminist therapy must, of necessity, be socio-political issues.

It is important to state at the outset that the radical nature of feminist therapy demands that there be no attempt to develop a closed system of theory or practice. Once any therapy is systematised, it immediately becomes limited by the dictates of the system. Because feminist therapy is committed to hearing women's *real* stories, to understanding the root causes of women's emotional distress, and to responding to women's experiences as they are presented, it is essential that it remain free to respond to whatever presents itself and to change as the need arises.

To this end, the following discussion of issues does not in any way attempt to develop a precise theory so that it could be said: This is *the* theory of feminist therapy. As a reading of each of the chapters will reveal, my intention here is simply to highlight important issues, the discussion of which, it is hoped, will precipitate the emergence of elements of a philosophical base for a feminist alternative therapy.

A brief comparison between feminist and mainstream therapies reveals marked differences in philosophy, in attitude toward recipients of therapy, and in the kinds of issues that form the basis of the actual therapeutic endeavour.

Philosophy

In terms of philosophy, therapists working in the psychoanalytic or humanist traditions take great care to point out that the science of psychology is concerned with the emotions and behaviour of individuals and not with social or political questions. They insist that the practice of therapy is, and must be, apolitical. An important element in the training of therapists is the insistence that the new recruits learn to be apolitical, unbiased, fair and balanced. A therapist is supposed to be able to see every side of every life story ever told to her. She is not supposed to have a bias but if she does, she must be careful not to let it show. She is not supposed to be moved to anger. She is not supposed to give her opinion. Above all, she must be balanced in her attitudes and encourage those who seek her help to be balanced also.

Early feminists like Kate Millett, Naomi Weisstein and Phyllis Chesler were among the first to point out that, far from being apolitical, traditional psychiatry, psychology and psychotherapy were very political indeed. It was a politics of conservatism designed to preserve the status quo. One only had to look at the role such therapies played in supporting and maintaining the subordination of women to find proof that their agenda was political.

While mainstream therapy still refuses to accept the fact of its political bias in favour of the status quo and continues to see itself as apolitical, feminist therapy is blatantly and proudly political. It begins with a socio-political analysis of women's oppression and sees the subordination of women as the root cause of individual women's psychological and emotional problems. Consistent with its analysis of cause, the goal of feminist therapy has two parts: one is the liberation of all women, collectively, from structural subordination (achievable only as women continue to work together to change the very foundations of patriarchy); and the other is the liberation of individual women from the belief that they have no alternative but to accept the inferior status assigned to them and to bear the consequences of their subordination in silence.[1]

Attitude

Given the difference in philosophy between mainstream and feminist therapies, it is not surprising that there is also a marked difference in attitude toward those who seek a therapist's help. Those working from a psychoanalytic perspective hold the attitude that anyone who feels the need for therapy or analysis is sick and in need of treatment. A recipient of therapy is, in fact, called a "patient", and is encouraged to acknowledge that the problem she is encountering comes from deep within her own psyche. She is psychologically disturbed.

Those working from a humanistic perspective have a more liberal attitude toward those seeking their help, but they still manage to place responsibility for the problem

---

1. While I am not claiming that all women would *accept* that the cause of their distress lies in their oppression or that there is a need for them to be liberated, it nevertheless remains that the primary goal of feminist therapy is liberation from oppression.

squarely on the shoulders of the "client" herself. Their attitude is that this person has a problem and is in need of help to deal with *her* problem.

The attitude of those working from a feminist perspective, however, is radically different from either of the above. The feminist attitude is that this person is oppressed and in need of liberation.[2] She is not sick. She does not have a problem that was primarily brought on by herself. She is suffering in the way that she is because, as a woman living in patriarchal society, she has been, and continues to be, oppressed.

Issues

The issues that inform the development of a feminist therapy are also very different from those of mainstream therapies. For psychoanalysis, the issues are: individual mental health, the authority and expertise of the analyst, and the need for the patient to trust and work with (not against) the analyst. For the humanistic therapies, the issues are: awareness of one's own potential, the need for individual empowerment, the freedom to do as one pleases, and the necessity of taking personal responsibility for the circumstances of one's own life.

In contrast to this individualistic emphasis where the task of therapy is seen to be that of helping individuals adjust to the various circumstances of their lives, a feminist therapy with its socio-political emphasis sees the initial task of therapy as that of helping women understand the pressures placed upon them by such circumstances and the extent to which those pressures are affecting their mental and emotional well-being.[3] Following that, the next task is to provide support and encouragement as women work to change the circumstances that have caused the problem. The socio-political emphasis is on *change* rather than *adjustment*, the need to get to the root of a problem and change it rather than simply learning how to adjust to and "live with" the problem, at a superficial level, so that the problem itself becomes more tolerable.

---

2. This is not to say that all emotional problems suffered by women are the result of direct oppression. Often a woman's distress is caused by circumstances beyond anyone's control (sometimes referred to as "fate"), for example, the death of a child or partner, news of her own or a loved one's illness, a deep sense of loneliness. The oppression many women experience in these circumstances is more correctly called indirect oppression, since it has more to do with society's expectations about how women ought to deal with their own distress than with the actual cause of the distress.

3. In addition to helping women understand the pressures they experience from external sources, from society in general, partner, children, parents, a therapist's task also includes helping women understand the nature and source of internalised oppression.

   Many women place themselves under enormous pressure to be all things to all people, to deny themselves in favour of others, to give of themselves and not expect anything in return, to care, to praise, to please, and then feel guilty if they fall short of their own standards of martyrdom.

   While such a situation appears to be the result of *internal* oppression and prompts libertarian feminists to call for women to stop oppressing themselves by getting in touch with their own power, it is in fact the result of *internalised* oppression.

   So strong is the conditioning of women in patriarchal societies that few of us escape the internalising of our own oppression. We willingly, and without question, demean ourselves and then wonder why our behaviour is often self-destructive. Many, through reading and involvement with other women, develop an awareness of the strength of their conditioning and take steps, themselves, to counter it, while others become aware of it for the first time as they talk with a feminist therapist.

There are five issues I have identified as important socio-political issues in the development of a feminist therapy. They are: oppression, access, honesty, passion and justice. Of course, one could argue for the inclusion of other issues as well, but these will be sufficient to enable us, at least, to begin to develop the theory or philosophy on which a feminist therapy must be built. A detailed discussion of each of these issues is contained in this and the following two chapters.

Oppression

An analysis of women's oppression is central to a feminist perspective on therapy because, without an acknowledgement of women's collective and individual oppression, it would be impossible to understand the real depth of women's pain and anguish. Women in therapy are very often the victims of "double oppression", that is, oppression first by society and then by the therapist.

The first point that needs to be discussed, then, is that *oppression is at the root of most emotional and psychological problems affecting women.*

The radical therapy movement of the 1960s led by R. D. Laing, Thomas Szasz and others insisted that *all* emotional and psychological problems affecting women and men were caused by society's oppression. Many who suffered from so-called "psychotic" conditions, however, questioned the validity and, indeed, the justice of such a sweeping statement.

In this present analysis of oppression, the word "most" is used rather than "all" in acknowledgement of the fact that it is not yet clear what is at the root of conditions such as schizophrenia and bi-polar disorder (manic depression). If the cause is some kind of chemical imbalance as is most often suggested, then it would be unfair and, in fact, oppressive, to suggest that sufferers from such psychoses simply needed to get to the root of their oppression and they would be healed. There is not enough known yet about psychotic conditions to make judgments of this kind.

One thing that is known, however, is that many people who are diagnosed as having a psychosis and prescribed mind-altering and mood-altering medication for life, are wrongly diagnosed. One or two schizophrenic episodes do not amount to schizophrenia, nor does the existence of mood swings amount to bi-polar disorder.

The kinds of conditions that often have oppression at their root are so-called "neurotic" conditions experienced by most women to varying degrees throughout their lives. A list of conditions that cause women to feel unable to cope and prompt them to seek the help of a therapist would include: depression, anxiety, eating disorders, excessive drug and alcohol consumption, unresolved grief, deep feelings of dissatisfaction, loneliness, disillusionment, emptiness, meaninglessness, low self-esteem, guilt, self-blaming, self-hatred, and so on.

The suggestion that oppression is the cause of most of the emotional and psychological problems that individual women experience makes it imperative that we examine both the collective and the individual oppression of women.

Collective oppression

The extent of the collective oppression of women in Western societies is now well known, thanks to the work of feminist researchers and writers in recent years. The following overview of feminist literature, demands and issues gives some insight into the extent of the oppression of women, and the determination of the feminist movement to expose such oppression and bring about change.

Feminist literature

Dale Spender's tireless work over many years has provided us with invaluable insight into the struggles and passions of many of our foremothers who spoke out against the oppression of women (Spender, 1982, 1983a, 1983b, 1984). Quotes such as the following are now commonplace in feminist circles:

> If all Men are born free, how is it that all Women are born slaves?   Mary Astill, 1700.

> The great social injustices are the subjection of labour and the subjection of women.
> Christabel Pankhurst, 1902.

> I myself have never been able to find out precisely what feminism is: I only know that people call me a feminist whenever I express sentiments that differentiate me from a doormat.   Rebecca West, 1913.

Writing about the feminist movement closer to our own time, Anna Coote and Beatrix Campbell remind us that even though the gap between those who identify as radical feminists and those who identify as socialist feminists "has seemed increasingly wide and unbridgeable", the one thing on which the two groups hold "strikingly similar positions" is "their understanding of the forces which perpetuate female subordination" (1982, p. 27). They quote from socialist feminist Juliet Mitchell's essay, "The Longest Revolution", published in *New Left Review* in 1966:

> "The problem of the subordination of women and the need for their liberation was recognized by all the great socialist thinkers in the nineteenth century," she wrote. "It is part of the classical heritage of the revolutionary movement. Yet today, the problem has become a subsidiary, if not an invisible element in the preoccupations of socialists. Perhaps no other major issue has been so forgotten" (Coote and Campbell, 1982, p.17).

Also, they include the following quote from Sheila Rowbotham's paper, "Women's Liberation and the New Politics", published in 1969:

> "Unless the internal process of subjugation is understood, unless the language of silence is experienced from inside and translated into the language of the oppressed communicating themselves, male hegemony will remain . . ." (Coote and Campbell, 1982, p. 17).

In their discussion of radical feminism, Coote and Campbell make the following comment on the original radical feminist groups of New York City:

Their most important contributions to feminist thinking, and the foundation stones of their own politics, have been their designation of women as an oppressed class and their formulation of the "pro-woman line" (Coote and Campbell, p. 27).

Also, they focus briefly on the work of Shulamith Firestone, a founder-member of Redstockings and author of *The Dialectic of Sex* (1971):

She argues that pregnancy and the dependence of small children upon their mothers put women at a disadvantage from the start of human society and make it possible for men to wield power over them. Since then, she says, those first causes of inequality have been overcome . . .

Yet men have maintained their supremacy by developing ideas and customs which enhance the dependence of children upon adults as well as that of women upon men (Coote and Campbell, p. 27).

Later expressions of radical feminism—which, they say, "were more determinedly separatist than the Redstockings' manifesto or the 1972 statement of UK radical feminists" (p. 30)—included the work of Sheila Jeffreys (1977) and the Leeds Revolutionary Feminist Group (1979). Again, the theme of women's oppression was central. Sheila Jeffreys, in her paper "The Need for Revolutionary Feminism", said the task of translating radical feminist political theory into a revolutionary strategy would include

the determination to wrest power from the ruling group and to end their domination. It requires the identification of the ruling group, its power base, its methods of control, its interests, its historical development, its weaknesses and the best methods to destroy its power (Coote and Campbell, p. 30).

It is apparent, then, that regardless of differences in manner of expression and degree of radicalism, the common themes running throughout all radical and socialist feminist literature in Western societies have been, and are, anger at the continued oppression of women and the call for the liberation of women from such oppression.

In Australia, Germaine Greer's *The Female Eunuch* (1970) shook the nation at its very roots and demanded that the second-class status of women be acknowledged and changed. She urged women to reject the status quo. She upset people by insisting that "women must learn how to question the most basic assumptions about feminine normality in order to reopen the possibilities for development which have been successfully locked off by conditioning" (p. 4) and, in a manner that was outrageous at the time, she spoke of "rebellion" and "revolution" (pp. 310–52).

The work of Anne Summers in *Damned Whores and God's Police: The Colonization of Women in Australia* (1975) emerged as an important historical account of the particular oppressions of Australian women since the early days of white settlement. She argued that the early stereotypes of women, either as "damned whores" (servicing the sexual needs of men) or as "God's police" (guarding the morals of the community), continue to keep women colonised today (pp. 197–263).

Feminist demands

The demands that feminist groups have made at different periods in history are revealing, also, because they reflect the particular areas of women's lives where the majority have experienced oppression.

Susan Faludi's historical overview in Chapter Three of *Backlash: The Undeclared War against Women* gives a brief account of the four most recent periods of feminist uprising in the United States and the backlash that followed each of those periods. This glimpse of the periods of feminist struggle throughout history is important for our purposes, because the demands made by women in each of these periods highlight the areas of women's oppression at that time.

First, Faludi points to the struggle for women's rights in the United States in the mid-nineteenth century, a high point of which was the Women's Rights Convention organised by Elizabeth Cady Stanton, Susan B. Anthony and others at Seneca Falls in 1848. The main issue on the agenda was women's suffrage, crucial in the fight against women's oppression because the right to vote meant the right to be recognised as an adult human being. Also on the agenda was discussion about women's rights in education, employment, health, dress reform, marital and property rights, and the issue of "voluntary motherhood" (Faludi, 1991, p. 69).

The next period of feminist uprising began early in the twentieth century when working women moved to form their own unions. The International Ladies' Garment Workers' Union was founded in 1900. Women workers went on strike, demanding decent pay and better working conditions. In addition to that, Margaret Sanger focused attention on another area of women's oppression by organising a nationwide birth-control movement aimed at freeing women from continual pregnancy and child-rearing (Faludi, p. 70).

Another period of feminist activity began in the 1940s as a direct result of World War II. With so many men away at the war, women were encouraged to join the work-force. In the United States, five to six million women poured into the workforce, two million of them into jobs in heavy industry. Women's involvement in employment outside the home revived their political energy. They saw the injustices, felt the oppression and began flooding into unions, demanding equal pay, equal rights in the workplace, child care and so on. When the war ended, millions of women were fired for no other reason than that the men needed their jobs. When it suited patriarchy, it was proclaimed that the "God-given" task of every woman was to stay at home, creating a happy, peaceful, harmonious atmosphere for her man, having babies and serving the needs of her partner and children happily and ungrudgingly (Faludi, pp. 71–3).

Women's discontent lay smouldering under the surface till the mid-1960s when authors like Betty Friedan, Germaine Greer and Kate Millett began writing courageously about women's subordination, women's oppression by men, and women's extreme disillusionment and unhappiness. So began another wave of feminist uprising that continues today, in spite of the fierce backlash that has made every effort to destroy it (Faludi, pp. 74f). At this time, women began talking to each other in earnest. Through consciousness-raising groups, many women had their eyes opened to the extent and multifaceted expressions of women's collective and individual oppression. It became obvious that the problems that each individual woman was experiencing at home and in the wider society, for which she had consistently blamed herself, were in fact problems that most women were having to contend with.

Women flooded into universities and into the workplace. They began speaking out against violence, rape, incest, injustice, racism, inequality and war. They began demanding a better deal in relationships with men. Divorce statistics rose. Sole-parent families became commonplace.

Women began demonstrating at political rallies, and the demands around which they united were an indicator of the major areas of women's oppression in the 1960s and 1970s. It was at this time that women workers in Australia became very active in the struggle for women's rights. In Zelda D'Aprano's account of her personal involvement in the trade union movement, *Zelda: The Becoming of a Woman* (1995), she describes the dawning of her awareness that trade unions in the 1960s and 1970s never concerned themselves with the pain or problems of women:

> It wasn't until I became a feminist that I was able to examine my union struggle as a woman, and this was a new aspect to me . . .
>
> I never once at a trade union meeting brought up the question of child care centres or pre-school facilities . . . No men ever brought this matter up either (p. 158).

In January 1969, Zelda began working in the office of the Sausage Workers' Union. At a Left Action Conference in Sydney, as the conference was gearing up to begin, she recalls, "I became aware that all the people assembled on the stage were men; there wasn't a single woman seated there although at least one third of the people at the conference were women." Realising this, Zelda then "approached the microphone and raised objections to the all-male panel on the stage and demanded woman representation". And, as she says, her demands were accepted and attended to (p. 164).

The demand for wage justice was another issue women workers were involved with at that time. When a test case for equal pay was to be heard before the Arbitration Commission, women were used by the sausage industry and the Australian Council of Trade Unions (ACTU) to support union demands. Zelda D'Aprano describes the mood:

> There was great optimism felt about the forthcoming case . . . The time of the case hearing was upon us and women from the sausage factories were brought into the court to support their claim. I was asked to go along with them and together we marched up and down the street in front of the court building, holding our placards and chanting slogans (pp. 165–6).

When the time came for the hearing, however, it was a different situation entirely. All the judges were male, Zelda noted, and all those arguing the case, for and against, were male. The role given to the women was as follows:

> The women sat there day after day as if we were mute, while the men presented evidence for and against our worth. It was humiliating to have to sit there and not say anything about our own worth. I found the need to sit there silent almost beyond my control (p. 166).

The final decision in the equal pay case, Zelda recalls, meant very little change for women.

> To the women in the sausage industry, the result meant an extra three per cent of women obtained equal pay, and as nine per cent were already getting equal pay, this meant a total of twelve per cent of women in the industry would now obtain wage justice (p. 168).

After that, "All was silent from the unions about the question of equal pay" (p. 169), a situation which enabled the women to see that "the question of equal pay was only being used by these men to further their own ends" (p. 170).

During a discussion "about all of these aspects" between Zelda and her friend Dianne Ronberg, who was a member of the Victorian Employed Women's Organisation Council (VEWOC), they agreed "that something more than just talking was needed to draw attention to the pay injustice meted out to women" (p. 170).

Believing that "the Commonwealth Government should set an example by giving equal pay to women in government employment", Zelda began to formulate a plan of action. What followed was the event for which Zelda D'Aprano is most remembered. She explains:

> Following the meeting [of the VEWOC] at the city square, several of the women accompanied me to the Commonwealth Building where within seconds I was chained across the doors. The other women walked up and down with the placards which called upon the government to grant women equal pay.
>
> I did not know how long I would be there, I was very nervous but it had to be done and I was prepared for anything (p. 171).

When the media asked her why she was protesting in this way, she explained that she was "protesting against the injustice done to women over the right to equal pay". When asked how she felt about being the only woman prepared to protest in this way, she said, "today it was me, tomorrow there would be two, then four women, and it would go on until all women were demanding their rights" (p. 171).

In other Western countries, courageous women like Zelda D'Aprano were also demonstrating and demanding changes be made to improve the situation of women. In Britain, the first International Women's Day marches in London and Liverpool took place in March 1971 in support of four basic demands: equal pay for equal work, equal education and job opportunities, free contraception and abortion on demand, and free 24-hour child care (Coote and Campbell, p. 24). In 1975, further demands were added: "'financial and legal independence', and 'an end to all discrimination against lesbians and a woman's right to define her own sexuality'." Then, at a national conference in 1978, the following demands were articulated:

> "freedom from intimidation by threat or use of violence or sexual coercion, regardless of marital status; and an end to all laws, assumptions and institutions which perpetuate male dominance and men's aggression towards women" (Coote and Campbell, p. 26).

Today, these same demands are still being made by women in all Western countries because, sadly, although much is said to have changed, there is much that remains the same. Women still do not receive equal pay for equal work. They still do not have equal opportunity in education or employment. Free—and safe—contraception and abortion on demand are still not available, and there is still a long way to go before free 24-hour child care is available. Women still do not have financial and legal independence. Lesbians are still discriminated against. Women are still not free to define their own sexuality. Violence against women in the form of intimidation as well as actual physical and sexual violence is still a reality. Male dominance and male aggression toward women are still encouraged and supported by society's male-dominated institutions: governments, universities, the law, the church. While such oppression of women continues, feminist demands will remain the same.

Feminist issues

The issues receiving particular attention by Australian feminists in recent years are another indication of the level of oppression that still exists for women despite our demands for change. We will look at several.

Violence in the home

Studies commissioned by federal and state governments in recent years reveal an alarming rate of domestic violence in Australian society and an alarming degree of acceptance of such violence by women and men alike.[4] Of concern to Australian feminists is the extent to which violence is condoned as an inevitable means of resolving disputes.

The Australian Institute of Criminology's second national conference on violence, held in Canberra in June 1993, heard that the rate of physical and sexual assault against women had increased sharply since the early 1970s and that the incidence of such violence in Australia was high by international standards. Senator Rosemary Crowley, then Minister assisting the Prime Minister on the Status of Women, raised the question of the role of those institutions concerned with law and order by querying the low arrest rate of male offenders in cases of violence against women. "If violence is considered a crime," she said, "why is it that so few arrests and convictions are made against perpetrators of violence against women?"

The fact is that *all* women are oppressed by violence and the threat of violence, and that that oppression is made worse when male violence against women is treated so lightly by those institutions in society that purport to be concerned with law and order.

---

4. One of several reports commissioned by the federal government is: Public Policy Research Centre, *Community Attitudes Towards Domestic Violence in Australia*, 1988. Examples of reports commissioned by state governments are: NSW Domestic Violence Committee, *Report of NSW Domestic Violence Committee to the Premier*, 1985; Women's Policy Co-ordination Unit, Department of Premier and Cabinet (Victoria), *Criminal Assault in the Home: Social and Legal Responses to Domestic Violence*, 1985; and *Beyond These Walls*, 1988 Report of the Queensland Domestic Violence Task Force to the Minister for Family Services and Housing.

Rape

In 1992, the Australian Institute of Criminology conducted a national survey about rape and sexual abuse in conjunction with an ABC TV documentary called "Without Consent". The responses of the women who courageously told their stories in that survey have been brought together by Patricia Easteal in her book, *Voices of the Survivors* (1994). This book is a powerful account of the experiences of almost 3000 respondents who spoke of having been raped by husbands, estranged partners, relatives, boyfriends, acquaintances, bosses, doctors, priests and strangers.

Although rape and incest are common experiences of women and girls, and despite the fact that they cause extensive emotional and psychological trauma to the victims, they are crimes that still go largely unreported due, it is suggested, to the oppressive attitudes of many police and judges. Jocelynne Scutt, in a paper titled "Language, Law and Liability: The case of the credible client" (Mayo lecture, James Cook University, 30 April 1993), commented on the incidence of sexual assault in Australia and, in particular, the attitudes of some judges toward the crime of rape. Some, she said, appeared to see rape and consensual sexual intercourse as almost interchangeable. One judge, she said, had suggested a rape victim was not traumatised because she had been knocked unconscious before being raped. In another case, the fact that the victim was a prostitute was held to be a mitigating factor. Yet another judge had commented that "no" from a woman often meant "yes".

Not only are rape and the fear of rape high on the list of atrocities that oppress women in Western societies, but so also is the treatment that rape victims often receive at the hands of doctors, police, lawyers and judges.

Pornography

The effect on women of the existence and growing acceptance of pornography has been spelled out by Sheila Jeffreys in her careful treatment of the so-called sexual revolution, *Anti-climax: A Feminist Perspective on the Sexual Revolution*. She says pornography was "derepressed" as a result of the "sexual revolution", and became a massive, multibillion-dollar industry (1990, p. 250). "Decensorship, which was based upon the derepression of sadomasochism and womanhatred, allowed pornography to come in from the cold" (p. 251).

It has been suggested by some that the sexual revolution played an important part in women's liberation, but feminist anti-pornography groups that formed in the late 1970s saw it differently. As Jeffreys points out:

> Pornography gave the lie to any idea that women were gradually achieving equality. Pornography made it clear that what constituted sex under male supremacy was precisely the eroticised subordination of women. Inequality was sexy and the sexiness of this inequality was the grease that oiled the machinery of male supremacy (p. 251).

Feminists concerned about violence exposed the link between pornography and men's violence against women:

Pornography could not be ignored by feminists who were concerned to end male violence. An examination of pornography revealed that all the varieties of male violence against women were depicted in pornography as pleasurable to men and to women too. Women raped and tortured in pornography claimed to love and seek their abuse. Incest was shown as harmless and good fun for all the family. It became clear that pornography provided a textbook for and justification of such violence (p. 252).

Sheila Jeffreys, Andrea Dworkin, Catharine MacKinnon and other feminists writing against pornography agree that "all pornography teaches the inferiority of women" (Jeffreys, p. 253).

Reproductive technologies

Another issue of concern to feminists is that of reproductive technology. Commenting on the oppressive nature of the reproductive technology industry, Robyn Rowland says: "In this field the social control of women through control over women's bodies and procreation is played out with a medical and social justification" (1988, p. 163).

Again, in her more recent book, *Living Laboratories: Women and Reproductive Technologies*, Rowland reminds us:

Men have always been concerned with controlling women's fertility and the "products" of that fertility. That control has ranged from laws which circumscribe women's access to contraception and abortion to religious and political controls which set the appropriate rates of reproduction for women (1992, p. 8).

In 1989, Renate Klein wrote about the use and abuse of women's bodies in the name of reproductive technology. She says: "what is claimed to be 'treatment' is, in fact, a process of trial and error, and women's bodies are the experimental test-sites" (1989c, p. 230). Also, women entering IVF programmes are rarely told the true statistics. Klein reminds us that an "Australian government report concludes that the success rate for an 'unproblematic live birth' is 4.8 per cent . . . That means that at least 95 out of 100 women will *not* have an unproblematic live birth!" (Klein, 1989c, p. 233).

Robyn Rowland, discussing "the fragmentation and dismemberment of women", says:

Reproductive technology concerns itself with the control and manipulation of women's bodies; it is based on an ideological assumption that woman equals (inefficient) nature and that male medicine can do better. It constantly fragments and dismembers women during this process, and it uses women as experimental subjects, without obtaining their educated consent (1992, pp. 215–16).

A woman's oppression does not end when she finishes with the IVF programme. Klein reminds us that, regardless of the low success rate associated with the IVF procedure, it is always the woman herself who is deemed to have failed, not the technology. According to the language of IVF doctors: she had "bad" eggs; her womb was a "hostile environment"; "nature's best incubator" failed. "The technology is never blamed for failing" (p. 230). Klein goes on to describe the trauma every woman experiences at this point:

The woman who has "failed", even with technology's help, is thrown by the way-side. She is only a "bad statistic"—no longer of medical interest, she is left to her own devices. After years of traumatic ups and downs, often with her career abandoned, the relationship with her partner sometimes strained to breaking point and now too old to be considered for adoption, she finally has to come to grips with the fact that she might never have her own (or another) biological child. She must go through the process of upheaval and grieving this entails and get on with her life (1989c, pp. 230–1).

The collective oppression of women through the existence of violence, rape, pornography, reproductive technology and all other situations where women are demeaned, is played out on a daily basis in the personal lives of individual women. Every day, individual women experience oppression in their homes, in the workplace, in education, and in society at large.

Individual effects of oppression

Recent studies by feminist theorists have enquired into the effect women's collective and individual oppression has on their psychological health. Three common problem-areas for women suffering the effects of oppression are: anxiety and panic conditions, depression and eating disorders.

Anxiety and panic conditions

My own research into anxiety disorders led me to the conclusion that anxiety and panic conditions in women are directly attributable to women's powerlessness, invisibility and emotional deprivation (1992, p. 49).

A puzzling fact about the prevalence of anxiety and panic conditions is that, even though women are said to be gaining more power as a result of the feminist movement, anxiety is becoming more prevalent rather than less. More and more women are finding themselves afflicted with this confusing, frightening, debilitating condition in an age when women supposedly have more power. An obvious explanation for such a situation is that, while it appears on the surface women have made great gains, in truth nothing has changed substantially. Anxiety is caused not by a woman's growing awareness of injustice, not by her anger, not by her involvement with feminism, but by an unconscious, inexplicable, empty feeling that "something is still not right" (p. 73).[5]

Depression

Feminist research into depression in women reaches similar conclusions about cause. To understand and deal adequately with depression, say Kathy Nairne and Gerrilyn Smith, it must be seen "both as an individual experience and a political process" (1984, p. 6). Their book, *Dealing with Depression*, makes a clear point about the connection

---

5. For a detailed discussion of powerlessness, invisibility and emotional deprivation as causes of anxiety, see Chapters Three, Four and Five of my book, *Overcoming Anxiety: A Positive Approach to Dealing with Severe Anxiety in your Life* (1992).

between depression and oppression. "Depression *is* connected to oppression", they say. "In effect, women are forced down to be kept down; depressed to be oppressed" (p. 7). They make the point that it is more correct to say women "are depressed" than to say "women 'get depressed' (as if we seek it out) or 'suffer from depression' (as if it were a physical illness)". The fact is that "women are depressed by their life experiences" (p. 7).

In a discussion of the psychoanalytic contention that depression occurs when one turns hostile feelings in upon oneself, they comment: "It is not surprising that women feel depressed when we live in a women-hating world. What is more puzzling is why some of us are not depressed" (p. 10).

Linda Bailey, in *How to Get Going When You Can Barely Get Out of Bed*, argues that it is the "female sex role", the training every girl receives from the beginning of her life, that "sets the stage for depression" (1984, p. 11). Through her socialisation, every woman "has been trained to forfeit her capacity to act in her own behalf or create the life she desires, an education which will predispose her to depression" (p. 13).

In stating the connection between depression and oppression so clearly, feminist therapy is offering a challenge to those who work with marginalised groups in any culture. If depression is a result of oppression, as we believe it is, then it is not unrealistic to assume that those who suffer a double oppression (for example, the combined effects of racism and sexism) have twice the chance of suffering from depression. Indeed, with every oppression one suffers, when marginalisation is added to marginalisation—on the basis of sex, race, class, disability, sexual preference, etc.—the potential for depression is magnified accordingly.

An Aboriginal woman who had been sexually abused from the age of four, who was physically and sexually assaulted by her husband for twenty years, who had known nothing but poverty all her life, and who turned to alcohol and suffered the humiliations that alcoholic women know so well, one day doused herself with petrol and set herself alight outside the shops in her community. Mainstream society expressed horror and asked "Why?", but to those who had any understanding at all of the connection between oppression and depression, between the lifetime of oppressions this woman endured and her deep unfathomable depression, the reason was all too clear.

Eating disorders

In addition to anxiety conditions and depression, eating disorders also are caused by women's oppression. Naomi Wolf, in *The Beauty Myth*, reminds us of some frightening statistics:

> 90–95% of anorexics and bulimics are women . . . the American Anorexia and Bulimia Association states that anorexia and bulimia strike a million women *every year* . . . Each year, according to the Association, 150,000 American women die of anorexia (1990, p. 148).

According to Wolf, it is no accident that so many women, now that we have the potential to be more powerful than we have ever been, are obsessed with notions of beauty. "We are in the midst of a violent backlash to feminism", she says, "that uses images of female beauty as a political weapon against women's advancement" (p. 2).

She points to research by Wooley and Wooley confirming that "concern with weight leads to 'a virtual collapse of self-esteem and sense of effectiveness'". Again, "Polivy and Herman found that 'prolonged and periodic caloric restriction' resulted in a distinctive personality whose traits are 'passivity, anxiety and emotionality'" (p. 153). Wolf goes on to say:

> It is these traits, and not thinness for its own sake, that the dominant culture wants to create in the private sense of self of recently liberated women so as to cancel out the dangers of their liberation.
>
> Women's advances had begun to give them the opposite traits—high self-esteem, a sense of effectiveness, activity, courage and clarity of mind. "Prolonged and periodic caloric restriction" is a means to take the teeth out of this revolution (pp. 153–4).

This look at the most common emotional and psychological problem-areas for women —anxiety and panic conditions, depression and eating disorders—shows clearly that these and other such problems are the result of women's collective and individual oppression in a society determined to keep women weakened and in an inferior position. When women take steps to improve our self-esteem and increase our power in society, the forces of the backlash simply work harder to undermine our emerging sense of self and put a stop to our progress.

The fact that *oppression is at the root of most emotional and psychological problems affecting women* makes it urgent that feminists develop an alternative therapy. It must begin with an analysis of women's oppression and proceed in a way that takes seriously the connection between the fact of women's oppression and the deep feelings of helplessness and hopelessness that prompt women to seek the help of a therapist.

The second point to be considered about oppression will simply be alluded to here and then discussed more fully in Part Three. It refers to what this book calls "psychoppression", by which I mean that *most therapies actually add to the oppression of women by encouraging them to look within themselves for the cause of their unhappiness and encouraging them to take full responsibility for their own pain and despair.*

Psychoanalysis, the humanist therapies, New Age therapies, popular psychology, and lesbian sex therapy, all place the focus on the individual. They insist that the problem is within the woman who is feeling badly, and any attempt to look at the context of her life is seen as a diversion.

Feminist therapy, however, insists that every woman who presents for therapy be seen in the context of her whole life, and that the problems she is experiencing in the present be seen in relation to the fact of her oppression. In contrast to other therapies that see women as "sick" or as being "responsible for their own problems", feminist therapy holds the view that every woman who comes for therapy has been and continues to be oppressed, and is in need of liberation. It is from that basic assumption that therapy proceeds.

Before leaving the issue of oppression and moving on to look at access, it is important to emphasise that the above discussion of oppression is vital to the development of a feminist therapy, in that it establishes the basic reason why the feminist movement must involve itself urgently in a therapy that is radical and political. Throughout this chapter, four important assertions have been made:

- the oppression of women in Western societies is a fact;
- oppression causes most of the emotional and psychological problems that prompt women to seek therapy;
- the more oppressions a woman suffers (on the basis of race, class, disability, etc.), the greater the potential for emotional and psychological distress; and
- traditional, New Age and popular therapies *add* to the oppression of women by encouraging them to blame themselves for the problems they encounter.

3

ACCESS AND HONESTY

While the issue of oppression stands by itself, in that it points to the actual cause of most of the emotional and psychological distress experienced by women, the other four—access, honesty, passion and justice—stand in relationship to each other, in that they refer to the actual practice of therapy. Though related in this way, each of the four issues will be discussed separately.

Access

Mainstream psychotherapy seems to operate on the assumption that all people have access to therapy if they want it but, as the following discussion reveals, such an assumption is not valid. Access to mainstream therapy is available only to those who fit comfortably into the mainstream therapeutic system presently being offered. This system is not readily accessible to those who are different in terms of race, ethnic background, physical and intellectual ability, sexual orientation and so on, nor is it accessible to those who refuse to play the therapeutic game the way mainstream therapies intend it to be played.

The question of access for members of marginalised groups is a difficult one in the development of a feminist therapy. It is imperative, here, that we avoid the simplistic response which insists that all therapists and all community agencies offering therapy be made accessible to anyone and everyone who wants to use whatever services they choose. Those who favour this approach must be warned that such a situation would serve the purposes of "equality" rather than "equity". It would open the way for dominant groups to take over (in the name of equality) those services that have been established (for the purposes of equity) to respond to the specific needs of oppressed, marginalised groups.

"Equality" demands that men have equal access to services offered at women's centres, that whites have equal access to services offered at Aboriginal and Islander centres, that people from English-speaking backgrounds have access to services for those of non-English speaking backgrounds, and that the able-bodied have access to services set up specifically to cater to the needs of those who have a disability. "Equity", on the other hand, demands that the effects of negative discrimination be reversed by a process of positive discrimination and that services be made available for the specific and exclusive purpose of responding to the needs of members of disempowered groups.

The issue in relation to access to therapy, then, is not that all therapy must be made accessible to all people at all times, but rather, that therapists be honest about the accessibility of the therapy they offer. Mainstream therapies are often not accessible to minority group members, nor are they necessarily appropriate since they tend to reinforce the existing power structures, and it is for these reasons that special services are required.

Inaccessibility on the basis of race is obvious when one considers that all Western therapies available to date, including radical therapy and feminist therapy, have been developed by middle-class whites with middle-class whites in mind and consequently are not readily accessible to anyone else. The answer to the access problem in relation to Aboriginal and Islander people, however, does not lie in all white therapists learning to do therapy the Aboriginal or Islander way. Such a response would be false. Rather, the answer lies in white therapists, first, being honest with ourselves about the accessibility of the therapy we offer; second, employing Aboriginal or Islander workers wherever possible, so that accessibility can become a reality; and finally, giving our support (whenever it is requested) to Aboriginal and Islander people and agencies who are working to develop counselling services within their own communities.

Gracelyn Smallwood, the first chairperson of the North Queensland Tripartite Forum set up to advise and assist governments in the formulation of policy to improve health among Aboriginals and Torres Strait Islanders, gave a paper at a conference in Brisbane in 1992. Toward the beginning of her paper, called "Cross Cultural Mental Health: North Queensland Perspective", Smallwood argued that "culturally appropriate services are urgently needed" to respond to the mental distress that is "a common and crippling problem for many Aboriginal and Islander people" (p. 2). She went on to say:

> While some progress has been made in resolving some mental health problems, there is still no culturally appropriate service for Aboriginal people in Queensland. Mental health services are co-ordinated and controlled by the dominant white society and do not take into account Aborigines laws, customs and beliefs. Service provision and delivery is based on the values of a dominant and ethnocentric Anglo-Saxon bureaucracy (p. 4).

To illustrate the urgent need for culturally appropriate mental health services, she gave the following example:

> In one North Queensland institution, a group of young Aborigines were diagnosed as being mentally unstable. As soon as the black nurse went in to visit them, the youths were open and responsive in their communication with her. It also became apparent in the course of the interaction with the nurse, that what they in fact required was someone who was genuinely empathic and could communicate at their level, someone who shared a similar

cultural orientation. The youths emphasised they did not want to talk to white people about their problems (p. 9).

The question of access is not simply about access to therapy. It is also about access to help through therapy, or more correctly, about access to liberation from oppression through therapy. With regard to women, feminist therapy makes it clear that, wherever possible, women should seek therapy from women, regardless of how "sensitive" or "understanding" a particular male therapist may appear to be. It is simply a contradiction to expect that an oppressed person will be liberated from her oppression at the hands of a member of the oppressing group. Similarly, for an Aboriginal or Islander person, access to liberation through therapy will not be readily available at the hands of a white oppressor.

To summarise, then, there is a need for white, middle-class therapists to be more honest with themselves about the degree of accessibility their therapy offers to people from non-mainstream groups in society and, in line with the concept of equity, give support to the setting-up of alternative services.

The other point about access that requires attention is the fact that mainstream therapy is accessible only to those who are prepared to play the therapeutic game as dictated by the "experts".

Psychoanalysis is accessible only to those who are willing to accept that they are sick and in need of treatment. It is accessible only to those who are willing to see the therapist as expert and to cooperate with the expert's interpretation of how therapy should proceed. The therapist is in charge, and anyone who seeks help must be committed to trying to understand and accept the expert's diagnosis and treatment. To want something different is called "resistance" and is taken as a further sign of mental instability.

Some humanist therapies are accessible only if a person, first, has the ability to understand and second, is open to learning the particular system used. Transactional Analysis with its system of interactions or transactions between people in terms of parent, adult and child, is one such therapy.

The problem for those therapies that depend on a particular system of knowledge or a particular therapeutic procedure is that, before a person can receive help, that person is required to learn how to be a good recipient of therapy. In other words, a woman has to move out of her own reality, her own normal way of thinking and relating, in order to gain any benefit from therapy. Such a situation speaks of a fairly serious access problem!

The feminist assumption is that, in order for a therapy to be accessible and helpful, it must exist totally to *respond* to whatever situation presents itself. It is not acceptable for a therapist to approach a therapy session either with a set of preconceived ideas about the person who has come for help, or with an agenda about how the session will proceed. The therapist's role, especially during the initial session, is to listen, empathise, be patient, be alert, and respond appropriately to the woman's expressed need. Feminist therapy, in contrast to mainstream therapies, begins with the assumption that one woman talking with another woman about a problem she is having is a normal occurrence in life. No therapeutic games are needed. What is needed is for the therapist to be real and for the situation to be as "normal" as possible.

Some women have experimented with alternative approaches to therapy. One alternative approach, which pays careful attention to the question of accessibility for all women, is that of Melbourne Women's Circus. Initially set up to work with survivors of sexual assault, it has effectively drawn in women from a range of backgrounds. The development of circus skills in a safe and uncompetitive environment has the effect of increasing women's self-esteem, thereby countering the effects of oppression. There are limits on the number of women able to join at any one time, but access is open to all women regardless of age, ability, background or sexual orientation.

Honesty

The third issue to be considered in the development of a philosophical base for a feminist therapy is honesty.[1] It may seem strange to speak of honesty as a radical political concept but, in the context of the ever-expanding psychotherapy industry, it seems that honesty is often not the first choice of many psychiatrists, psychotherapists and counsellors and must, therefore, be given special attention here.

The following is a discussion of the kinds of dishonest attitudes and practices that exist in mainstream and New Age therapies today.

Ignoring the reality of oppression

In the early 1970s, Phyllis Chesler criticised psychotherapy because of its dishonesty in dealing with women. Those therapists who focused on inner dynamics and ignored the reality of women's oppression set up a situation, she said, where women were never able to have "real" conversations with their therapists. When one is discouraged from talking about that which is real in one's life, for the reason that it is not judged to be appropriate material for a therapy session, then the whole therapeutic encounter is based on unreality (Chesler, 1972, p. 110).

The most notable of therapists who chose not to believe women's stories in therapy, particularly those that told of childhood sexual abuse, was Freud. It seems that the real stories of women's lives were not appropriate in his view, and so he turned them into something else (see Chapter Five).

While therapists today are more likely to believe women's stories of abuse and oppression because of the general acceptance in Western societies that such things do happen, many of them nevertheless still question a woman's perception of the extent of the abuse. Women are often accused of "exaggerating" or of "over-dramatising". Indeed, it is not unusual to hear therapists comment to their colleagues: "It couldn't

---

1. The need for honesty was highlighted by Adrienne Rich (1979) in her now classic selection of articles on the ways in which women are lied to, mystified and ignored: *On Lies, Secrets and Silence: Selected Prose 1966–1978.*

have been as bad as she made out", or "If he's really as violent as she says, she would have left him long ago." Such trivialising of women's experiences in the minds of therapists results in therapy sessions that deal with something other than the "real" problems of women.

Another form of ignoring women's oppression occurs when both the therapist and the woman who has come for therapy pretend the problem is something other than what they both know it is. The simplest form of this is when a woman insists on taking the blame for a bad relationship even though it is clear that it is her husband who is mostly at fault. The therapist and the woman are both aware that the only way this relationship will ever improve is for the husband to make some major changes in attitude and behaviour, but since he refuses to accept any blame at all for his partner's distress, the only way to proceed is to work *as if* it is the woman herself who is at fault. This sort of pretence is extremely dishonest, for two reasons: first, because it encourages the woman to believe it really is *she* who is at fault and that there may be something *she* can do to change the situation when, in fact, the therapist knows there is not; and second, because it allows the one who is causing such distress to continue in his destructive ways believing that his partner's dissatisfaction with the relationship is all in her head and has nothing to do with him.

Mystification

Mystification is another dishonest practice adopted by many mainstream therapists. Mystification, which is "the act of making mysterious", is designed to give the mystifier power over the mystified. A therapist who practises mystification has a need to outwit or outsmart the one who has come for help. The attitude is: what you say about your life, and what your instincts tell you about what is going on in your life, are not as significant as what I (the therapist) "know" about you.

Therapy, in most instances, is a reasonably simple process, but the need many therapists have to feel "clever" causes them to practise mystification, that is, to turn the therapeutic process into something much more complicated than it ought to be.

Labelling is the most common form of mystification. Therapists of all persuasions are taught, in their training, that one of the first things they must do with patients/clients is "assess" them. If therapists get the assessment right, then they will be able to attach the right "label" and, having attached the right label, they will have no trouble "treating" the condition.

One of the problems with labelling is that it serves to depersonalise interactions. For many doctors and psychiatrists, attaching a label to someone after the initial therapy session means it is then not necessary to listen to what that person may want to say in subsequent sessions. Drugs to suit the label are prescribed and all that is seen to be required after the initial session is a series of fifteen-minute appointments to check on how the drugs are working, and to change the drugs or the dosage whenever required.

As well as depersonalising interactions, the act of labelling gives tremendous power to the labeller, particularly when the labeller is a psychiatrist. The increasing importance placed on psychiatrists' reports in legal circles is a good example. The trend towards lighter sentences for serious crimes when a psychiatrist's report is given to "explain" the perpetrator's behaviour is worrying.

While it is important that courts do not ignore psychological evidence that enables real justice to be done, as in the case of women who murder their husbands after years of violent abuse, or of sons who murder their fathers after a prolonged history of sexual abuse, it is nevertheless a concern that such psychological reports can also be used in the service of injustice. Lawyers defending men charged with serious crimes such as assault, rape, attempted murder and murder invariably seek a psychiatrist's report as evidence in defence of their client's "innocence" or "diminished responsibility".

The label "dissociation" has become a favourite in recent times. A man who rationally and deliberately placed a knife in his briefcase, drove to his ex-wife's home and stabbed her several times before leaving her to die, was said to be "dissociated" at the time of the stabbing, according to a newspaper report. The very light sentence he received makes it obvious that the psychiatrist's report claiming dissociation carried more weight than the glaring evidence of intent.

Again, a man on trial for the shooting murder of another man who, he said, had made sexual advances toward him, was analysed by a psychiatrist who then testified that he could have been in a "dissociated state" at the time of the shooting. The psychiatrist was quoted in a local newspaper as saying: "When we take action we are governed by our feelings, whether they are good feelings or bad feelings. In that case I don't think a person could make a willed choice." There is something very unjust about using psychiatric labels in defence of someone who, in full command of his senses, went and got a gun, went back to the man who had offended him to demand an apology, and then shot him.[2]

What does "dissociate" really mean? What do any of the labels really mean— personality disorder, borderline personality, hypomania? That psychiatric labels are used at all indicates an intent to mystify, and such mystification places amazing power in the hands of psychiatric professionals.

The power of labelling given to psychiatrists can and often does result in feelings of utter powerlessness and untold misery for those being labelled. The confidential nature of psychiatric reports means that even the one who is the subject of one of these reports can have great difficulty gaining access to it. Consequently, those who write them are rarely held accountable for what they write.

The following is an analysis of a psychiatrist's report shown to me by the young woman about whom the report was written. According to the young woman (who has

---

2. While I am aware of a number of cases, during my lifetime, where women have been charged with murdering their male partners after years of abuse, I cannot recall one case in which the psychiatric label of dissociation was used as a defence. Even when a defence of provocation is allowed, women are judged to have acted in full control of their senses. Are we to believe it is only men who "dissociate", or is that just a convenient label when no other explanation is apparent?

given permission for the report to be discussed in this context), her employer insisted she see the psychiatrist when her "depression" began interfering with her work. The report, written by the psychiatrist after only one session with her, began: "[She] presented as a thin thirty year old woman . . . She impressed as being very dependent."

The label "very dependent" is the first of many labels throughout the report, and even though it is rightly expressed as an impression and not as a psychiatric diagnosis, there is no doubt (because of the power given to psychiatrists and their reports) that it would be read by her employer as a definitive diagnosis.

Reference is made in the report to two previous psychiatric reports the writer had access to. The result was a highly damaging profile of a woman who, in my estimation, could be said to be simply lonely and depressed due to the alienating circumstances of her life. In addition to "very dependent", other labels in the report were: "depression", "mood instability", "perceived rejection by her mother", "affective disorder", "the possibility of hypomania", "allows herself to be exploited (by men)", "obsessed", "very poor self-image" and "a suggestion of mood elevation".

The dishonesty inherent in such labels lies in the fact that they do not tell the real story. Indeed they give, if not a totally false picture, then certainly a distorted one. The result is mystification, alarm, caution in the minds of those who read the report. The damage such labelling invariably does to one's reputation and career opportunities, as well as to one's own self-esteem, is not difficult to imagine.

To illustrate how different this particular report could have sounded if it had been presented without the use of destructive labels, the following (in italics) is an alternative way of expressing the same facts:

- "Depression": While the word "depression" is acceptable because of its now common usage in our vocabulary, it should only be used if accompanied by an explanation. *She is depressed because the men she has been involved with thus far have used and abused her and then cast her aside.*

- "Mood instability": *She smiles and laughs a lot because she has learned that people expect women to be pleasant and positive. At other times, she cries a lot because she is deeply sad.*

- "Perceived rejection by her mother": The word "perceived" implies that it did not really happen, that the young woman simply made it up, but the facts reveal something quite different. *When she was six years old, her mother disappeared out of her life. At sixteen, after finally tracking her mother down, she made contact only to be told by her mother to leave her alone because she did not want to be a mother to anybody. She suffered actual rejection by her mother.*

- "Affective disorder": Similar to "mood instability".

- "The possibility of hypomania": The label "hypomania" means "mild, short-lived highs". To those not familiar with psychiatric jargon, it sounds much more serious than it actually is. Consequently, it is a highly damaging label to include in a report, particularly when it is merely a "possibility". Omit altogether.

- "Allows herself to be exploited by men": *On several occasions she has been a victim of male arrogance and exploitation.*
- "Obsessed": *When a man uses her and then throws her out, she has difficulty letting go. This proves highly inconvenient for the men involved.*
- "Very poor self-image": *The number of rejections she has suffered throughout her life have left her with a very poor self-image.*
- "A suggestion of mood elevation": *Occasionally she feels extraordinarily happy.*

As these alternative expressions illustrate, the presentation of psychiatric reports without the use of labels would make the reports sound very ordinary indeed. The problem with that for those professionals who enjoy the elevated status of powerful, clever, mysterious demi-gods is that ordinary-sounding reports give the impression that the writers themselves are ordinary people. Is it any wonder, then, that the psychiatric profession persists in using labels and, indeed, works to create new and more mystifying labels as a necessary ongoing activity of the profession?

Therapy under duress

All therapists know, or ought to know, that therapy under duress does not work, yet many agree to requests from police or parole officers that amount to nothing more than enlisting the therapist's help in attempting to force people to change their behaviour. A therapist who agrees to work with someone knowing that that person has not freely chosen to seek therapy, and knowing also that therapy under such conditions is a pointless exercise, is operating from a position of blatant dishonesty.

Another example of therapy under duress occurs when distraught parents bring their teenager for "help" when all else has failed. The problem again is that, if the teenager does not want "help", the therapy is doomed to failure. It may be important to arrange one therapy session to allow for the possibility of the teenager warming to the therapist and beginning to open up, but if that does not occur, it must be explained to the parents and to the teenager that any further sessions would be pointless. To continue, knowing that no progress is possible, would be extremely dishonest.

The most difficult situation involving duress occurs when a woman comes with a request that a therapist help her satisfy her husband's demands even though she does not want to. Such a request in therapy commonly involves the husband's sexual demands, either in terms of frequency or experimentation. When a woman refuses to be available for sex as often as her partner wants it, or when she refuses to go along with his desire to experiment with the different kinds of sex he reads about in pornographic magazines, many men threaten to "find someone else". In a desperate attempt to "keep the marriage together", a woman in this situation often seeks the help of a therapist for "her" problem.

To agree to work with her in order to help her feel better about allowing herself to be degraded and exploited, to help her put aside her own wishes and desires, to help her act against her own moral standards, amounts to nothing more than colluding with her husband to oppress her further. To use therapy in this way is dishonest in the extreme.

The honest response would be to explain to the woman that it simply would not work; that, even if she stayed in therapy for years, the time would never come when she would *want* to be degraded and exploited; and that you, the therapist, are not willing to assist in her husband's oppression of her.

All you are prepared to do in your role as therapist is work to help her learn to be more assertive, to help her feel good about saying "no", to help her gain the confidence to insist that her husband change his attitude toward her, and also, if he does not change, to help her find the courage to leave him when she feels ready to do so.

To engage in therapy knowing that a person has come to you under any form of duress is to use therapy in an oppressive and dishonest way.

Misuse of drugs

One of the most frightening examples of dishonesty in therapy occurs in relation to the use and misuse of drugs. Many doctors and psychiatrists prescribe drugs for depression, anxiety and other emotional distress as a matter of course. In many instances, there seems to be no thought given at all to possible alternative treatments nor to the possible negative effects of prescribing drugs for emotional difficulties.

Criticisms of such flippant and irresponsible use of drugs range from supportive and understanding to angry and outraged. Critics who prefer to soften their criticism with supportive comments are quick to point out that doctors in busy practices are under extreme pressure. Allowing a woman to talk about her depression takes time, they say, and time is something busy doctors do not have. They prescribe medication, therefore, as a quick response to emotional suffering. Outraged critics, on the other hand, call it "malpractice". Beatrice Faust, in her courageous and powerful exposé of the medical and pharmaceutical industries, calls it being "abused by someone we trust" (1993, p.16).

Speaking of her own five-year search for help with "a series of unfamiliar and disturbing symptoms", which she herself eventually diagnosed as the effects of benzodiazepine (Ativan) addiction, she says: "That none of the thirty or so GPs and consultants ever did query the Ativan is proof of the ignorance and complacency of the medical profession" (p.14).

If doctors and psychiatrists are so busy that they do not have time to listen to their patients, there are two obvious alternatives to the irresponsible and dishonest prescribing of drugs: either to schedule fewer patients in a day, or to refer patients on to someone who does have the time.

The need for long-term therapy

There is a mistaken belief, fostered by some therapists, that in order for therapy to be effective, it must be long term. Psychoanalysis, in particular, stresses the need for long-term therapy. People go "into" psychoanalysis and, in many cases, do not "come out" of it for years.

To present therapy as something that can solve all of one's problems, resolve all of the repressed material from one's past, and take away all imperfections if only one perseveres long enough, is dishonest. The truth is that most problems for which people seek help require only short-term therapy (two to four sessions, sometimes six). The only cases in which longer-term therapy is appropriate are those involving the need to work through and try to understand crippling events from the past. The practice of encouraging women to continue in therapy when it is not needed is dishonest and exploitative.

Everyone needs to be in therapy

Another form of long-term therapy is that which encourages people to believe everyone needs therapy and that everyone really ought to be involved in some form of therapy throughout their entire lives.

Those New Age and other modern therapy movements that seek to convince us we are all "codependent" or deficient and, as such, need to engage in a life-long quest for "healing" are dishonest (see Chapter Seven for a more detailed discussion of this point). *Therapy is not a substitute for living.* To suggest everyone needs to be in therapy is to advocate that people spend their lives standing off and observing the way they are living, instead of just getting on with it. In actual fact, the most effective therapy occurs when it is seen as nothing more than an occasional aid to be called on when it is needed throughout a person's life. To suggest otherwise is misleading and dishonest.

The above examples of dishonesty remind us of the fact that when honesty is not passionately pursued as a basic principle of therapy, the pretence that masquerades as therapy is simply another form of oppression of those already oppressed. It is imperative that feminist therapists, realising the ease with which oppression can occur in therapy, constantly examine our own attitudes and practices to make sure honesty is always a prevailing principle.

4

PASSION AND JUSTICE

Passion

Any discussion of feminist therapy must include the issue of passion. Without real passion, a person (or, indeed, a society) has no depth, and without depth, we are no more than hollow shells.

In many ways, women are set up in Western societies to be passionless. Emotions are encouraged, of course. We are permitted to be emotional, to have feelings, but we are not permitted to be passionate because a passionate woman, that is, a woman whose passions are not reined in, poses a real threat to the dominant male culture. The expectation is that women will keep their passions subdued and, being committed to pleasing others, most women work hard to oblige.

It is not surprising, then, that a common reason for women to seek therapy is the desire to try to understand and find relief from emptiness and meaninglessness, most often experienced as depression. Life is dull. Nothing is exciting. All their endeavours are experienced as futile. To make it worse, they blame themselves for the state they are in, and feel guilty.

When a depressed woman goes to mainstream therapists or doctors, many so-called professionals have a bag full of "reasons" why she might feel the way she does, and they simply put their hand into the bag and pull out one of their superficial, ill-considered diagnoses. "You're just going through a bad patch", they say. Or, "Maybe you should find something else to occupy your mind." Or, "Your hormones are all messed up." Or, "You're just getting older."

The unacceptable fact is that the normal experiences of women's lives—ovulation, menstruation, pregnancy, birth, post-natal experiences, menopause, old age—are increasingly being seen by mainstream medicine and psychiatry as problematic and, therefore, requiring medication.

From the perspective of feminist psychotherapy, the reason for such an emphasis on the part of medical and psychiatric "experts" is that it then allows them to ignore the *real* cause of the deep sense of desperation that so many women live with. Overwhelmingly, the real cause of a woman's deep depression and despair is the emptiness and meaninglessness that results from having to deny her true self and her passions.

This present work on the development of a feminist therapy owes much to Mary Daly for her important contribution on "passion". While I do not mean to claim Mary Daly's support for the development of a feminist therapy, her work on passion nevertheless offers important insights for those of us who still see some value in striving to develop a feminist therapy that is radically political.

In *Pure Lust*, Daly's examination of passion begins with the writings of medieval scholastic philosophers, moves to a discussion of two types of pseudopassion used for the purpose of crippling and freezing women's real passion, and ends with a call for us to purge ourselves of these poisonous pseudopassions through "Naming/Realizing" so that our lives can be "moved" by real passions (1984, pp. 197–216).

Her choice of medieval philosophers as a starting point "for the dis-covering of deep Elemental Passion", which she names "E-motion" (p. 198), was made on the basis of "a refreshing vigor, clarity, bluntness, and complex simplicity in that analysis that is lacking in contemporary psychobabble" (p. 198). Contemporary psychotherapy is lost in its own "mire of muddled therapeutic jargon" (p. 199). Its superficial and never-ending focus on "feelings" has the effect of preventing a clear focus on passion.

An important aspect of medieval theory, according to Daly, is the fact that

passions were understood to be *movements* of a faculty known as the "sensitive appetite", which tends toward the good and shrinks from the evil as perceived by the senses. Essential to this analysis is the idea that passions are *caused* by something that is perceived. They are movements rooted in knowledge and are not static, inexplicable blobs of "feeling" (p. 198).

The medieval philosophers named eleven passions. Six of them "are said to be movements of . . . the more basic 'part' of the sensitive appetite" (p. 198). They are *love*, *desire*, and *joy* which tend toward the good, and *hate*, *aversion*, and *sorrow* which tend away from the evil. Each passion is related to another, and each pair exists as a pair of opposites in accordance with the opposition of good and evil. Love seeks that which is perceived to be good for the person; hate rejects that which is perceived to be bad for the person. Desire moves toward the good; aversion moves away from the evil. Joy is a response to the good; sorrow is a response to the bad (p. 198).

The remaining five passions, according to medieval naming, are *hope*, *despair*, *fear*, *daring* and *anger*. Hope and despair are related in opposition to each other in the sense that hope indicates a movement toward the attainment of some perceived good, and despair indicates a shrinking from it. Fear and daring are related in the same way, but to evil rather than to good. Fear shuns evil, while daring stands up to it.

The one passion that has no opposing passion is anger. Anger is caused by an evil already present, and there is no other appropriate related or opposite passion. When a wrong has been done, one does not have the option of withdrawing because one cannot ignore an evil that is already present. The only options are either to succumb and be overwhelmed by it, or to engage in "a movement of attack on the hurtful evil, which movement is that of anger" (p. 199).

These eleven passions are said to be real passions in that they are "*caused* by something that is perceived" (p. 198). They are not static. They are movements. "Real passions are movements within us, and they move us" (p. 200).

From this discussion of "such truly moving passions", Daly goes on to expose two types of "pseudopassions which are the products of patriarchy, which paralyze women, containing and concealing our Fires, our true desires" (p. 200). The first type she calls "plastic passions" and the second, "potted passions".

Unlike real passions, which are movements connecting a woman with others and with the world in which she lives, plastic passions have no movement. They are static. They are just "there", keeping women separated, disconnected, alone. Plastic passions demand to be "dealt with" endlessly, and the more they are dealt with the more they need to be dealt with, because their function is to keep a woman frozen at that level by hiding from her the real reason for her despair. In Daly's words, "They function to hide the agents of her oppression/repression." In addition she says: "Since they have no perceivable causes, they function to serve the mechanisms of 'blaming the victim'" (p. 201).

Daly names some of the plastic passions as follows: "*guilt, anxiety, depression, hostility, bitterness, resentment, frustration, boredom, resignation, fulfillment*" (p. 201). As any therapist will readily admit, these are the "feelings" which prompt many women to seek the help of a therapist. Daly does not deny that these "unmoving, paralyzing feelings" exist. They do exist but, she says, they are not real in the sense of being "natural". They are man-made. They are "sickening substitutes that poison our powers", preventing us from experiencing real passion (p. 201).

Mainstream psychotherapy encourages a woman to focus on such feelings, to talk about them, to express pent-up emotions with a view to releasing the hold these feelings have over her life. It must be said that if such therapy is done with awareness, patience and sensitivity, it most often results in the woman feeling better, being able to resume her day-to-day activities, and participating more honestly and wholeheartedly in her relationships.

To most, that sounds like "successful" therapy which, in mainstream terms, it is. It has achieved the central aim of mainstream therapy, which is to "fix" things in the short term so that a woman can resume the part she has always played in propping up patriarchy. Moreover, if this therapy has done its job properly, she will now be even more subservient to the dominant culture. She will have learned the "value" of endlessly focusing on how she feels and will not realise that such focusing functions to keep her real passions frozen. She will not know that "her true passions . . . are being choked by these synthetic substitutes" (p. 203).

Feminist therapy must go further than simply helping a woman release her feelings. An important and necessary role for feminist therapists is that of helping raise a woman's consciousness to the way plastic passions operate to keep her paralysed, and therefore obedient, and therefore depressed or anxious or obsessive, etc. When a woman comes to the realisation that her true passions have been frozen by endless focus on pseudo-passions, and when she then finds the courage to name her true passions, she has begun a process which will free her "from the lethal fix that is freezing her" (p. 203).

Using one of the true passions (anger) as an example, Daly explains that when a woman finds the courage to name her experience of *real anger*, she is then able to see clearly the process that kept her frozen for so long.

> A woman then recognizes that when she experiences real anger—that is, Rage—at her oppressor/suppressor she is moved to action by her Rage. She sees that in contrast to this, if she is merely frozen in states that can accurately be labeled "hostile", or "bitter", or "resentful", she is not moved to act. She sees also that . . . [they] are constantly trying to convert her Rage into plastic by labeling it as "hostility", "bitterness", et cetera. They work to label it out of existence, converting it into these plastic passions . . . She sees also that these sickening substitutes are blended with anxiety, depression, guilt, frustration (p. 203).

A woman focusing endlessly on her pseudopassions is no threat to the patriarchy because all her energies are taken up with the task of striving to "understand herself" and "deal with her feelings". On the other hand, a woman who is experiencing real anger at her oppressor and who is "moved to action by her Rage" presents a real threat, because a woman stirred to action by rage will demand change.

From her discussion of plastic passions, Daly moves on to discuss the other type of pseudopassions which she refers to as "potted passions". *Potted* means "planted or grown in a pot". Potted passions are "stunted, artificially contained . . . twisted and warped versions of genuine passions". Likening them to "the nine-inch-high potted bonsai tree that could have grown eighty feet tall", she says, "these passions are dwarfed; their roots are shallow" (p. 206).

Referring to potted passions as "feelings that fragment and distort the psyche, masking Passion", Daly describes what happens to women and their "emotions":

> women are intimidated, tracked, and trained to love, desire, and rejoice in the wrong things, hate, have aversion to, and be sad over the wrong things, hope for and despair over the wrong things, fear and dare the wrong things, be angry over the wrong things. These passions are "real" in a sense (like the bonsai tree or canned orange juice) but they are less than they should be and therefore dysfunctional, potentially deadly . . . They are incomplete, and, like lies which are partial truths parading as the whole, they are substitutes for genuine e-motions, deceiving their subjects and those with whom they are connected/disconnected in this deceptive way (pp. 206–7).

Mary Daly's call for us to purge ourselves of these poisonous pseudopassions through naming/realising, thereby freeing ourselves up to be "moved" by our real passions, is not at all a simple matter, as Daly makes obvious in every page of *Pure Lust*. The pressures on women, the snares, the entrapment, the mechanisms of control over women's lives, which feminism recognises are at the base of women's pain and confusion and despair, are intense and powerful forces.

The task of feminist therapy, then, clearly begins with the need to help women confront the fact of the fragmenting and distorting of their psyches by a society that keeps power in the hands of men by conning women into believing their "happiness" and "fulfilment" lie in denying themselves and living for others. The political imperative inherent in a therapy that is feminist demands that a therapist see her task as that of helping women, first, to understand why they, so much of the time, feel separated from their real passions and, subsequently, to have the courage to name the cause of their emptiness and despair, to name their oppressors. Then, having freed themselves from endless involvement with pseudopassions, women are able to find "room for movement, for passions that are contagious, that fuel the Fire of other Furies" (p. 205).[1]

Daly's important work on passion leads us, now, to examine the situation of women in Western societies with a view to discovering the variety of ways women are robbed of passion. The following examination will, on the one hand, demonstrate the connection between a lack of real passion and the problems that prompt women to seek the help of a therapist and, on the other hand, highlight the inadequacy of the goals of mainstream therapy.

Moderation and self-control

There is a requirement in Western societies that women live their lives moderately and with self-control. This means that in social situations they do not engage in loud talking or loud laughing, they drink and eat in moderation, they do not argue, they do not contradict others (especially their male partners), and they do not feel or speak passionately about anything. The requirement is that women will suppress their opinions, emotions and inclinations, as well as their expectations of being equal members in any group of peers. Women are continually being told they are too talkative, too emotional, too enthusiastic, too involved. When giving an opinion, they are told they "sound ridiculous" and they "make fools of themselves".

Most women learn quite early in life that being passionate about anything is unacceptable because it is "unfeminine". Women who live with men, and women who are mothers, are usually discouraged from expressing opinions openly and passionately because many male partners and children find it embarrassing when a woman stands up and insists on being heard on an issue. Not wanting to offend or shame the ones they love, many women stifle their passion, especially their anger, and then wonder why they experience life as boring, bland, spiritless, passionless. The requirement to be moderate and self-controlled robs women of passion.

Repression of anger

Not only are women expected to suppress their anger on a day-to-day basis: they are also expected to keep anger from the past repressed. As more and more women admit to having been sexually abused in childhood and name their fathers, stepfathers,

---

1. For later reflections by Daly on Passion, see her autobiography, *Outercourse: The Be-Dazzling Voyage* (1992).

brothers, uncles, grandfathers or "friends" as their abusers, they are often advised to "keep quiet" about it and also, to "keep calm". Being angry about something that happened ten, twenty or thirty years ago will serve no useful purpose, they are told. They are urged to try to understand that he must have been "sick" to do such a thing, and that it is better to pity him than to be angry at him. The obvious question is: Better for whom? It is certainly not better for the woman concerned, because repressed anger causes depression, dramatically reduces motivation and takes away her ability to be passionate about anything.[2]

Women, too, who have been subjected to years of emotional, physical, sexual abuse at the hands of their male partners and who have years of repressed anger stored inside themselves, are often advised to keep it inside for the sake of the relationship. A tactic of some mainstream therapists is to divert attention from the expression of anger, counselling a woman to see the value of being "positive", being calm, keeping the peace. Such a tactic, of course, works in favour of the perpetrator and against the victim. The requirement to keep anger repressed robs a woman of passion.

One of the most important tasks of feminist therapy is to develop ways of enabling women to express their anger from the past, to unleash it and direct it in such a way that justice is served.

Libertarian values of fairness and tolerance

Western societies in the late 1970s adopted the philosophy and values of the liberal humanist movement almost without question. Such values as fairness, tolerance, openness, personal growth, individual enhancement, fulfilling one's own potential, and taking responsibility for one's own life were seen as inherently good values. After the first flush of feminist agitation and anger in the early 1970s, women in particular were attracted to the libertarian values of the humanist movement. For many, being a feminist lost its political emphasis and took on the meaning of being a free, independent woman seeking her own individual advancement and fulfilment.

The libertarian era, with its emphasis on individuals "feeling good", encouraged a focus on pseudopassions, and consequently the 1980s will go down in history as a decade where individual self-awareness and self-enhancement took precedence over any sense of commitment to or responsibility for others. The messages bombarding everybody for the past fifteen to twenty years have been: Keep a balanced view in all things. Be fair. Be calm. Be moderate. Be accepting. Be tolerant. Passion, blame, anger, rage are not appropriate in an era when every individual is called upon to take responsibility for the circumstances of her or his own life.

The New Age movement, with its emphasis on "positivity", appeared as a natural extension of the liberal humanist movement. Any attempt to focus on, or be angry about, old hurts and resentments is not acceptable. The message is: Be positive and heal yourself. Say affirmations. Forgive everyone who has wronged you (whether or

---

2. For examples of women who have spoken out, see Patricia Easteal (1994), *Voices of the Survivors*.

not they have admitted their wrongdoing). Holding grudges or seeking revenge is not helpful. The focus is to be on healing yourself.

There seems to be no acknowledgement at all among New Age gurus that "healing" cannot take place in a vacuum. Any attempt to "heal oneself" or "heal one's relationships" without reference to the *source* of the "illness" will be nothing more than an exercise in superficial self-conning. Ignoring one's deep hurt and rage and attempting to heal oneself through positive thinking and affirmations will have about as much effect as applying a bandaid to a sore that will not heal. The bandaid does not stop the pain, the festering, the poison. It just keeps the sore out of sight and gives the appearance that it does not exist.

Since feminism in the 1980s was strongly influenced by libertarian and New Age philosophies, it is not surprising that postmodernism also emerged for a time as a popular philosophical stance among feminists in academic circles. From the "anything goes" philosophy of the humanists it is only a small step to the "everything is all right so long as you deconstruct it" philosophy of postmodernism.

What is missing in libertarianism and postmodernism is the passion, the anger, the fury that marks feminism as a political movement determined to bring about real change for women. A feminist therapy must demolish the superficial focus on pseudopassions which has come to represent psychotherapy under the liberal humanist regime, and help women in their struggle to acknowledge and express their real passions.

Therapy as a way of life

In her book, *A Passion for Friends: Toward a Philosophy of Female Affection*, Janice Raymond laments the fact that feminists in great numbers have moved away from a passionate political stance and moved toward what she calls "therapism" or "therapy as a way of life". By that she means: women who stay in therapy for years, incorporating it into their lives as a necessary part of their living, women for whom therapy or "healing" is a primary focus in life; and also, women who give their relationships with other women a therapeutic context, as in co-counselling, where the emphasis is on total self-exposure and where, instead of simply *having* feelings, the emphasis is on "feeling oneself feeling" (1986, p. 157).

Such an emphasis on feelings and self-disclosure distorts reality, Raymond says. "Life acquires reality mainly in the course of confessing it and subjecting it to a constant psychological probe. Not the emotions themselves but the telling of emotions becomes definitive for reality" (p. 157).

As mentioned in Chapter One, Raymond objects to the fact that "the women's movement, like society at large, has fast become a therapeutic society . . . [where] women engage in massive psychological strip-teases that fragment and exploit the inner life" (p. 156). Drawing on the work of Hannah Arendt, she goes on to say that psychological introspection "thingifies" subjectivity by "externalizing and wrenching the inner life out of its depths". As a consequence, she says, "true and deep subjectivity is hard to find" (p. 157).

Therapism robs a woman of real passion or, in Janice Raymond's words, "Therapy as a way of life filters out the passion and lets the feeling through." The result, she says, is "the loss of the passionate Self" (p. 159).

These are just a few of the many ways women in Western societies are robbed of passion. The requirements are that women be moderate and self-controlled; that we repress and suppress our anger; that we be fair and tolerant and balanced and calm at all times; and that we focus on our own therapy, our own "healing", by engaging in an endless analysis of our feelings. Such endless preoccupation with self and "feelings", encouraged by mainstream and New Age therapies, ensures that a woman looks only within herself for the cause of her problems and remains oblivious to the real cause, namely, her oppression. Thus, the agents of her oppression are able to continue their destructive work undisturbed, and the psychotherapy industry continues to boom.

In developing a feminist therapy that does not result in the kinds of psychoppression evident in other therapies, it is crucial that we pay attention to the insights of Mary Daly and Janice Raymond on passion, and acknowledge the distinction between real passions and pseudopassions. If all we strive to do as therapists is help women talk about their feelings in order to get in touch with them, our aim as feminist therapists is no different from that of mainstream therapists. What we need to do is incorporate into our role such activities as: the raising of women's consciousness to the fact that plastic passions function to keep them paralysed; encouraging women to name their oppressors as a step toward freeing themselves from their oppression; and also, supporting women as they find the courage to acknowledge and express their true passions. If we do this, the primary aim of feminist therapy, which is the liberation of women from the specific oppression/s designed to keep them in a state of emotional ill-health, will be achieved.

Justice

The final socio-political issue to be considered in the development of a feminist therapy is justice. A search of the literature spanning one hundred years of psychoanalysis and thirty years of liberal humanistic therapy reveals a lack of any real focus on justice. While such a situation is not surprising, given the deliberate focus on the individual as the source of her own problems, it nevertheless represents a serious omission on the part of mainstream therapy. One wonders how dedicated students of human behaviour and the human psyche could miss what simple common sense reveals, that *emotional and psychological health is not possible when justice is not done.*

Consider the situation of a woman who goes to a therapist to try to get some relief from her depression. She confides in the therapist that she was sexually abused in childhood and thinks that this may have something to do with her depression. She talks, also, about the anger that is beginning to rise up in her. A psychoanalytic psychotherapist would focus on the woman herself and encourage her to talk about her own sexuality, including her feelings for her father, with the aim of helping her to see that her depression comes from within herself. Similarly, with a liberal humanist therapist, the focus would be on the woman herself. She would be encouraged to take full responsibility for her own depression because, she would learn, it is unhelpful to blame someone else for one's own unhappiness. The aim would be to have her commit herself to working towards personal empowerment and a positive attitude.

The feminist response to such therapeutic procedures is, of course, to warn that only one person benefits from focusing on the woman herself as the source of her own depression: the perpetrator of the sexual abuse. When the onus is on the victim to take responsibility for her own feelings, the perpetrator is in fact relieved of responsibility for his actions and a situation of injustice prevails. Given that mental health is possible only when justice is done, the pursuit of justice in therapy is crucial. A feminist therapist, therefore, would encourage the woman to talk about her intuitions regarding the cause of her depression, to talk about her sexual abuse, to name, to blame, to be enraged. It is only as she is enabled freely to explore the events of her past in this way that she will begin to experience a sense of justice.

The following discussion highlights four important issues pertaining to the pursuit of justice in therapy. They are: guilt, forgiveness, blame and anger.

Guilt

Guilt is a topic most women are familiar with, and one which needs urgent attention if women are to be freed from the compulsion to feel guilty. Mary Daly says: "Of all the damaging and continually embedded pseudopassions, the most poisonous probably is guilt" (1984, p. 215).

In our attempt to understand women's relationship to guilt, it is important here to recall how pseudopassions work, and to remind ourselves that we feel guilty most of the time not because we *are* guilty, but because women are expected to feel guilty. The pseudopassion of guilt works to keep us looking inward, focusing on ourselves, using up our energy trying to "deal with" our guilt. Such activity is designed to take away our strength and render us harmless in the face of those who are really guilty. When we are preoccupied with feeling guilty, our real passions are denied and our mental and emotional health is in jeopardy.

Looking at the relationship between guilt and mental health, it is clear there are at least three circumstances in which guilt is harmful to one's mental health:

- *When we* are *guilty but refuse to admit it to ourselves and others.* Such a situation is particularly harmful because it necessitates living in pretence and unreality, which is itself a state of mental ill-health.
- *When we* are *guilty and do admit it to ourselves and others, but refuse to move beyond it.* To wallow in one's guilt by talking about it and berating oneself endlessly is harmful to one's mental health. Guilt that is real must be acknowledged, worked through, and let go.
- *When we are* not *guilty but choose to* feel *guilty.* Such a situation is harmful to one's mental health because, like the first option, it necessitates living a lie.

The third of these options is as common among women as the first is among men. In fact, there appears to be a connection between the two, in that when men refuse to accept responsibility for their behaviour, there always seems to be a woman ready to step in and take on the responsibility. "Someone has to feel guilty," women seem to say, "so why not me?"

The reason women do this, of course, is that we have been socialised to be martyrs and rescuers of men, and most of us do it almost without thinking. Traditional therapies tend to agree with public opinion in viewing the tendency for women to take on guilt for men's behaviour as something positive, caring and even noble. Feminist therapy, on the other hand, warns of the serious consequences of such "caring" and "noble" behaviour.

Two of the consequences have already been mentioned. One is that feeling guilty serves to keep women preoccupied with themselves and saps them of their power to confront those who are really guilty. The other is that taking on guilt that belongs to someone else necessitates living a lie. A third consequence, and one that is perhaps not often considered, is that when a woman takes on guilt for something she did not do, she is in fact colluding with the forces of injustice, supporting and encouraging the moral bankruptcy of the one who is really guilty, and assisting in the development of her own and the other's emotional ill-health.

An important task for feminist therapy surely is that of helping women sort out their complex relationship to guilt. Mostly the reason for our taking on other people's guilt is not because we *want* to feel guilty. It just seems to happen, almost automatically, due no doubt to the strength of our socialisation.

Mary Daly suggests that one way to overcome the pseudopassion of guilt which is so firmly embedded in our psyches is to work to develop "the Courage to Sin". She says:

> The Courage to Sin . . . is precisely about being true and real ontologically, about refusing to be "a player of the [patriarchal] female part" . . . To Sin is to trust intuitions and the reasoning rooted in them. To Sin is to come into the fullness of our powers (p. 152).

One "sin" we definitely need to learn to commit is that of absolutely refusing to take responsibility for the sins of others. This involves a determination to make a clear assessment of who is guilty and who is not, in every instance, and to refuse to feel guilty unless we *are* guilty. The Courage to Sin against patriarchal expectations is difficult but essential if justice is to be done.

Forgiveness

Just as women are expected to take on the guilt of everyone around them, so we are expected to forgive those who have wronged us, and our forgiveness is to be automatic and unconditional.

Under the influence of humanist and New Age philosophies, interactions between people in Western societies have become riddled with injustices. It is a commonly held belief, for example, that if we do not forgive others, we will become "bitter and twisted".

We are advised: "make peace with your parents", forgive them, forgive everybody. It is said to be crucial that we not hold grudges, no matter what evil has been perpetrated against us. Find a way to forgive the man who rapes your little daughter. Find a way to forgive the man who harasses you, rapes you, beats you. Find a way to forgive the woman who betrays you. Try to understand, we are told. Try not to be angry at those who hurt you, intimidate you, ignore you, brush you aside. "Forgive and forget." "Think positively." "Love everybody." "Build bridges, not walls." These are familiar sayings. We are bombarded with them, and we sometimes feel guilty when we cannot oblige.

What we must see in the context of developing a radical, political feminist therapy is that the expectation to forgive unconditionally in fact serves the cause of injustice rather than justice, and results in ill-health rather than health.

If we look back in history in search of the original meaning of the word "forgiveness", before it became contaminated by libertarian and New Age interpretations, we are led inevitably to certain passages in the Bible. The Old Testament with its philosophy of "an eye for an eye and a tooth for a tooth" certainly could not be said to advocate forgiveness at any price. The New Testament, on the other hand, does recommend forgiveness, but not in the unconditional way some would have us believe. The following examples from New Testament writings reveal that there are, in fact, conditions that have to be met before forgiveness is appropriate.

In the first example, Jesus says to his disciples: "If your brother sins, rebuke him, and if he repents, forgive him" (Luke 17: 3, Revised Standard Version). Forgiveness here is clearly conditional, and the condition in this instance is *repentance*. Note that the appropriate response to a person who has perpetrated a wrong against oneself is to "rebuke" that person, to confront, to express anger. Forgiveness is appropriate only when the sinner repents.

The second example is a prayer spoken by Jesus from the Cross. He asks: "Father, forgive them for they know not what they do" (Luke 23: 34). Again, forgiveness is conditional and, this time, the condition is *ignorance*. From the biblical account, it seems Jesus was prepared to forgive those guilty of murdering him because it was his sincere belief that they did not understand what they were doing. For feminist therapy, the plea of ignorance presents some difficulties in the sense that, if it is to be acceptable as a condition for forgiveness, the perpetrator must clearly have been unaware of what he was doing, and this is often hard to ascertain. Very common amongst women is the desire to find excuses for other people's bad behaviour, and "ignorance" is a popular choice. In response to a man's violent and oppressive behaviour, for example, a woman will often say: "He mustn't have understood what he was doing"; "He'd had too much to drink"; or "He was in such a rage. He wouldn't have done it in his right mind." Forgiveness based on wishful thinking does not make the forgiveness appropriate or just. The fact remains that, unless the perpetrator actually was unaware of what he was doing, forgiveness on the basis of ignorance is inappropriate.

A third example comes from the pen of the writer of the first epistle of John. Speaking of God's forgiveness, the writer says: "If we confess our sins, he is faithful and just, and will forgive our sins and cleanse us from all unrighteousness" (1 John 1: 9). The condition for forgiveness in this instance is *confession* of sin.

What these examples show is that, in biblical terms, it is inappropriate to offer forgiveness when there is no admission of guilt, no repentance, no sorrow for the sin, no confession and no desire for forgiveness, unless the sin was committed in total ignorance. To forgive or not to forgive is a very serious matter and must never be decided lightly.

Another crucial point about forgiveness relates to the confirmation of guilt. Justice demands that guilt be confirmed before forgiveness is even considered. Both victim and perpetrator must acknowledge and confirm that the wrong was in fact done by the perpetrator, because *without confirmation of guilt as a starting point, there can be no real forgiveness.* What seems to happen with many women is that we offer forgiveness almost before the sin has been committed. At least while a sin is in the process of being committed, or immediately afterwards, women find themselves saying: "It's all right. I forgive you. I know you didn't mean it." The problem with such a situation is that, in our haste to offer forgiveness, we do not allow time for the proper processes of guilt and forgiveness to take place. Where there is no acknowledgement of guilt, there can be no forgiveness.

Another common practice amongst women is that we *say* we forgive someone who has wronged us, when deep in our hearts we know we do not forgive that person, and perhaps never will. In terms of our own mental health, it is better to admit that we do not forgive than to pretend that we do. It is better to maintain our anger forever than to pay lip-service to forgiveness simply because others expect it of us.

One more point about forgiveness is that it is not necessary to offer forgiveness simply because someone asks for it. Indeed, it is important psychologically that we not try to forgive someone who has wronged us until we are ready, realising, at the same time, that we may never be ready. For those who believe there are some crimes or sins that are unforgiveable no matter how sorry the perpetrator says he is, any attempt to offer forgiveness would be inappropriate. In these instances, while forgiveness is not necessary, finding a way to put the matter behind you so that it does not dominate the rest of your life is critical.

Blame

Blame has already been discussed to some extent, but it is important to reiterate what has been said. If blame is not directed appropriately, then justice is not done and emotional and psychological health is not possible, either for the victim of a wrong-doing or for the perpetrator.

Blame is crucial to the success of therapy in many instances. Feminists call it naming—finding the courage to name those who perpetrate injustices against us. Because women have been conditioned into believing that, above all else, we must be kind and caring, we have tremendous difficulty when it comes to blaming. It seems so unkind and uncaring and consequently, there is a strong compulsion to protect perpetrators of evil, even those who have done their destructive worst to us.

Naming and blaming our oppressors is essential if we want to rise above the effects of the wrong they have done to us. Consequently, naming and blaming are important issues for feminist therapy. Even though it might not always be comfortable for the therapist, it must be a part of a woman's working through her pain. One of the characteristics of blame in therapy is that we have to work with a woman till she gets the blame right. Women commonly get the blame wrong. When their male partner treats them badly, for example, they often blame their mother-in-law for not bringing her son up properly. As a matter of fact, the blaming of a perpetrator's mother is a common response to male violence and is often supported by mainstream therapists.

In a 1994 documentary called *Deadly Hurt*, written and directed by Melbourne filmmaker Don Parham and shown on SBS TV, a child psychiatrist was among those interviewed in relation to the violent murder of a woman by her husband, and his subsequent suicide. One would have thought that any therapist working with the couple's three teenage daughters who, in their short lives, had witnessed fairly constant violence by their father against their mother, would have found the issue of blame reasonably straightforward. But no. The psychiatrist, in her work with the girls, helped them to see that the one to blame was not their father, but their father's mother! *She* had "dominated" him all his life. *She* had not allowed him to find himself. *She* was the cause of all the violent acts he had committed against his wife throughout their marriage, and *she* was the cause of the frustration that led him to commit the final act of murder. As a viewer, it was interesting to observe how "satisfied" the psychiatrist, the three daughters and several of the other women and men interviewed on the programme seemed to be with that explanation.

Sadly, because the daughters were not encouraged to blame the one who was actually blameworthy and, in that way, express their rage at their father's despicable act, they were robbed, at that time, of the opportunity to acknowledge their rage, work through it, and come to an honest resolution of this terrible tragedy that had occurred in their lives. Unless they do find a way to blame their father, they will never be able genuinely to forgive him, even if they want to. Undoubtedly, there will be opportunities in the future for each of them to get the blame right so that they can begin rebuilding their memories of their mother and, also, of their father.

Another way women often get the blame wrong is by blaming themselves. We often name ourselves as the cause of hurtful and harmful things done to us and then wonder why the problem persists.

Psychological release will only come when a woman finally discovers who it is that she is really angry at and directs her blame appropriately. It is very important, therefore, that therapists encourage the kind of exploration that leads a woman to the truth. Justice, as a psychological issue, demands that we help a woman move in therapy to the point where she can and does blame the one who is blameworthy. It is then that emotional and psychological health will be possible.

Anger

Many women are still reluctant to allow their anger to surface, but it must be stressed here that *the ability to be angry is central to the mental and emotional health of all oppressed people.* One cannot free oneself from oppression without some degree of anger. Blaming and naming are not possible without anger. A woman must first acknowledge her anger, and then express it in whatever way feels right to her. If the expression of anger is to lead to the resolution of one's own unfinished business, however, it is important that it be expressed assertively and not aggressively. Rather than being a thoughtless act of self-indulgence, the expression of anger must serve justice if it is to facilitate mental and emotional health.

According to Mary Daly, anger is one of our *real* passions. The experience of most women is that, all through our lives, we have been encouraged to water down our anger, to call it "annoyance" or "resentment" or "frustration". Women are commonly heard to say they feel "cross" or "cranky" or "grumpy", because pseudo-anger is somehow more acceptable for women than real anger.

There are two results of watering down our anger and calling it something more acceptable: one is, it causes us to pretend our real anger does not exist and sets the stage for depression and anxiety; and the other is, it allows the perpetrators of evil to continue in their morally corrupt ways, hurting us and others over and over again, with no suggestion of accountability for their actions.

When a woman finds the courage to name her experience of real anger and is "moved to action by her Rage" (Daly, 1984, p. 203), she experiences real freedom from the pressures that imprisoned her for so long.

The process, then, in order that Justice be done and mental and emotional health made possible, is as follows: a woman refuses to feel guilty when she is not guilty; she refuses to forgive unless forgiveness is appropriate; she names and blames those who have wronged her; and she acknowledges and expresses her anger in clear and deliberate ways. Then, being mobilised to action by her Rage, she demands justice—for herself and, by extension, for all women.

Having discussed Oppression, Access, Honesty, Passion and Justice as socio-political issues that inform the development of a philosophical base for a feminist therapy, attention must now focus on the question of practical application. A detailed discussion of the practice of a feminist alternative therapy will follow in Part Four. Prior to that, however, it is important that we take a closer look at those therapies which have been the subject of consistent criticism by feminists since the early 1970s. The main criticism of psychoanalysis, the humanistic therapies, and the more recent New Age and popular therapies, including lesbian sex therapy, is that they all depend for their "success" on blaming the victim. The following chapters will present a feminist perspective on each of these oppressive therapeutic regimes.

PART THREE

BLAME-THE-VICTIM THERAPIES

5

FREUD AND PSYCHOANALYSIS

While the act of "blaming the victim" started long before Freud's time, there is no doubt that he enshrined the practice into psychological law and gave it such a legitimacy that it survives today as a central feature in the practice of mainstream therapy. The victim, seeking the help of a therapist in dealing with the effects of her victimisation, is further victimised by a therapy that blames her for her own distress. When women went to Freud for psychoanalysis, his practice was to focus only on the inner dynamics of his patients and ignore the social context in which they lived; thus he held them responsible for the problems they were experiencing. In addition to his own practice of blaming of the victim, at the same time he developed elaborate theories to make sure that the psychoanalysts who followed him did the same.

Freud's refusal to acknowledge the devastating effect women's enforced inferiority had on their mental health caused feminists, in the early years of Second Wave feminism, to speak out strongly against Freudianism for its role in the continued subordination of women. Their courageous attacks on Freud and his theories were made in full cognisance of the reverence with which he was regarded in the Western world. Shulamith Firestone put it very aptly when she said: "Freudianism has become . . . our modern Church" (1970, p. 46). She expressed her amazement that, even though

> psychoanalytic therapy has been proven ineffective, and Freud's ideas about women's sexuality literally proven wrong (e.g., Masters and Johnson on the myth of the double orgasm), the old conceptions still circulate. The doctors go on practising (p. 47).

Firestone knew, as indeed all who have a feminist analysis of society know, why "the doctors go on practising" a therapy that is absurd in so many ways: it suits a male-dominated society very well to hold on to a system of thought that so convincingly "proves" the inferior status of women.

While some feminists support Freud and argue for a more "rational" analysis of his work, the great majority of them accuse him of leading the backlash against women's burgeoning independence in the late nineteenth and early twentieth centuries and for providing the framework for women's continuing oppression to this day. Generally speaking, criticism of Freud during this Second Wave feminism has occurred at the instigation of three different groups: the early feminists, those writing about childhood sexual abuse, and feminist therapists intent on exposing the oppressive nature of Freudian psychoanalysis.

Criticism by the early feminists

The first group, the early feminists, criticised Freud's image of women, his "discoveries" about female sexuality and his method of research. In so doing, they deliberately exposed him and his followers as advocates and supporters of the subordination of women.

His image of women was, glaringly, one of inferior beings who, no matter what they did, could never qualify as full human beings. Simone de Beauvoir, writing as early as 1952 about Freud's view of women, commented that "man is defined as a human being and woman as a female—whenever she behaves as a human being she is said to imitate the male" (1952, p. 47). The label devised for this kind of "illness" in a woman was "masculinity complex". De Beauvoir pointed out that women had two choices in Freud's system and both led to emotional ill-health. "Woman is shown to us as enticed by two modes of alienation", she explained. "Evidently to play at being a man will be for her a source of frustration; but to play at being a woman is only a delusion" (p. 46). No matter what choices a woman made in life, she would never experience the satisfaction of being a whole human being.

After a revealing discussion of Freud's letters to his wife in the years before their marriage, Betty Friedan describes Freud's image of women in the following ways:

> The fact is that to Freud . . . women were a strange, inferior, less-than-human species. He saw them as childlike dolls, who existed in terms only of man's love, to love man and serve his needs (1963, p. 96).

Again, "It was woman's nature to be ruled by man, and her sickness to envy him" (p. 97). A woman was "inferior, childish, helpless, with no possibility of happiness unless she adjusted to being man's passive object" (p. 106). Freud and his followers saw their task in therapy as that of helping women get rid of "their neurotic desire to be equal . . . [and to] find sexual fulfilment as women, by affirming their natural inferiority" (p. 106).

Kate Millett added to the discussion of Freud's image of women by pointing to his belief that "modesty and jealousy" were "two aspects of woman's character" and that such characteristics were "directly related to penis envy". A woman's modesty is a sign of her "self-despair over the 'defect' of her 'castration'" (1972, p. 188). In an attempt to expose the total absurdity of Freud's notion of penis envy, Millett reveals:

> When Freud suggests that modesty in women was originally designed "for concealment of genital deficiency" he is even willing to describe pubic hair as the response of "nature herself" to cover the female fault (p. 188).

Female jealousy, too, springs from penis envy. When a woman complains about her husband's sexual freedom, it is because women generally have "little sense of justice". It is penis envy that causes women to resent the freedom their husbands enjoy (p. 189).

Phyllis Chesler put it succinctly:

> The "Freudian" vision beholds women as essentially "breeders and bearers", as potentially warmhearted creatures, but more often as cranky children with uteruses, forever mourning the loss of male organs and male identity (1972, p. 79).

In addition to their criticism of Freud's image of women, the early feminists also raged against his "discoveries" in relation to female sexuality. Particular targets for their rage were the Electra Complex (the female version of the Oedipus Complex) and the notion of penis envy.

In Freud's own analysis of his childhood experiences, which he delved into after his father's death, he became aware that he had loved his mother and hated his father. As a result of his analysis of himself, he came up with the idea that *all* boys probably loved and desired their mothers and *all* boys probably hated and feared their fathers because fathers were seen as rivals for their mother's love. Soon after these thoughts had occurred to him, he developed what he called the theory of the Oedipus Complex and claimed this as an explanation of infantile sexuality. Of course, there was no proof at all that it explained the early development of male sexuality except, perhaps, in his own particular case. Even less did it explain the early development of female sexuality, but he came up with the Electra Complex anyway. As de Beauvoir points out: "Freud never showed much concern with the destiny of woman; it is clear that he simply adapted his account from that of the destiny of man, with slight modifications" (1952, p. 34).

Shulamith Firestone agrees. "It is generally believed," she says, "that the Electra Complex is less profound a discovery than the Oedipus Complex, because, like all Freud's theories about women, it analyses the female only as negative male: the Electra Complex is an inverse Oedipus Complex" (1970, p. 56). Friedan commented that, to Freud, a woman "is merely . . . a man with something missing" (1963, p. 102).

It was the notion of penis envy, or feminine castration complex, developed by Freud as part of his explanation of the beginnings of female sexuality, that received the most attention from the early feminists. De Beauvoir disputed his theory by suggesting that there are many different ways little girls respond to the presence of the penis and it is not readily apparent that "envy" is one of them:

> To begin with, there are many little girls who remain ignorant of the male anatomy for some years. Such a child finds it quite natural that there should be men and women, just as there is a sun and a moon . . . For many others this tiny bit of flesh hanging between boys' legs is insignificant or even laughable . . . It may even happen that the penis is considered an anomaly . . . it can inspire disgust . . . Finally, the fact is that there are numerous cases where the little girl does take an interest in the penis of a brother or playmate; but that does not mean she experiences jealousy of it (1952, p. 254).

Kate Millett reminds us that Freud's understanding of the female personality "is based upon the idea of penis envy" and is, therefore, negative. In other words, "what she is is the result of the fact that she is not a male and 'lacks' a penis" (1972, pp. 179–80). She continues:

> Freud assumed that the female's discovery of her sex is, in and of itself, a catastrophe of such vast proportions that it haunts a woman all through life and accounts for most aspects of her temperament. His entire psychology of women, from which all modern psychology and psychoanalysis derives heavily, is built upon an original tragic experience—born female (p. 180).

Many of the early feminists commented on the fact that if Freud had had a better understanding of women, he would have written about "power envy" rather than "penis envy".[1] If girls and women are envious of anything about boys and men, they insisted, it is the power, the freedom and the status men and boys enjoy by virtue of the fact that they are male (Friedan, 1963, p. 104). While a boy is encouraged to "assert his subjective freedom" a girl is taught "she must try to please, she must make herself [an] object; she should therefore renounce her autonomy" (de Beauvoir, 1952, pp. 261–2). Kate Millett argues:

> Confronted with so much concrete evidence of male's superior status, sensing on all sides the depreciation in which they are held, girls envy not the penis, but only what the penis gives one social pretensions to. Freud appears to have made a major and rather foolish confusion between biology and culture, anatomy and status (1972, p. 187).

In simple terms, women's envy derives from the fact that they are "born female in a masculine-dominated culture" (p. 180).

Another area of Freud's work that was the subject of much criticism in the early years was his method of "research". He, literally, made his theories up. They were developed in his own mind, sometimes in response to his work with patients, often in response to memories of his own childhood experiences and, with no attempt at all to test his theories, he proceeded to present them as "scientific" fact. Firestone reminds us that "Freud's theories are not verifiable empirically" (1970, p. 47). It is a mistake to take his theories literally, she says, because "his ideas, taken literally, lead to absurdity —for his genius was poetic rather than scientific" (p. 50).

In de Beauvoir's words, Freud presumed "the prestige of the penis" and, from that presumption, proceeded to develop his theories. She says:

> psychoanalysis fails to explain why woman is the *Other*. For Freud himself admits that the prestige of the penis is explained by the sovereignty of the father . . . [but] he confesses that he is ignorant regarding the origin of male supremacy (1952, p. 44).

---

1. Over the years since then, feminists have made light of Freud's suggestion of penis envy by inventing terms such as "womb envy", "menstruation envy", "venus envy", etc.

She concludes: "We therefore decline to accept the method of psychoanalysis" (p. 44).

Millett, writing about the subjectivity and the consequent masculine bias of Freud's theories, says:

Indeed, since he has no objective proof of any consequence to offer in support of his notion of penis envy or of a female castration complex, one is struck by how thoroughly the subjectivity in which all these events are cast tends to be Freud's own, or that of a strong masculine bias, even of a rather gross male-supremacist bias (1972, p. 182).

While it is generally agreed that Freud's method of "research" and his consequent psychological "discoveries" are highly suspect, his theories, nevertheless, continue to be accepted as the basis for much of what passes for psychological and psychiatric practice even today. "The doctors [and therapists] go on practising" and women go on being blamed for the devastating effects of their subordination.

Criticism of the cover-up of childhood sexual abuse

While feminists have found much to criticise in Freud's writing, the vast majority agree that there is no area of his work more deplorable, more worthy of total condemnation and outright rejection, than his cover-up of the fact of childhood sexual abuse. As Florence Rush explains:

Sigmund Freud, whose theories have had such enormous influence on modern thinking, knew that the sexual abuse of children existed, but he could not reconcile the implications of that abuse with either his self-image or his identification with other men of his class, and thus he altered his telling of reality (1980, p. 82).

Such tampering with the truth, such downright dishonesty, has had serious repercussions in the lives of women and girls for almost a century and for that, many feminists agree, Freud cannot be forgiven.

There are those, on the other hand, who argue that it is unfair to call into question all of Freud's work on the basis of his abandonment of the seduction theory. This way of thinking, they say,

leaves no room for the possibility that Freud could make an error of judgment, perhaps a grave one . . . without this compromising the whole fabric of psychoanalytic thought and its development by subsequent generations of analysts (Scott, 1988, p. 91).

What Ann Scott is suggesting is that, instead of focusing on Freud's possible "error of judgment" and the effect his "error" has had on women ever since, we ought to be "exploring what becomes of key aspects of psychoanalytic theory" if incest is, in fact, a real event and not imagined. The important issue, in her opinion, is not the implications of what feminists call Freud's "cover-up" but rather, "how much or how little, at the level of mental structure, depends on the reality or fantasy of a special kind of experience" (p. 91).

The view of a radicalised feminist therapy is that such a deliberate cover-up does, in fact, call into question all of Freud's theories. As a matter of fact, justice demands that we name Freud and Freudianism; that we tell the story of the cover-up; that we expose his motives; and that we point to the effect his altering of reality has had on women (particularly victims of childhood sexual abuse) ever since. Our naming must also include a call to women to avoid therapists who continue to practise in the Freudian or psychoanalytic tradition.

The following account of the events surrounding Freud's reversal of his seduction theory is compiled from the writings of those who are themselves victims/survivors of childhood sexual abuse, and of others who are sympathetic to the feminist stance.

In *The Best Kept Secret: Sexual Abuse of Children*, Florence Rush devotes a chapter to a discussion of "The Freudian Cover-up". Her study of Freud's papers and, in particular, his letters to his friend Wilhelm Fliess, has enabled her to set out chronologically the events leading up to and including the cover-up.

In 1896, in a letter to Fliess, Freud wrote about his frightening discovery that many children are victims of adult sexual molestation, and "that anxiety is to be connected, not with a mental, but with a physical consequence of sexual abuse" (Rush, 1980, p. 87). In that same year, Freud set out his seduction theory in a series of three papers which he called "The Aetiology of Hysteria". His main theme in these papers was that "Hysteria originated in a sexual seduction at an early (prepubescent) age" (Masson, 1988, p. 87), and also that the perpetrators were in most cases "close relatives, a father or a brother" (Bernheimer and Kahane, 1985, p. 13).

To Freud's great disappointment, his colleagues had a severe adverse reaction to such suggestions and, one by one, they began rejecting his ideas and his friendship, and he became increasingly isolated. Rush writes: "Despite continued evidence [of childhood sexual abuse], Freud never again, after the 1896 presentation, publicly promoted his seduction theory" (p. 88), though he did continue to discuss it privately in his correspondence with Fliess. There is a suggestion by some that isolation from his colleagues probably had something to do with his reluctance to speak publicly, but Rush is of the opinion that it was more likely due to his own concerns about naming fathers as seducers. "Though staunch on sexual trauma as the cause of neurosis," she says, "he was extremely unhappy with the idea of father as seducer" (pp. 88–9).

Another significant event around the time of his presentation was the death of his father in October 1896. Freud admits that he was not prepared for the intensity of his grief and suffering. Writing to Fliess, he said "at a death a whole past stirs within one. I feel now as if I had been torn out by the roots" (Rush, 1980, p. 90). His "intense conflict and suffering" led him into a period of self-analysis which included interpretation of his dreams (p. 90).

His self-analysis took him back to "memories of childhood experiences" and he was able to recall a desire for his mother and hostility toward his father. As he agonised over his feelings for his father, he continued to struggle with his thoughts about the apparent extent and regularity of sexual molestation of children by their fathers. In February 1897 he confided in Fliess that "the number of fathers named by his patients as sexual molesters had truly alarmed him" (Rush, 1980, pp. 90–1). He found himself making a connection between the stories he heard from his patients and his own "paternal death wish". His thoughts went to "some hysterical features in his brother and several sisters" and he inferred from that that his father, too, had been a sexual molester (p. 91).

In May 1897, Freud wrote to Fliess telling him of a dream he had had in which he recognised "affectionate" feelings toward his eldest daughter, Mathilde, aged eleven. He said: "Not long ago I dreamt that I was feeling over-affectionately towards Mathilde." After a brief discussion of the dream, he concluded: "The dream of course fulfills my wish to pin down a father as the originator of neurosis and put an end to my persistent doubts" (Rush, 1980, p. 91).

This marks the beginning of Freud's turn-around on his seduction theory, the beginning of his rejection of the numerous stories his patients had told him. He explained it all away by reasoning that, because of his own "unconscious paternal death wish", he had *wanted* to blame fathers as seducers. And since he had a need to blame his father, "he presumed all his patients had the same need". This realisation then enabled him to see that the stories of fathers as seducers, which he had initially believed, were in fact "defensive fictions" (p. 91).

In relieving himself of guilt and anxiety in relation to his own father and, indeed, in relation to his own "complicity in male fantasies of seduction" (Bernheimer and Kahane, 1985, p. 14), he "simultaneously relegated his patients' testimony to fantasy, discarded his seduction theory and replaced it with the incipient Oedipus complex" (Rush, 1980, p. 91).

In September 1897, Freud explained his turn-around to Fliess:

> I no longer believe in my neurotica . . . I shall start at the beginning and tell you the whole story of how the reasons for rejecting it arose. The first group of factors were the continual disappointment of my attempts to bring my analyses to a real conclusion, the running away of people who for a time had seemed my most favorably inclined patients, the lack of the complete success on which I had counted . . . Then there was the astonishing thing that in every case . . . blame was laid on perverse acts by the father . . . though it was hardly credible that prevented [*sic*] acts against children were so general . . . Thirdly, there was the definite realization that there is no "indication of reality" in the unconscious, so that it is impossible to distinguish between truth and emotionally-charged fiction (Rush, 1980, p. 92).

Freud's astonishment, his inability to believe that fathers would behave in such "perverse" ways, led him to develop a theory that "seduction scenes are infantile wish fulfillments, fantasies rather than memories". In other words, he simply reversed the direction of the lustful energies. "Seduction now originates with the child's perverse desire, stimulated by autoerotic activity, of which the parent is no more than the passive object" (Bernheimer and Kahane, 1985, p. 14).

Commenting on what she calls "Freud's Big Breakthrough into Fantasyland" (p. 109), Elizabeth Ward says in *Father–Daughter Rape*:

> Freudianism holds that girl-children unconsciously desire intercourse with their fathers: thus we have the sexualisation of girl-children as a reason for their being raped by the Father. By this and several other means, Freud managed to blame the victim (1984, p. 102).

Ward quotes Mary Daly who drew attention to Freud's misnaming and misdefining in order to obscure "his own active role [as a therapist] in the repetition of . . . [his patient's] violation" (p. 103). Ward draws attention to Freud's misnaming in his use of words like "infantile sexual experience" and "seductions" to name what was actually father–daughter rape (p. 104). He spoke of "the ill-matched pair" conducting "their love-relations" (p. 105). His misdefining of father–daughter rape included the use of words like "emotionally charged fiction", "fantasy" and "universal fantasies" (p. 109).

From the moment Freud decided to abandon his seduction theory, he worked at developing his theory of the Oedipus Complex. Elizabeth Ward sums up the anger of all feminists who reject Freud's attempt at a convenient explanation for father–daughter rape, when she says of the Oedipus theory:

> This device enabled him to turn . . . concrete reality . . . into the theory of a fantasy wish for sexual pleasure with the father (i.e. men). We still see the effects every day: "You're making it up!"—an especially common response to girl-children who complain of sexual assault. The most abiding myth about rape, "You must have asked for it" . . . [was given] scientific credibility . . . through the theory of Oedipal fantasy (which women could not refute since it resided in the unconscious) (p. 107).

Freud's reversal of the blame for childhood sexual abuse is no more clearly illustrated than in the account of his work with his best-known and most-studied patient, Dora. While feminists have told Dora's story many times and been enraged by it each time, it is important to tell at least part of it again in this context.

Dora was first brought to Freud by her father, against her will, in October 1900. She was eighteen years old. "Her main 'symptoms', (presumably according to the father) were depression . . . and a change in her character." Also, she had developed "a nervous cough, hoarseness, and loss of voice" (Masson, 1988, p. 87).

Dora's father told Freud that he had formed an "intimate friendship" with the K family. Frau K had nursed him through "a long illness" and, he explained, "Herr K was always most kind to Dora" (p. 87). When Dora was sixteen she and her father visited the Ks at a summer resort. Suddenly Dora told her father she was leaving. A few weeks later she revealed to her mother

> that Herr K had made sexual advances to her on a walk after a trip on the lake. Herr K vehemently denied Dora's accusation, saying that he knew from his wife that Dora read books about sexuality . . . and that she had merely "imagined" the whole scene she described (p. 88).

Dora's father told Freud:

> I have no doubt that this incident is responsible for Dora's depression and irritability and suicidal ideas. She keeps pressing me to break off relations with Herr K and more particularly with Frau K . . . But that I cannot do. For, to begin with, I myself believe that Dora's tale of the man's immoral suggestions is a fantasy that has forced its way into her mind (p. 88).

During analysis, Dora told Freud that this was not the first incident with Herr K. When she was fourteen, he had

> contrived to be alone with her in his office, and "suddenly clasped the girl to him and pressed a kiss upon her lips". Dora had "a violent feeling of disgust, tore herself from the man", and left (p. 88).

She never told anyone about it till she confided in Freud.

Originally, Freud agreed with Dora that these two incidents were real and not imagined but then, influenced by his own theories about female sexuality, he changed his mind and made the following assumption. Referring to the "kiss", he said "this was surely just the situation to call up a distinct feeling of sexual excitement in a girl of fourteen who had never before been approached" (p. 92). As Masson comments, one wonders "how Freud (or anyone else) could know this" (p. 92). Freud, then, based on his own assumption, based on a theory he had simply *made up*, goes on to give his "clinical diagnosis". He says:

> In this scene . . . the behaviour of this child of fourteen was already entirely and completely hysterical. I should without question consider a person hysterical in whom an occasion for sexual excitement elicited feelings that were preponderantly or exclusively unpleasurable (p. 92).

Daly comments:

> Clearly, Freud assumes that any woman who "is approached", that is, sexually accosted, should respond with uncontrollable visceral desire for the male who mauls and violates her. Thus, Dora's normal reaction of disgust and Self-salvation is negated (1979, pp. 266–7).

Referring to Freud's labelling of her as "hysterical", Daly says:

> In this maze of obscene babble the great mind-shrinker announces that any woman who does not enjoy rape is hysterical. He reduces deep existential disgust to an "unpleasurable feeling" . . . [Dora] is blamed for being a victim who did *not* "ask for it," and who did *not* love being violated (p. 267).

Criticism of oppressive therapeutic practices

Feminists who reject the techniques and practices of psychoanalytic psychotherapy agree that the "cure" may be worse for a woman than her original feelings of distress. To diagnose a woman's personal conflicts as "wholly individual and personal" when in fact they are "systematically socially produced", they argue, is to encourage her to blame herself for the situation she finds herself in. Miriam Greenspan explains:

> In learning to see ourselves as men see us, we have learned to devalue, limit, and hate ourselves. The dilemma of being a man-made woman has been experienced in isolation, as a personal problem. The internalization of the cultural tension between the attainment of

femininity and personhood in the modern age of psychology has been manifested in what appear to be irrational, personal conflicts or "symptoms".

. . . The symptoms [of femininity] are systematically socially produced. Yet they are experienced as, appear to be, and are diagnosed as wholly individual and personal. Thus the "cure" that traditional therapy peddles for the relief of these symptoms is part of the problem. Traditional therapy confirms the man-made woman in her most deeply internalized conviction of personal failure (1983, pp. 96–7).

This theme, reiterated in more recent times by Janice Raymond (1986), Celia Kitzinger and Rachel Perkins (1993) and others, was also expressed in 1970 by Shulamith Firestone. In her usual powerful style, she puts it this way:

Freudianism in clinical practice has led to real absurdities . . . in fact as early as 1913 it was noted that psychoanalysis itself is the disease it purports to cure, creating a new neurosis in place of the old (we have all observed that those undergoing therapy seem more preoccupied with themselves than ever before, having advanced to a state of "perceptive" neurosis now, replete with "regressions", lovesick "transferences", and agonised soliloquies) (1970, pp. 47–8).

The more specific criticisms of the therapeutic practices of Freud and of psychoanalysis have centred on issues such as: the therapist as expert, the role of the unconscious and the need for transference.

The therapist as expert

Miriam Greenspan's analysis of the issue of the therapist as expert begins with a discussion of the "myths of psychiatric theory and practice" contained in the "Freudian approach" (1983, p. 16).[2]

Myth 1: "It's all in your head"

She calls this "the myth of intrapsychic determinism" which insists that "personal reality is essentially determined by unconscious forces within a person's mind" (p. 16). This belief, Greenspan says, ignores the fact of the interdependence of social and personal reality.

It views the private, personal realm of the individual as one polarity and the public, social realm of society as another. In isolating one polarity from the other, it misses the interdependence of each on the other . . . Instead, a person's emotional problems are divorced from any current social, historical, or economic context (pp. 16–17).

In encouraging women "to see the socially produced symptoms of sexual inequality as their own solely individual pathology" (p. 21), this myth is extremely destructive of women. It adds to a woman's self-loathing by encouraging her to lay the blame for her problems squarely on her own shoulders.

---

2. The wording of the titles is from Greenspan (1983), pp. 16, 21, 26.

Myth 2: *"Human emotional pain is a medical problem"*

When a woman experiences emotional pain and distress, she is seen by psychoanalysis to have an illness or a disorder that must be "treated" professionally.

> The assumption . . . is that . . . [a] woman's problems can be diagnosed and treated in a way that is analogous to the diagnosis and treatment of, say, influenza. Furthermore, the assumption is that such treatment will effectively help her with the daily concerns that have brought her to therapy—that fixing this woman's head will fix her life (p. 23).

Myth 3: *"Only an expert in diagnosis and treatment is equipped to offer a cure"*

The therapist as expert "is based on a fundamental inequality of power between doctor and patient" (p. 32) and, as such, Greenspan points out, the expert–patient relationship of psychoanalysis is one which women fit into much more comfortably than men, based as it is on the model of normal male–female relationships in our society. She says, "women are already socially prepared to accept as natural a relationship in which we see ourselves as inferior to and reliant upon an authoritative, powerful male figure" (p. 32).[3] It follows that

> In adapting to the Father Knows Best style of inequality in traditional therapy, women are positively reinforced to accept social domination in the rest of our lives . . . In effect, women are taught by the medium of therapy itself to collude in our own continued social subordination (p. 33).

Many of the techniques of psychoanalysis are designed to ensure the expert maintains his—and sometimes her—power. The requirement that the expert maintain a "posture of distance" (p. 28) from the patient is one such power technique. Greenspan points out that women who are patients learn to expect and adjust to "the blank stare of the therapist . . . to the absence of any sense of relationship . . . to the familiar silence . . . To the scrutiny of your words with no counter-balancing words of support" (p. 29). Also, the power of the expert is enhanced by the act of diagnosing and labelling patients. In a system set up to ensure that the expert is always right, any "disagreements with his superior knowledge are . . . construed as resistance—a manifestation of your illness or neurosis" (p. 30).[4]

---

3. While it is true that all women are "already socially prepared to accept as natural" a situation in which we see ourselves as inferior to men, heterosexual women are much more likely than lesbians to "fit comfortably" into that kind of therapeutic relationship. The choice of a lesbian lifestyle is a rejection (either conscious or unconscious) of the male/female power dynamic into which all women are conditioned.
4. In choosing to use male pronouns, Greenspan does not mean to imply that all psychoanalysts are men. It is the system of psychoanalysis (with its emphasis on the need for an expert who is powerful and withdrawn, and whose role is to scrutinise, make judgments, and come up with a diagnosis) that is male. Any woman working as a psychoanalyst has made the choice to work within that system.

The unconscious

The theory of "the unconscious" is one of the concepts available to the expert to use to enhance his own power. Though Freud wrote at length about the role of the unconscious, the truth is that there is still no evidence that it actually exists. Its use in therapy, therefore, is open to all kinds of misinterpretation and abuse. Elizabeth Ward articulates the feminist concern:

> The problem that feminist theorists face is not the theory of the unconscious but how it has been applied within male supremacist social structure: because we find that the *specifics* of what women or men, girls or boys, might fantasise about or act upon have been predetermined *by the tenets of male supremacy* (1984, p. 107).

Ward points to the situation of childhood sexual abuse as a concrete example of how the theory of the unconscious has been used against girl-children:

> psychoanalysis *expects* that girl-children, at a certain age, will be experiencing (and repressing) a desire to be possessed by their fathers . . .
>
> The Daughter who cries rape must have desired her Father and therefore, say the Freudians, she *imagines* (turns the desire into a fantasy reality) that she has had sexual relations with him (p. 107).

In a "male supremacist social structure," the theory of the unconscious can always be used to benefit the agents of oppression and blame the victim.

Transference

Finally, the psychoanalytic expectation of transference in therapy is another of Freud's theories that has come in for serious criticism from many in the feminist movement. Transference, when it happens naturally in therapy, can be a quite harmless aspect of the therapeutic relationship. It can, in fact, offer an opportunity for insight, provided the dynamics that are occurring are analysed and discussed openly between the therapist and the one who has sought her help. The main problem with the psychoanalytic understanding of transference, however, is that it is not simply accepted as a natural happening but, rather, is seen as something to be used and manipulated for the therapist's own ends.

Greenspan, in her account of the training she herself received as an intern in clinical psychology and community mental health (1983, pp. 39–86), recalls her introduction to the concept of transference. It was defined as "the process by which the patient transferred to the therapist feelings and attitudes that were not appropriate to the therapist but belonged instead to significant figures in her early life" (p. 80). It is interesting to note here Shulamith Firestone's description of transference, including her final remark expressing her opinion of its worth as a therapeutic tool:

> [The] therapy process is entered into with the help of a psychoanalyst through "transference", in which the psychoanalyst substitutes for the original authority figure at the origins of the repressive neurosis. Like religious healing or hypnosis . . . "transference" proceeds by emotional involvement rather than by reason. The patient "falls in love" with his analyst;

by "projecting" the problem on to the supposedly blank page of the therapeutic relationship, he draws it out in order to be cured of it. Only it doesn't work (1970, pp. 49–50).

From Greenspan's recollection of her training in "the workings of the transference relationship between patient and therapist", the emphasis, she says, was on "how to manipulate it" (p. 80).

> To further the therapy . . . it was considered essential for the therapist to maximize or enhance the transference. To do so, interns were instructed to take an "abstinent" posture toward the patient . . . withhold any opinions, feelings, and responses . . . *don't give her what she wants!* . . . Instead, the therapist must invite the transference by *intentionally frustrating the patient* (pp. 80–1).

Sandor Ferenczi, according to Jeffrey Masson, was "Freud's most beloved disciple" (Masson, 1988, p. 115); he made it clear that transference was not just something that was allowed to happen or not. In 1932, he wrote: "Psychoanalysis entices patients into 'transference'" (Masson, 1988, p. 121).

The emphasis on enticing, manipulating, frustrating those who seek the help of a therapist has made transference a very dangerous mechanism in the hands of those who are not without problems of their own. It gives to therapists the kind of power that enables them to do whatever they want and then to explain it away in terms of transference or countertransference. Since countertransference refers to "the therapist's feelings provoked by the patient's transference" (Greenspan, 1983, p. 84), the blame for anything that happens in therapy can be, and almost always is, laid on the shoulders of the victim. A recipient of therapy is conveniently blamed for anything from Greenspan's example (from her internship training) of a therapist's falling asleep during a therapy session to the much more destructive situation of sex between therapist and patient. The therapist who fell asleep is reported to have said to his patient the following week: "There must have been something in what you were saying or doing that made me fall asleep. What do you think it might have been?" Similarly, many unscrupulous and self-serving therapists who have sex with their patients turn the blame around and say: "There must have been something in what you said or did that seduced me into having sex with you. What do you think it might have been?"

Transference, if it has a place at all in therapy, is only acceptable when it occurs naturally, and only helpful if it is discussed and interpreted at the time of its occurrence. Countertransference, on the other hand, which refers to a situation in which the therapist uses the recipient of therapy for his or her own ends, for the working out of his or her own problems, is never acceptable and has no place at all in a therapy that is concerned with helping women find release from their oppression.

In sum, a feminist therapy based on a socio-political philosophy rejects the concept of "the therapist as expert", finds the concept of "the unconscious" highly questionable, and names the concept of "transference" a dangerous device open to misuse by unscrupulous therapists.

Jacques Lacan

Freudianism in its various forms has dominated psychiatry and psychology for the past hundred years. A new movement in psychological thought, the human potential movement, came into prominence in the 1950s and early 1960s. While the human potential and humanistic therapies held much promise and quickly gained an enthusiastic following, psychoanalysis was by no means dead. In fact, with postmodernism and, in particular, the work of Jacques Lacan, Freudian psychoanalysis has experienced a new lease of life in recent years. Amongst feminists, too, as Elizabeth Grosz points out, there has been "a dramatic turn-about in attitude towards psychoanalysis". Even a superficial survey of feminist literature over the last twenty years, she says, reveals "the re-evaluation of positions" on psychoanalysis, "the positive affirmation of a theory previously reviled" (Grosz, 1990, p. 19).

Focusing on the relationship between feminism and the work of Jacques Lacan, Grosz speaks of "contradictory evaluations" of his work by feminists. Some defend his theories and see his work as a significant feminist breakthrough, while others "are extremely hostile to it, seeing it as elitist, male-dominated, and itself phallocentric" (p. 147). Grosz continues:

> It is never entirely clear whether he is simply a more subtle misogynist than Freud, or whether his reading of Freud constitutes a "feminist" breakthrough. The utility of psychoanalysis for feminist endeavours remains unclear. It is a risky and double-edged "tool" (p. 147).

Somer Brodribb is one feminist who experiences no such ambivalence in relation to the work of Lacan or, indeed, to any of the theories of poststructuralism or postmodernism. She says:

> I define poststructuralism/postmodernism as a neurotic symptom and scene of repression of women's claims for truth and justice. Postmodernism is the attempted masculine ir/rationalization of feminism. I prescribe a listening cure for this masculinity *in extremis*, this masculine liberal philosophy in totalitarian form (1992, p. 20).

What is needed, she says, is "feminist thinking that does not take on the masculine construction of a question . . . We need women's work that . . . refuses the silencing of women by the masculinization of the feminist project."

She goes on to remind us that "A feminist sensibility [is one which] proceeds from a different understanding of psyche, consciousness and value than sexist non-sense" (p. 147).

One of the criticisms feminists make of Lacan's work is that it is deliberately obscure. It is described by Hazel Rowley and Elizabeth Grosz as "a labyrinth of puns, alliterations, and neologisms. Colloquialisms, slang, and coarse humour appear beside highly abstruse allusions" (Rowley and Grosz, in Gunew, ed., 1990, p. 183). Again, in *Jacques Lacan: A Feminist Introduction*, Grosz says, "Lacan cultivates a deliberate obscurity" (p. 13), and in a comparison with Freud, she says:

Lacan seemed to actively court controversy . . . [He] works largely by indirection, circularity, ellipsis, humour, ridicule, and word-play . . . [He] seems to go out of his way to flirt, mock, seduce and insult . . . [He] plays the gigolo (p. 14).

It is this, she says, that "makes his work all the more fascinating, all the more luring and ensnaring for feminists, seeing he so actively courts (and baits) them" (p. 14).

It is this arrogance that also turns many feminists off. I argue that a style that is "deliberately provocative, stretching terms to the limits of coherence, creating a text that is difficult to enter and ultimately impossible to master" (p. 17), has nothing of any significance to contribute to the resolution of women's day-to-day struggles.

A feminist therapy that is radical and political rejects the work of Lacan, not only because of its arrogance and deliberate obscurity, but also because of its reformulation and revitalisation of Freud's emphasis on the phallus and his rejection of women.

In Lacan's essay "The Meaning of the Phallus", he argues that "the phallus is the primordial signifier". Brodribb explains:

Lacan refutes the work of Melanie Klein on the centrality of the mother in theories of symbol and sublimation and replaces her mother with his Phallus. The centrality of the mother as *imago* appears in the work of Irigaray and Klein.

As Brodribb continues, Lacan's attitude toward women is made clearer:

Lacan regretted that the father of psychoanalysis left it in the hands of women, who "are beings full of promise, at least to the extent that they have never kept any yet" . . . It is the phallus that Lacan wants to put in the minds and hands of women (p. 95).

He claimed that "the phallus was most symbolic: it is naturally the privileged signifier . . . Women can only come to culture and language by wearing the phallus, and then always inadequately and incompletely" (p. 95). Brodribb goes on to say:

This rejection of women, material and abstract, is nowhere more evident than in Lacan's view of *vulva*. First, he suggests that the name derives from the universal sound men make during intercourse. The vulva is a void and void of meaning. All it signifies is being empty of a penis (p. 95).

He refers to the "feminine sexual organ" as "the form of openness and emptiness . . . a gaping opening . . ." (Lacan, quoted in Brodribb, p. 96).

Even this brief glimpse of Lacan makes it clear that a feminist therapy, concerned as it is with the liberation of women from oppression, must reject the oppressive attitudes and theories of Lacan, and with them the practice of Lacanian psychoanalysis.

6

HUMANISTIC THERAPIES

The human potential movement of the 1960s marked the beginning of a courageous break from the old, oppressive, therapist-centred model of traditional psychotherapy and the development of a new, "liberating", client-centred model that came to be called "humanistic therapy". A reading of the early literature leaves one in no doubt that the founders of humanistic therapy or "third force", as it is sometimes called,[1] were attempting to provide a therapy that was very different from the "blame-the-victim" emphasis that had dominated psychology and psychiatry since the nineteenth century.

A study of the work of the early humanists reveals that they did, indeed, provide a therapy that was different but that, in their attempt to eliminate the injustices of the past, they inadvertently introduced new ways of blaming the victim.

The problem was that, in insisting that liberation was available to all, this new therapy, based as it was on middle-class, white, male values, failed to take into account the total lack of power, the total lack of freedom of choice that is a daily fact in the lives of the oppressed. In proclaiming the myth "that only individual merit and perseverance determine success, that people are essentially free, as individuals, to overcome completely the social obstacles in their path" (Greenspan, 1983, p. 140), the humanists set up a situation where those whose circumstances made it impossible for them to choose to be empowered were seen to have failed. Once again, the victim was blamed.

The label "humanist" or "humanistic" includes the following therapies and their (all male) founders: the human potential movement (Carl Rogers, Rollo May, Abraham Maslow, Gordon Allport), Gestalt (Frederick Perls), Transactional Analysis (Eric Berne, Claude Steiner), psychodrama (Jacob Moreno), psychosynthesis (Roberto Assagioli), and primal therapy (Arthur Janov).

Humanist therapy placed positive emphasis on self-awareness, self-esteem, personal growth, empowerment, and individual achievement.While it was embraced whole-

---

1. The term "third force" distinguishes humanistic therapy from the first and second forces, namely, psychoanalysis and behaviourism.

heartedly by many feminists, there also emerged a strong feminist case against it. To begin with, there was an almost celebratory emphasis, as illustrated by the titles of the books that emerged: "Women as Winners", "Born to Win", "Body Work for Women", "Superwoman", "The New Assertive Woman".[2]

After the initial euphoria wore off, however, some of us began to see what the promises of individual freedom and empowerment actually meant for women. They offered very little of any positive value. For the majority of women, they meant simply more frustration, more self-blame, more guilt, more feelings of inadequacy and personal failure, brought about by the fact that their social situation made it impossible for them to achieve that which everyone now believed was "freely available to all". All a woman had to do was *choose* freedom, and she would be free. All she had to do was *take responsibility* for her own happiness, and she would be happy. All she had to do was *respond assertively* to whatever life sent her way, and she would be a "winner". Easy!

Miriam Greenspan spoke of humanist therapy's "false promises of power" (1983, p. 124) to those who were socially powerless. She and other feminists pointed out that no amount of personal, individual awareness would change the oppressive structures of a society bent on keeping one group in power at the expense of other groups. Social power was simply not available to women, racial minorities, the poor, those with disabilities; any therapy that proclaimed the universal availability of freedom and power and happiness was simply ignoring the fact of oppression.

Before presenting the major feminist objections to the humanist orientation, so clearly expressed by Greenspan, it seems important, first, to remind ourselves of the basic tenets of humanist therapy. Such a task can best be done by reference to the work of Carl Rogers, who is usually identified as the founder of this new movement in therapy.

Carl Rogers (1902–87) and his colleagues were responsible for the new emphasis that began to emerge in therapy in the early 1960s. Describing the change in attitude that took place in himself and his work, Rogers says:

> in my early professional years I was asking the question, How can I treat, or cure, or change this person? Now I would phrase the question in this way: How can I provide a relationship which this person may use for his own personal growth? (1961, p. 32).

The change was no less than remarkable. It rejected totally the idea of the therapist as the expert whose task it was to analyse, diagnose and treat the "patient" who was "sick". Instead, the therapist was simply a "facilitator of personal growth" whose role was to provide an environment and a relationship in which the "client" could do her own growing. Rogers stated his overall hypothesis as follows:

---

2. Dorothy Jongeward and Dru Scott (1976), *Women as Winners*; Muriel James and Dorothy Jongeward (1971), *Born to Win: Transactional Analysis with Gestalt Experiments*; Anne Kent Rush (1973), *Getting Clear: Body Work for Women*; Shirley Conran (1979), *Superwoman in Action*; L. Z. Bloom, K. C. Coburn and J. Pearlman (1975), *The New Assertive Woman*.

If I can provide a certain type of relationship, the other person will discover within himself the capacity to use that relationship for growth, and change and development will occur (p. 33).

In describing what he meant by "a certain type of relationship", he discussed three attributes or skills that a therapist must bring to every counselling relationship. They were: realness, an attitude of unconditional positive regard, and a sensitive empathy (pp. 33–4).

If therapists were careful to provide such a climate, Rogers insisted, changes would automatically occur in their clients' lives. To illustrate his point, he wrote about the trends he "noticed" occurring in the lives of his own clients which (not inconveniently) just happened to coincide with the aims of the humanist therapy he was developing. The trends, he said, were:

- *Away from façades:* "I observe first", Rogers said, "that characteristically the client shows a tendency to move away . . . from a self he is *not*" (p. 167).
- *Away from "oughts":* Moving away from "oughts" and "shoulds", particularly those absorbed from one's parents, was seen to be a sign of maturity, of taking charge of one's own life (pp. 168–9).
- *Away from meeting expectations:* "Other clients find themselves moving away from what the culture expects them to be", said Rogers. "Over against . . . pressures for conformity, I find that when clients are free to be any way they wish, they tend to resent . . . [any attempts] to mould them" (p. 169).
- *Away from pleasing others:* "I find that many individuals have formed themselves by trying to please others," he said, "but again, when they are free, they move away from [the need to please]" (p. 170).

Already it is clear that, right from the beginning, the aims of humanist therapy ran contrary to society's expectations of women. If women were not content with their lot in life, they were expected to pretend contentment—to live a façade—so that the lives of their partner and children were not disrupted. Women's lives were full of "oughts". They learned at an early age that being female meant living one's life according to other people's expectations. Pleasing others was the activity that gave them the few rewards they ever received. The suggestion that women could be "free to be any way they wish" was a totally foreign concept to most women because their experience was one of being trapped in the expectations of a society that needed to keep them in a subordinate position in order that men, and the society men had created, could continue to be serviced.

It is clear, also, why humanist therapy was embraced so enthusiastically by feminists. Feminists saw it, in those days, as the key to releasing women from the bonds of society's oppressive expectations. It was the firm belief of some early feminists (and some feminists ever since) that women ought to be "free to be any way they wish" and here was a therapy that promised to show the way. The promises were many, as a further look at the trends Rogers noticed in his clients will reveal. Not only were there trends "away from . . .", but there were also trends "toward":

- *Toward self-direction:* "the client moves toward being autonomous", Rogers commented. "By this I mean that gradually he chooses the goals toward which *he* wants to move. He becomes responsible for himself" (pp. 170–1).
- *Toward being process:* Using the kind of therapeutic language for which Rogers became known, he said, "Clients seem to move toward more openly being a process, a fluidity, a changing . . . They are in flux, and seem more content to continue in this flowing current" (p. 171).
- *Toward being complexity:* Here he refers to one's "desire to be *all* of oneself in each moment—all the richness and complexity, with nothing hidden from oneself, and nothing feared in oneself" (p. 172).
- *Toward openness to experience:* He said, "the individual moves toward living in an open, friendly, close relationship to his own experience . . . he is opening himself to internal feelings". There is also "a similar openness to experiences of external reality" (pp. 173–4).
- *Toward acceptance of others:* Rogers also noticed that "As a client moves toward being able to accept his own experience, he also moves toward the acceptance of the experience of others" (p. 174).
- *Toward trust of self:* Here he speaks of having noticed that "simple people become significant and creative in their own spheres . . . [due to the fact that] they have developed more trust of the processes going on within themselves, and have dared to feel their own feelings, live by values which they discover within, and express themselves in their own unique ways" (p. 175).

Apart from Rogers' rather patronising tone, at times, and the beginnings of a language that was soon to develop into rampant psychobabble, the promises of individual freedom, personal choice, self-awareness and self-direction were intoxicating for many feminists who were therapists. As a matter of fact, much of what passes for feminist therapy to this day actually brings together a humanist-feminist philosophy with humanist therapy techniques.

Greenspan warns against such a marriage. She says: "The danger of a feminist therapy based on a humanist orientation to the self and society is that it ends up creating new myths for women to live by" (p. 140). Under the influence of Rogers' self-theory, of Gestalt, of Transactional Analysis, humanist feminists have preached the message that women can be free if they want to be; that women can be successful if they believe enough in themselves and their own abilities; and that women can be powerful if they have the courage to tap into their own personal power sources. Greenspan comments:

> some of the current feminist ideas about "empowering" women through therapy reflect a confusion about what power is and how women can attain it. There is a difference between an individual woman's psychic sense of her own power, and the social power of women as a group (p. 141).

The ideology adopted by many feminists who are therapists seems to ignore this difference. Greenspan goes on to explain:

> This difference is obscured by the humanist-feminist ideology that says that a woman can be "empowered" through a strictly intrapsychic process—that is, by liberating her mind and ignoring the systematic and institutionalized lack of power and access to power that is woman's lot in this society. This line of thinking inevitably, if unwittingly, results in educating women to model themselves on male styles of power and success (p. 141).

A therapy that encourages women to aim for empowerment and success in their individual lives creates a situation where women compete with and judge each other. "If I made it to the top, then there's no reason other women can't do the same." "There's nothing standing in women's way, except women themselves." "All women can be successful, if they put their mind to it." "All women can be confident, assertive, powerful, if they want to be." These attitudes often expressed by women about other women come out of what is essentially "a masculine sense of power . . . based on hierarchical divisions between individuals", whereas what is needed is a situation of "women overcoming a common social condition together" (p. 141).

While not wanting to minimise the importance of helping women feel confident and empowered, Greenspan nevertheless issues the following warning to feminists who are therapists:

> if therapists train women to have different attitudes about their power as women and do not simultaneously work (and help their clients to work) to alter the institutionally built-in socioeconomic oppression in the society that awaits them, then therapists will end up merely creating a different kind of blame-the-victim myth: that if a woman doesn't make it, doesn't succeed, doesn't integrate herself, it is because she is not Superwoman enough, not liberated enough to do so (p. 143).

If feminist therapy is to avoid the humanist tendency toward blaming individual women for the problems they experience as a result of their oppression, the emphasis must be on the collective empowerment of women. As Greenspan says: *The ultimate goal of a genuinely feminist therapy must be to help a woman see how her own power as an individual is inextricably bound to the collective power of women as a group* (p. 142).

The following is a more detailed analysis and critique of humanist therapy with particular reference to the influence of Gestalt and of its founder, Frederick Perls. The analysis will be undertaken by highlighting some of the best-known themes of the humanist movement and pointing to the main concerns and criticisms voiced by feminists since the early 1980s.

"You are you and I am I"

This sentiment, which is sometimes expressed as "doing your own thing" or "you do your thing and I'll do mine", represents the central theme of the humanist orientation, which is *extreme individualism*. As Greenspan comments:

> The essential core of the humanist theory and practice of therapy is an unshakeable belief in the individual's capacity to create himself and his life . . . The idea here is the simple proposition that you are responsible for your own reality—not society, not the environment, not the past, but you as a person right now (pp. 123–4).

The problem such an individualistic focus presents for women, feminists argue, is that it serves to keep women separated from each other and, therefore, from the power that is available to us through solidarity and connectedness. There is no clearer expression of the "me" emphasis of humanist philosophy than that found in the so-called Gestalt "prayer", as follows:

> I do my thing and you do your thing.
> I am not in this world to live up to your expectations.
> And you are not in this world to live up to mine.
> You are you and I am I,
> And if by chance we find each other,
>   it's beautiful.
> If not, it can't be helped.

Greenspan refers to "this little ditty" as the ultimate expression of "the humanist view of the self". She describes it as:

> a spinning center with no particular connection to any other spinning center except, perhaps, if one such center should happen—by chance—to collide with another. Should such a meeting take place, so much the better. If not, the self spins off, happily ensconced in its warm cocoon (p. 127).

Without a doubt, the humanist orientation, with its total lack of any sense of inter-relatedness, any sense of responsibility for the situation of others, has had a profound influence on all aspects of Western culture. The "me" generation, as it is often called, has produced a society where "people are neither politically nor morally nor personally responsible for one another". The important thing seems to be that "you satisfy yourself and 'do your own thing'" (p. 127).

Greenspan draws attention to the fact that, even though there is an "enormous difference between the traditional and humanist views of the individual, both rely on . . . the myth that 'it's all in your head'". Consequently, she says, clients of humanist therapy are as adversely affected as clients of traditional therapy, because both are encouraged to "blame themselves for lacking total control over their own lives" (p. 124).

"I'm not responsible for how you feel"

This sentiment follows directly on from the previous one. If "you are you and I am I", and if I am in this world "to do my thing" and you are in this world "to do your thing", then it follows that I am not responsible for how you feel when my "doing my own thing" bothers you.

A fact that seems not to have been apparent to the early humanist therapists was that when one person in a relationship (usually the man) insists on doing his own thing all the time because that is his "right", then the other person in the relationship is forced to adjust her own wishes and desires to fit in with his. The humanist theory is presented as if it is possible for both parties to do their own thing but, in practice, if there is to be a continuing relationship, one partner, usually the woman, has to be prepared to put her own "thing" aside in order to preserve the relationship.

Why is it, we ask, that the humanist philosophy seems to have worked reasonably well for men, but not so well for women? The reason, which appears quite obvious in hindsight, is that humanist philosophy was aimed at men. It was *men* who were to be free to do their own thing, not women. Sentiments like: "I'm not responsible for how you feel" very conveniently provided a legitimation of existing male behaviour or, at least, of the kind of behaviour men always believed to be their right. Thanks to the humanist movement, men now had permission to do whatever they wanted without having to consider the consequences to others. If anyone objected, that person could now be told: "That's your problem! I'm not responsible for how you feel."

One of the tasks adopted by humanist therapists was that of helping women, in particular, acknowledge that their unhappiness was indeed their own problem. Blaming your partner's behaviour for your own unhappiness was simply unacceptable. When a woman sought the help of a therapist, it seemed to be assumed that her partner had a right to do whatever he was doing and that her inability to cope with his behaviour was a sign that *she* was the one with the problem. No consideration was given to the woman's need for the therapist's confirmation that her partner's behaviour was oppressive and was, in fact, the cause of her distress. The issues of justice and honesty seemed to have no place in the therapeutic context. Rather, the focus was on helping her to adjust so that she could cope better with his behaviour and, as a result, feel that she had achieved something for herself.

"If it feels good, do it"

This sentiment came to prominence with the rise of humanism and has been the hallmark of libertarian philosophy and lifestyle ever since. "If it feels good", don't let issues of justice and morality stand in your way. "If it feels good", don't stop to consider the effect your behaviour may have on someone else. Just go for it. Do it.

Most often, this sentiment was linked to sex, though it was also seen to legitimate all kinds of other indulgences as well, such as drinking, eating and drug-taking. Regarding sex, many encounter group experiences, human relationship groups and marathon week-ends, so popular during the 1960s and 1970s, had an air of "sexual freedom" about them. The future was not important. It was only the "here and now" that mattered. The inevitable consequences of one's actions were not a consideration. The only thing that mattered was letting go of your inhibitions and following your impulses in the here and now. "If it feels good, do it" and if, on returning home, your spouse is distressed and devastated at your betrayal, you are not responsible for how he or she feels. If your partner is upset, then it is your partner who has the problem.

The sexual revolution, as this change in sexual relations is often called, had a huge effect on women, but the effect was usually negative. Women were encouraged to be more sexually liberated. Women were encouraged to get in touch with their own bodies, to see sex as something to be enjoyed, to know what they wanted out of sex and to "demand" their right to be sexually satisfied. Women were encouraged to make use of pornography, to expand their sexual horizons by discovering sex-aids such as vibrators, dildos and other sex toys. Women were encouraged to experiment with sado-masochistic fantasies and practices as a way of increasing their sexual appetites and of making sex more exciting.

While many who identified as feminists saw the "sexual revolution" as an important opportunity for women, others saw it as a backlash against women's increasing independence. Sheila Jeffreys argues that

> the increasing independence of women [at the time] provided a direct threat to the maintenance of male power and privilege. That no such threat did materialise . . . owes a great deal to the success of the sexual revolution."

She goes on to say: "The science of sexology was founded on the assumption that sex played a crucial role in maintaining women's subordination" (1990, p. 93).

One of the most popular sex books ever written was Alex Comfort's *The Joy of Sex*. It is, in many ways, synonymous with the sexual revolution of the 1960s and 1970s. Every page advocates, "If it feels good, do it"—oral sex, anal sex, group sex, pornography, bondage, any kind of sexual experimentation you may want to indulge in. Some sexologists even argue for a more tolerant attitude toward practices such as sex with children and necrophilia. "Whatever turns you on" is their catchcry. The libertarian emphasis on total sexual freedom which focused initially on heterosexual sex has, in recent years, been taken up by gay and lesbian sex therapists. The discussion of lesbian sex therapy in Chapter Eight will reveal the same philosophy of "whatever turns you on", together with similar victim-blaming tendencies.

While humanist therapists encourage "sexual freedom" by saying "if it feels good, do it", feminist therapists call for integrity and justice. They say to women, "If it doesn't feel good, don't do it", and also, "If it doesn't fit with your own ethical and political standards, don't do it."

"Everything is relative"

Humanism, with its "live and let live" philosophy, discourages anything that appears to be judgmental. The effect of this in Western societies, so dominated by humanist theory and practice, has been to replace the values of justice and truth with pleas for tolerance and permissiveness. "Everything is relative", we are told. Postmodernism, too, presents a latter-day version of this same philosophy with its theory of "multiple positionings". Taking a stand on an issue is not important. In fact, nothing matters except, perhaps, texts, language and deconstruction. There is no such thing as "bad" behaviour. Different behaviours reflect different subjectivities. In humanism and postmodernism, this means all behaviours, including the sexual abuse of children and violence against women, are to be seen as relative to other behaviours on a continuum.

It is for this reason that feminists need to be wary about using the "continuum" argument as a way of making the statement that harassment, verbal intimidation and threats against women are all, in their own way, acts of violence against women.

While there is no doubt that harassment, intimidation and threats are acts of violence in their own right, to present them in terms of a continuum of violent behaviours enables the advocates of tolerance to take the feminist argument and use it in support of their theory that violent physical and sexual abuse of a woman is simply an extreme version of a verbal argument. A recent newspaper article about the murder of a woman by her husband reported a male police officer as saying: "It's a tragedy. It looks like a 'domestic' gone wrong." Feminists ask: Is there ever a time when a "domestic" could be said to have "gone right"? Is murder simply a little worse than physical abuse?

The continuum argument works like this: murder is a little worse than physical abuse; physical abuse is a little worse than verbal abuse; verbal abuse is a little worse than a "tiff". Since murder and a "tiff" are on the same continuum, a tiff must be regarded more seriously than it appears and murder less seriously. Everything is relative.

Greenspan comments on the philosophy of relativism by stating that when the emphasis is on "doing your own thing", it follows that "One thing is . . . as good as another . . . All values are leveled and equated" (p. 128).

Sexual liberalism, too, Sheila Jeffreys reminds us, was based on the "everything is relative" premise. "Some of the sexual revolutionaries did not seem to draw the line at any form of sexual practice", she says, and cites the sexual abuse of children as one such practice (1990, p. 97). The fact that sex with children was quite acceptable in some countries, the sexual revolutionaries argued, was proof that it was only a problem when people sought to make it a problem. The focus is placed on "the prudery of the victim" rather than the perpetrator's abuse of power. "In other words sexual abuse does not really exist except in the minds of people who are irrationally prejudiced" (p. 98). In the minds of sexual libertarians, "All sexual practices are seen as equally morally neutral" (p. 98).

In a society where everything is relative and where tolerance and a non-judgmental attitude are given top priority, there is no room for "shoulds" and "oughts". No one has the right to judge another person's behaviour, we are told. No one has the right to judge what another person should or should not do. Humanist therapists insist that words like "ought", "should", "right" and "wrong" have no place in our vocabulary because they limit us. "Every time we use 'should'," Louise Hay counsels, "we are either making ourselves wrong, or someone else wrong" (1984, audiotape). Does Hay really believe that "we" are never wrong or that "someone else" is never wrong? Voicing their objection to such a non-moral, non-principled stance, Celia Kitzinger and Rachel Perkins insist:

> Men oppressing women is *wrong*, apartheid in South Africa is *wrong*, millions starving to death while others live in affluence is *wrong*. Struggling against oppression is *right*. Treating each other with respect is *right*. Trying to build community is *right* (1993, pp. 71–2).

The liberal humanist sentiment that "everything is relative" and the corresponding belief that nothing is "bad" in and of itself, led to a situation where previously identified moral and criminal offences came to be labelled "sick". Expressing her disgust about the attitude of some mental health professionals to the crime of incest, Louise Armstrong said (as we saw in Chapter One), "We called it criminal, they called it sick." She continued:

> "Sick" became so thoroughly ingrained as the correct way to "understand" that even the appearance, in 1980, of a group of perfectly respectable doctors and professors under the banner of the "pro-incest lobby" could not shake the public's need to disbelieve the obvious. These men were passionately promoting the healing powers of "positive incest": they sought an open permission for sex with their children . . . And the media and the populace looked at these perfectly normal men and as one voice they cried, "Sick! That's sick!" (1990, p. 50).

Armstrong points out that the liberal humanist ideology, which views childhood sexual abuse in terms of "illness and cure, rather than crime and accountability", provides

> a new shield of protection of offenders. The mental health "understanding" has generously given them a new framework for denial, a new justification for retaliation and vengeance toward child-victims and women who break the silence (p. 52).

Phyllis Chesler reminded us, as early as 1972, of the need for therapists to be careful not to "banish the concepts of good and evil from the arena of human responsibility" (1972, p. 66n).

In replacing justice and truth and accountability with tolerance and permissiveness and understanding, humanist therapy has made it impossible for women and men to confront the real issues of their lives. Instead of encouraging people to search for the truth and, in so doing, to tap into their real pain and passion, humanist therapy encourages a superficial focus on individual personal responses. The message to women is: learn to accept whatever is, because people (men, at least) have a right to do their own thing and not be judged or held accountable for it. Therapy is there to help you adjust.

"Let it all hang out"

With humanist therapy's emphasis on group experiences came the pressure for people to make public what had, up till then, been privately held thoughts and feelings. "Get in touch with your feelings", we were told. "Talk about how you feel." "Get it out."

Janice Raymond warns women against what she calls "psychological hypochondria" (1986, pp. 155–6). With the pressure to "show and tell all", she says, "women engage in massive psychological strip-teases that fragment and exploit the inner life" (p. 156). Tragically, when "the inner life becomes the outer life", the inner self of a woman is wrenched out of its private depths and put on display for all to see. "Thus an inner life is reduced to an exercise in therapeutics" (p. 157).

Raymond observes that the humanist emphasis on feelings has encouraged women "to believe that what really counts in their life is their 'psychology'" (p. 155) and that, consequently, therapy has become a way of life to them. Miriam Greenspan comments that the concept of "therapy as a way of life" is encouraged and exploited by those who stand to gain from what has become a huge therapeutic industry:

> Growth becomes another market commodity necessary for our physical and mental well-being. Like a good laxative, growth therapy purges you of the garbage of the past and makes it possible for you to be open to consuming more and more growthful experiences (1983, p. 126).

Humanist therapy with its promise of liberation has, in fact, enslaved many people by creating a situation where the personal meaning of their lives is dependent upon finding new and better "growth" experiences. Greenspan puts it this way:

> Growth psychotherapies . . . often help to create not strong individuals but compulsive therapy consumers: people desperately in search of the new therapy or new pop psychology book or new technique that will finally set them free; people urgently seeking to buy what can be won only through the collective task of transforming the social world (p. 129).

While it cannot be denied that the humanist movement ushered in an era in psychotherapy that had the potential for being less oppressive and more liberating than traditional psychoanalysis, the fact is that it was aimed at white, able-bodied and mostly middle-class men, and not at women or other marginalised peoples. It was applicable only to those for whom personal and social freedom was a real possibility, and not to the oppressed, for whom real personal freedom will never be a possibility until it goes hand-in-hand with a radical change in oppressive social institutions and attitudes.

The central emphases of the humanist movement, as revealed in this discussion of its popular sentiments, were: the value of the individual, personal empowerment, doing one's own thing, taking responsibility for oneself, sexual freedom, sexual experimentation, satisfying one's impulses in the "here and now", replacing justice and accountability with tolerance and understanding, labeling moral and criminal offences "sick" for the purpose of encouraging sympathy rather than outrage and, finally, the recommending of therapeutic activity for everyone.

In the humanist therapies, those "clients" of therapy who benefited from the liberalism of the humanist movement were those whose social standing already allowed them the freedom to "be any way they wished". Women and other oppressed people did not enjoy that freedom and, consequently, humanist therapy became another vehicle of oppression for those already oppressed. As Greenspan explains:

> For most women—as well as for the economically and racially oppressed of both sexes—the myth of individual freedom sold by the new growth therapies is yet another betrayal. The impotence of the oppressed individual totally to alter the painful aspects of her existence *by herself* is not only ignored but perpetuated by an ideology that urges people to reject any forms of collective responsibility for one another's pain and to embrace instead absolute individual responsibility for one's own life. Thus the humanist orientation is ultimately useless to the oppressed. It becomes another blame-the-victim hype (p. 129).

The widespread appeal of the humanist orientation to therapy meant that there was no shortage of attempts to develop it further. On the one hand, there were those who, because of their own experience of "healing" through therapy or involvement in growth groups, genuinely wanted to find ways of making that experience available to more and more people. On the other hand, there were those who simply saw the personal growth movement as presenting them with a new entrepreneurial opportunity. Regardless of motive, what followed was the appearance of an extensive array of therapeutic opportunities, some of which came to be called New Age therapies and others, popular psychology. These two movements which, it will be seen, perpetuated the blame-the-victim emphasis of the humanist therapies, are the subject of the following chapter.

7

NEW AGE AND
POPULAR PSYCHOLOGIES

Since the line between New Age psychology and popular psychology is becoming more and more difficult to draw, it is important, for our purposes here, to deal with them together. Both movements have developed as extensions of humanist therapy and both, as will be seen, emphasise positivity, personal affirmation, empowerment and the need for healing.

The New Age movement in Western societies has been associated, at least in its beginnings, with alternative lifestyles and communities, while popular psychology has tended to be associated with the mainstream. New Age philosophy is expressed through a wide range of therapies as well as through literature, while popular psychology is expressed mostly through literature. The overwhelming majority of consumers in each case has been female.

The major focus of this chapter will be on reviewing two of the most popular books to emerge from those movements and analysing them, from a feminist perspective, in terms of their tendency to blame the victim. Before discussing the literature, however, it will be helpful to take a look, first, at some of the practical "therapies" that have come to prominence under the umbrella of the New Age movement.

Massage, massage therapy, therapeutic massage, remedial massage, to quote a few of its many names, has been used for centuries to relieve stress and promote relaxation. It gained renewed popularity in Western cultures with the onset of the New Age movement. Amongst feminists, too, it has been particularly popular and it cannot be denied that, if used only when needed, it can be a very useful practice. A problem arises, however, when the proponents of the "healing" nature of massage encourage a moving away from stressful activities and a moving toward a greater and greater focus on one's own relaxation and well-being. It was just such an attitude that was responsible for large sections of the feminist movement turning away, in the 1980s, from the difficult and extremely stressful work of raging against patriarchy and of fighting to change the oppressive structures of society. The move made by so many feminists away from stressful situations and toward their own personal comfort represented a considerable drain on feminist resources. For many, the need to be perpetually personally relaxed took precedence over the need to continue fighting at the front line of a very stressful battle.

When massage is advertised, as it was in a brochure on display at a women's centre recently, as taking "time out to relax and pamper yourself", as something that ought to be "a key part [of] your weekly body maintenance regime", it is in danger of becoming an activity for the self-indulgent. In a popular feminist newsletter emanating from a major Australian city, massage is advertised regularly as something that will "help you relax and unwind at the end of the week". It is said to be "for stress relief, re-balancing and the promotion of health and well-being".

Reiki is another of the New Age therapies that has risen to prominence in recent years and is also popular with feminists. It is said to be a "natural flow of energy that cannot be influenced by the mind" and gives one "the feeling of being reconnected to [one's] source of energy". The brochure continues:

> It accelerates the body's ability to heal physical ailments and opens the mind and spirit to the causes of disease and pain, the necessity for taking responsibility for one's life and the joys of balanced wellness.

The kinds of concepts used in Reiki publicity are: being fully in touch with the energy, feeling whole, reawakening one's innate power, taking responsibility for one's life. Implicit here is the sense that those who do not succeed in experiencing and making positive use of Reiki "energy" are somehow to blame for their own emotional or physical pain.

Body therapy, too, has been given a new lease of life with the New Age movement. At least one body therapist refers to herself in a feminist newsletter as an "optimal well-being consultant".

Rebirthing has also been very popular in recent years. Through special breathing techniques, one is said to be able to get in touch with one's earliest emotions and relive the trauma of one's birth. Why anyone would actually want or need to do that is not immediately obvious, but some people make a habit, through continual rebirthing experiences, of going back to what they believe are the early days and months of their lives. One rebirther, advertising in a feminist newsletter, refers to it as "a pathway to self-knowledge, aliveness and compassion".

Other therapies identified with and influenced by New Age philosophy are the natural therapies, herbalism, Bach flower remedies, reflexology and aromatherapy. In addition to the array of therapies, there is also extensive use of Tarot cards, palm reading, crystals and runes.

The term "attitudinal healing" seems to be used freely in the various New Age therapies. When a person is in pain and distress, for whatever reason, it is her own "attitudes" that need to be "healed". Such healing of attitudes involves perpetual positivity, unconditional forgiveness, making peace with your parents, saying affirmations and praising your pain. Feminist therapy's emphasis on reality, on the need for justice, anger, blaming and honesty, in order that emotional health may be restored, would be labelled "negative thinking". In New Age philosophy, reality and truth are replaced by positivity and pretence.

The message of the New Age therapies is clear: if you have a problem, it is *your* problem. It is not helpful to analyse the context of your life, the dynamics of your relationships, the unfair pressures you are placed under, the injustices, the oppression, the victimisation you are experiencing. Such analysis is called "negative thinking". You must keep the focus on yourself, your inner dynamics, your inability to think positively, your unwillingness to see yourself as a "beautiful person". The answer lies simply in your learning to affirm yourself, to take responsibility for your own healing, and to be happy. If your problems persist, *you* are to blame. It is because you are not working hard enough at healing your attitudes, not thinking positively enough, not saying affirmations enough. The victim is to blame.

To illustrate the "blame-the-victim" theme of New Age therapies, attention will be focused now on one of the most popular books to come out of the New Age movement, namely, Louise Hay's *You Can Heal Your Life*. The following discussion of this remarkably popular book[1] will proceed by analysing, first, its appeal and, then, its victim-blaming.

Louise L. Hay, You Can Heal Your Life *(1984)*

The appeal

It is not difficult to see why a book like this one has such appeal to people who are struggling to survive physically, emotionally, spiritually or economically in a society that favours the few at the expense of the many. It is no wonder that women, for example, are the major consumers of all New Age material because women are particularly vulnerable in a society that sets them up to be powerless, invisible, dependent, compliant, and then despises them either for fulfilling society's expectations and being exactly the way they are supposed to be, or for rebelling and refusing to fulfil the stereotype. Caught in an unwinnable situation, most women at different times in their lives experience feelings of worthlessness, emptiness, hopelessness, guilt, despair. It is not surprising, then, that a book which promises freedom and power and personal control is very attractive to women.

We will look at the reasons for the book's appeal.

Its language is spiritual

Throwing all modesty aside, Hay claims for herself the authority of a prophet or a divinely chosen mediator. Her heavily spiritual tone gives the impression that her words have the ultimate stamp of approval, that her promises are, in fact, promises from God. Not lacking in confidence for one moment, she speaks of her gratitude to "the Divine Infinite Intelligence for channeling through me that which others need to know" (1984, p. 210).

---

1. The 1988 edition, which was the first Australasian edition, boasts "over 1.5 million sold".

In her "treatment" paragraph at the conclusion of Chapter One, which she suggests people read several times a day, readers are encouraged to think of themselves, too, as channels of spiritual energy. They are to say: "I believe in a power far greater than I am that flows through me every moment of every day" (p. 15).

There is no doubt that people who are searching for something to give meaning to their lives can be drawn in quickly, first by the "divine authority" of the one making the proclamations, and second by the thought of having such divine power flow into and through themselves.

It emphasises the positive and discourages the negative

Each chapter begins with an "affirmation" which readers are encouraged to say over and over again. The following are some examples:

> The past has no power over me (p. 32).
> I am in the rhythm and flow of ever-changing life (p. 55).
> I cross bridges with joy and with ease (p. 70).
> The answers within me come to my awareness with ease (p. 81).
> All my relationships are harmonious (p. 103).
> I am deeply fulfilled by all that I do (p. 109).
> Every Experience is a Success (p. 113).

Anyone having difficulty coming to terms with oppressive events from their past, anyone longing for peace and harmony, anyone looking for answers, anyone in difficult or abusive relationships, anyone looking for fulfilment, anyone bogged down with feelings of failure, will find such affirmations very attractive indeed.

The total emphasis on positivity makes it clear that nothing "nasty" is ever acceptable—no criticising, no blaming, no judging. Contrary to biblical teaching about the role of God as Judge, Louise Hay pontificates that "The Universal Power Never Judges or Criticises Us." All we have to do is stop judging ourselves and repeat often the affirmation "Love is everywhere, and I am loving and lovable." Before long, Hay promises, loving people will come into our lives, those already in our lives will become more loving to us, and we will find ourselves easily expressing love in return (p. 8). Everything is wonderful!

Its message is simple

Hay has succeeded in reducing the complexities of life's problems to one simple requirement: loving oneself. "When people come to me with a problem," she says, "I don't care what it is—poor health, lack of money, unfulfilling relationships, or stifled creativity—there is only one thing I ever work on, and that is *loving the self*" (p. 14).

Just as understanding everyone's problem is simple, so is finding the answer to everyone's problem. Speaking of the "power greater than I am" as the "One Intelligence in this Universe", she says: "Out of this One Intelligence comes all the answers, all the solutions, all the healings, all the new creations" (p. 15). The absolute simplicity of this message is very attractive to many people.

It promises power

In addition to divine power, readers are promised absolute power in their daily lives. "We are 100% responsible for all of our experiences", she says. All we have to do is change our thought-patterns, release the past, forgive everyone, learn self-love, self-approval and self-acceptance, and we will find that "everything in our life works" (p. 5). If we accept the responsibility that is ours, we will experience the power to be and to do anything we want.

Another of Hay's treatment paragraphs that readers are encouraged to read over and over says:

> I am one with the very Power that created me and this Power has given me the power to create my own circumstances. I rejoice in the knowledge that I have the power of my own mind to use in any way I choose (p. 6).

The promise of power includes absolute power to change one's life, and also absolute power to choose. Even though her promises in both areas are no less than preposterous, people in distress want to believe such claims because they offer a hope where all seemed hopeless.

The power to change is a theme running throughout the book. Hay claims without reservation that, regardless of the circumstances of our lives in the past or the present, "we can totally change our lives for the better" (p. 4). We even have the power to change any and every physical illness that besets us. "We create every so-called 'illness' in our body", she says, and it follows that we also have the power to change that which we have created. The message to cancer-sufferers is: you created your own cancer, now you can change it simply by releasing your resentment. "Releasing resentment will dissolve even cancer", she says with all the confidence of a miracle-worker with divine powers of healing (p. 5).

Her message to AIDS-sufferers, too, is preposterous but appealing to those whose illness gives them little hope of a long life. She begins by placing total responsibility for AIDS on the shoulders of gay men. She says "gay men created a disease called AIDS" (p. 137). Then she goes on to argue that because youth and beauty are so important to gay men, "the experience of getting old is something . . . [many gay men] dread. It is almost better to die than to get old. And AIDS is a disease that often kills." Because gay men are afraid of getting "older" and of feeling "useless and unwanted", she says, it appears that many have decided, "it is . . . .better to destroy themselves first" (p. 138).

After stating, "We need to make some mental changes", she concludes her section on AIDS by saying:

> This is a time for healing, for making whole . . . We must rise out of the limitations of the past. We are all Divine, Magnificent expressions of Life. Let's claim that now!

While a gay man in the midst of a happy, productive life might find Hay's claims preposterous, that same man with the AIDS virus might cling to her words as his last opportunity to be cured. All he has to do is "make some mental changes" and seek "healing" and wholeness.

Just as everyone has the power to *change* their lives, so everyone also has the power to *choose*, according to Hay. Some of the claims she makes about the power we all have to choose our own lives are quite astounding but, again, they are so striking and written with such unquestionable authority that they are very appealing to many people. Under the heading "I Believe That We Choose Our Parents", she says:

> Each one of us decides to incarnate upon this planet at particular points in time and space. We have chosen to come here . . . We choose our sex, our color, our country, and then we look around for [a] particular set of parents (p.10).

The parents we select, she says, are those we think will help us with the work we have to do in this particular reincarnation. How does she know this? How can she claim this with such absolute authority? Her message, of course, is that, since we chose our parents, we cannot blame them for our own shortcomings.

We choose our thoughts, we choose to feel the way we do about ourselves, we choose our attitude to the past, we choose our physical and emotional illnesses, we choose to be happy or unhappy. If we can believe that everything in our lives is there because of our own choices, then we must also believe that we have total power to change what we have chosen as well as the effects of those choices.

It calls for understanding and forgiveness

Most people want to believe that it is possible to forgive those who have acted destructively toward them. Those who have tried to forgive but are burdened with guilt because they know they still hold resentment toward a particular person are encouraged by Hay's command to forgive. They now know it is possible. All they have to do is try harder.

If we are having difficulty forgiving someone, she says, it is probably because we have not tried hard enough to "understand" the one who has hurt us.

> How hard it is for most of us to understand that *they*, whoever they are we need most to forgive, were also in pain. We need to understand that they were doing the best they could with the understanding, awareness, and knowledge they had at that time (p. 14).

To ensure readers get her message about the need to forgive, she provides some pretty strong incentives. She says: "Resentment that is long held can eat away at the body and become the disease we call cancer. Criticism as a permanent habit can often lead to arthritis" (pp. 12–13). With no thought at all about the appropriateness or inappropriateness of forgiveness in any particular situation, she gives readers an exercise to help them forgive. You are simply to say the person's name and then say, "I forgive you for ——". You are to do it over and over again, and then imagine the person you are forgiving saying to you, "Thank you, I set you free now" (pp. 77–8). It is all so simple!

In one of her "treatment" statements, she adds: "I now look at the past with love and choose to learn from my old experiences. There is no right or wrong, nor good or bad. The past is over and done" (p. 205).

It is easily applied in practice

Another point to be made about the appeal of Louise Hay's book is its practical applicability. Readers do not have to think or analyse or reason or worry. Hay does all that for them. She sets out affirmations to say, exercises to do, "treatments" to read over and over again (self-hypnosis). She tells readers exactly how to read the book, what to think, what to believe, and also, she promises rewards. It is all very practical and easy to follow.

It makes promises that are difficult to resist

Finally, the promise of miracles is very appealing indeed.

> Loving and approving of yourself, creating a space of safety, trusting and deserving and accepting, will create organization in your mind, create more loving relationships in your life, attract a new job and a new and better place to live, and even enable your body weight to normalize.

She goes on to explain that "Self-approval and self-acceptance in the now are the main keys to positive changes in every area of our lives" (pp. 14–15).

In case all these promises are not enough, who could resist her other, very personal, promise that "when you work with these ideas my loving support is with you"! (p. 4).

Many of the features of this book that make it attractive and appealing to women are the same points that are identified as contributing to its victim-blaming.

The victim-blaming

The ways in which this book blames the victim are similar to those discussed in the previous chapter dealing with the humanist therapies. New Age therapies in general, and Louise Hay's in particular, blame the oppressed for being oppressed and also for their inability to rise above the effects of their oppression.

The positive theme of "you can do it if only you will learn to love yourself" runs throughout Hay's book; it is a classic example of psychoppression. From the title, *You Can Heal Your Life*, through to the last page, the message is clear: you *can* heal yourself, make yourself free, give yourself power, success, happy relationships, have a satisfying job, lose weight, etc., and *if you do not achieve those things, it is your fault.*

The emphasis on the individual and the requirement that the individual accept total responsibility for all her experiences (p. 5) is a heavy burden for those whose experiences in life are actually the effect of social oppression. Hay's writing, in effect, calls on women to ignore their oppression (because it does not really exist), and believe that life is and can be whatever they make of it.

Another blatant example of victim-blaming is the suggestion that we are each responsible for creating every illness that we have (p. 5). Thanks to Louise Hay, terminal cancer-sufferers who believe what she says, now approach their death with a huge degree of guilt, in addition to all the other concerns one has in such circumstances. If they accept her evaluation of their situation, they will believe, not only that they caused their own cancer but, also, that the reason they have not been able to find a cure is due to their own shortcomings.

AIDS-sufferers endure the physical and emotional pain of an approach to death over which they have no control; in addition, they must feel guilty because they "chose" to get AIDS in the first place, and then were not able to love themselves enough or take charge of their lives enough to be cured.

Hay's requirement of forgiveness is another example of her willingness to blame the victim. The emphasis is on the need for the victim to try to "understand" what motivated the perpetrator and then, regardless of what his motivation was, "forgive" him (p. 14). Feminist therapy's insistence that forgiveness ought not to be offered unless it is appropriate to do so, that is, unless the perpetrator is truly sorry and is taking steps toward making amends, is the total antithesis of Hay's call for unconditional forgiveness. A careful reading of her discussion of forgiveness reveals that she actually changes the focus of the injustice that occurs. Instead of the perpetrator being blamed for the injustice committed against the victim, she focuses on the victim as the one who commits an injustice by refusing to forgive. She says to the victim: "Search your heart for the injustices you still carry. Then let them go" (p. 78). Her advice to victims to do her exercise on forgiveness over and over again "to clear out any remaining rubbish" is an obvious indication that it is the victim who is blamed. It is the *victim* whose life is full of "rubbish" that needs to be cleared out. It is the *victim* who is full of injustices. There is not even a hint of blame directed at the perpetrator.

Not only is the oppressed blamed for her own oppression in Hay's scheme of things: she is also supposed to be understanding and forgiving so that the oppressor does not have to cope with being blamed.

While the confidence with which Louise Hay makes her diagnoses and offers her treatments is appealing to many who long to enjoy the same kind of confidence, *You Can Heal Your Life* essentially adds to the oppression of those already oppressed. It makes promises that it cannot fulfil. It encourages people who are already victims to blame themselves for not being able to achieve that which is unachievable. It calls on victims to ignore the real causes of their problems, to give up the search for a true and just explanation of their pain and distress and, in the manner of pretence, to be happy to operate at a superficial level: "everything's wonderful so long as you don't think too deeply".

While it does seem clear that Louise Hay had no intention of oppressing anyone through the system of "healing" that she developed, her work is, nevertheless, a classic example of the blame-the-victim approach of all New Age therapies.[2]

---

2. A more recent example of New Age literature and its appeal to women is Marlo Morgan's *Mutant Message Down Under* (1991), in which she purports to describe her journey through the Australian desert and her involvement with Aboriginal spirituality. Susan Hawthorne, in a hard-hitting review, refers to it as "A Case of Spiritual Voyeurism". In pointing out some of the many "factual errors", "borrowings", "misrepresentations" that appear in Morgan's book (which is being promoted to
cont. next page

Focusing attention, now, on the literature which has come to be known as popular psychology, it will be seen that it, too, follows the humanist tradition of blaming the victim. While less spiritual and more down-to-earth than New Age material, popular psychology also places the blame squarely on the shoulders of those who are searching for answers to the distress they experience. This strategy actually sells books. Women, in particular, because of their socialisation, are only too pleased to learn that it is they who are to blame, and only too willing to accept the blame and to work endlessly at "improving" themselves in the hope that that will change their presently unbearable situations.

Robin Norwood, Women Who Love Too Much (1985)

This book is representative of the popular psychology movement that has swept through countries like the United States, Britain and Australia since the early 1980s. It also focuses on women in those situations where women's oppression is greatest, and represents another aspect of victim-blaming.

The appeal

This book has been enormously successful in terms of sales as evidenced by the number of times it has been reprinted. From conversations with women, it is apparent that there is a great demand for it amongst middle-class women in Western countries and that the majority of women who read it seem to find it helpful, especially in relation to gaining a better understanding of the dynamics of their relationships with men. Norwood courageously exposes the all-too-common behaviours of men in heterosexual relationships as self-absorbed and oppressive, and women who are victims of such male arrogance are relieved to find a book that discusses their own situation so openly. In the United States, in particular, there has developed what could almost be called a cult following.[3]

Its title is alluring

In a society where women have been trained since infancy (when they received their first doll) to love and care for others, there is something quite satisfying about being told that your unhappiness and distress spring from the fact that you are doing exactly what you are supposed to do, but that you are doing it too well. There is something noble and good about the charge of loving *too much*.

---

2. *cont. from previous page*
   American women as an experience of personal and spiritual healing), Hawthorne expresses a concern that readers are being misled. "Morgan's book", she explains, "presents an unreachable group of people —all the more seductive to the rootless, confused, alienated-from-nature, stressed American buyer of this book—as a panacea for all of earth's ills" (1994, p. 33).
3. As well as the book introducing readers to the problem which Norwood calls "women who love too much", there are support groups for women who love too much and finally, there is a follow-up book called *Letters from Women Who Love Too Much* (1989).

It focuses on experiences common to women

Most women who have been, or are presently, in relationships with men can identify immediately with what Norwood is saying about the way women behave in response to the attitudes and behaviours of the men in their lives. Most can relate to the case studies either from first-hand experience or from their knowledge of the experiences of friends and relatives.

It is full of case studies

The first line of Chapter One begins: "It was Jill's first session, and she looked doubtful." After about twelve lines, Norwood has Jill beginning to tell her story in a way that would capture any heterosexual woman's attention: "I'm doing this—seeing a therapist, I mean—because I'm really unhappy. It's men, of course. I mean, me and men" (pp. 5–6). A woman whose primary relationships are with men is reminded, as she reads case study after case study, of her own sometimes desperate attempts to please the man in her life, to get him to communicate, to have him listen and understand what she is saying. She is reminded of how much and how often she has had to compromise herself, knowing that the word "compromise" is not in his vocabulary. She is reminded of all the effort she has put into preserving the relationship and for little, if any, return.

One of the attractions of so many case studies is that they allow readers to compare their own situation with the situations of the women whose stories are being told, and to conclude that their own experience is "not so bad". Norwood actually warns readers in her preface that that is a common reaction but, she says, it is one that readers should be wary of. She says it is common for a woman to believe

> that her problem is "not that bad", even as she relates with compassion to the plight of other women who, in her opinion, have "real" troubles . . . It is one of the ironies of life that we women can respond with such sympathy and understanding to the pain in one another's lives while remaining so blinded to (and by) the pain in our own (p. 4).

Regardless of Norwood's warning, the opportunity to compare oneself with the women in the case stories and "feel better" about one's own pain is one of the appealing aspects of this book.

It blames women

It seems strange to say that a book is attractive to women because it blames women for the problems they are experiencing, but it is true. Prior to reading this book, a woman may actually have believed that her husband's violent and abusive behaviour toward her was the cause of her distress, but once she is "enlightened" by Norwood's thesis, she realises it is her own behaviour that is causing her distress. He is not to blame, which is just as well because he has no intention of changing. She herself is to blame because she "loves too much".

To blame oneself has the effect of making the problems in the relationship appear manageable. All a woman has to do is change her thought-processes, change her attitudes, think of herself as "sick" and commit herself to a process whereby she will "get well". Blaming women is appealing to women because it gives the impression that, once a woman "gets well", the relationship will automatically "heal" itself.

It releases women from guilt by labelling them "sick"

In the preface, Norwood explains that, by reading this book, "We will come to understand how our wanting to love, our yearning for love, our loving itself becomes an addiction" (p. 1). Likening the experience of many women to that of alcohol addiction or drug addiction, she says "many, many of us have been 'man junkies' and, like any other addict, we need to admit the severity of our problem before we can begin to recover from it" (p. 2).

We can learn, she says, from co-alcoholic women "about why we have developed our predilection for troubled relationships, how we perpetuate our problems, and most importantly how we can change and get well" (p. 3).

It offers a programme of "recovery"

The programme of recovery outlined in Chapter Ten is offered with absolute confidence and is, therefore, very convincing. Norwood claims:

> in my personal and professional experience, I have never seen a woman who took these steps fail to recover, and I have never seen a woman recover who failed to take these steps.

How could any woman who is experiencing problems in her relationship resist such pressure? Then she adds: "If that sounds like a guarantee, it is. Women who follow these steps will get well" (p. 198).

The programme, based as it is on the premise that women are to blame for problems in their relationships and that all they have to do is acknowledge that they are "sick" and seek to be "well", is as follows:

1. Go for help.
2. Make your own recovery the first priority in your life.
3. Find a support group of peers who understand.
4. Develop your spiritual side through daily practice.
5. Stop managing and controlling others.
6. Learn to not get "hooked" into the games.
7. Courageously face your own problems and short-comings.
8. Cultivate whatever needs to be developed in yourself.
9. Become "selfish."
10. Share with others what you have experienced and learned (1985, p. 198).

It promises rewards for "recovery"

The book is full of promises about the miraculous changes that will take place in a woman who pursues a programme of recovery. A promise made in the preface is that when a woman sets out on the road to recovery, she will "stop the pain" in her life. "If you choose to begin the process of recovery," Norwood says, "you will change from a woman who loves someone else so much it hurts into a woman who loves herself enough to stop the pain" (p. 4).

Then there is the promise of "true intimacy". Speaking about the "thrill and excitement that comes . . . from knowing and being known", she concludes: "For a woman who loves too much, developing true intimacy with a partner can only come after recovery" (p. 45). While she does not actually promise that true intimacy will occur, there is no doubt that her intention is to give that impression.

Also, there is the suggestion that a woman on the road to recovery will be able to learn "how to live a healthy, satisfying, and serene life without being dependent on another person for happiness" (p. 59).

The promised rewards for recovery, running throughout the book, are actually summed up by Norwood in a list she refers to as "the characteristics of a woman who has recovered from loving too much" (p. 241). In an abbreviated form, they are:

1. Self-acceptance, self-love, self-regard.
2. Acceptance of others as they are.
3. Awareness of one's own feelings and attitudes.
4. Cherishing and validating oneself.
5. High self-esteem, so that one "does not need to be needed in order to feel worthy".
6. Allowing oneself to be "open and trusting with *appropriate* people".
7. Questioning the value of one's relationship: "Does it enable me to grow?"
8. The ability to let go of a destructive relationship and to seek support from friends.
9. Valuing her own serenity.
10. Awareness that "a relationship, in order to work, must be between partners who share similar values, interests and goals" (p. 242).

As with Louise Hay's book, it must be said again that many of the features of Norwood's work that make it attractive and appealing to women are those that also represent its victim-blaming, as the following discussion makes clear.

The victim-blaming

Robin Norwood's stated purpose in *Women Who Love Too Much* is: "to help women with destructive patterns of relating to men recognize that fact, understand the origin of those patterns, and gain the tools for changing their lives" (p. 3). While there is no attempt here to suggest that Norwood does not achieve her stated objectives, a feminist analysis reveals that it is what she *omits* from her discussion that allows her then to blame women for their own unhappiness.

There is nothing inherently wrong with the ten steps she sets out as a "program of recovery" but, because the focus of her programme is limited to the personal dynamics of each individual woman, it results, unavoidably, in the oppression of women. It is simply not enough to focus on a woman's "patterns of relating", a woman's need to understand her patterns, a woman's need to learn how to change her life, without any significant reference to the unjust and oppressive behaviour of her male partner.[4] In

---

4. Norwood's focus throughout is on heterosexual relationships, but unjust and oppressive behaviour is not confined to relationships between women and men. Some lesbian relationships which are not built on feminist principles can also be very oppressive.

line with all humanist therapies, the whole issue of the role of justice in mental health is ignored in Norwood's work.

The most blatant example of victim-blaming which, incidentally, is characteristic of all popular psychology movement literature aimed at women, is the labelling of "women who love too much" as "sick". A woman who finds it difficult to release herself from the need to "love" a man even though he consistently treats her badly, is said to be suffering from a "disease". She has an "addiction" (pp. 163–75). She is called upon to try to understand her "condition" (p. 4) and to stop behaving in those ways that keep her "sick" (p. 205). If she wants to "recover" from the "disease" of "loving too much", the requirement is that she follow the programme of recovery set out in the book.

The suggestion that those who are victims of other people's oppressive behaviour are, in fact, sick and need to involve themselves in a programme of recovery only serves to encourage victims to ignore the injustice of their situation and blame themselves for the way they are feeling. Justice demands, and psychological health requires, that the one who is blameworthy be blamed; but Norwood clearly disagrees. She says: "No matter how sick or cruel or helpless her partner is, she . . . must understand that her every attempt to change him, help him, control him, or blame him is a manifestation of *her* disease" (p. 185). It is not seen to be legitimate, or helpful, to focus blame on the blameworthy. Rather, the victim is blamed.

Another example of victim-blaming is the call for victims to change their behaviour while perpetrators, presumably, are free to continue in their destructive ways. One of the marks of a "recovered" woman is that she "accepts others as they are without trying to change them to meet her needs" (p. 242). The only demand for change the victim has a right to make, it seems, is of herself.

Finally, instead of encouraging a victim to leave the one who is oppressing her in a bid to free herself from his victimisation, Norwood seems actually to discourage such a move. She says: "When women come to see me, they often want to leave their relationship before they are ready." Avoiding the question of whether it is better for a woman to leave or stay, Norwood says: "As you follow [the process of recovery] . . . the relationship will take care of itself." Clearly she is saying that it is not the relationship that is the problem. It is the woman, the victim, who is the problem. Fix the "problem" and everything else will fall into place. As a woman follows the ten steps of the recovery programme, she says, "Being with him ceases to be the The Problem and leaving him ceases to be The Solution" (p. 201).

In summary, any system that encourages a woman suffering the effects of oppression in her relationship with her male partner to view herself as "sick", that encourages her to focus attention on her own need to "recover", that discourages her from blaming her oppressor, that discourages her from calling on him to change, and that discourages her from leaving him, is a system which clearly and blatantly blames the victim.

One other popular movement that needs to be discussed here is that referred to as "codependence" or "codependency". The terms "co-alcoholism" and "co-addiction", discussed by Norwood (p. 115), prompted the emergence of the term "codependency". Originally coined to refer to the problems faced by women married to alcoholics, the term was "discovered" by pop psychologists in the early 1980s and they have since turned it into a multimillion-dollar industry.

The all-embracing nature of codependency, as defined by pop psychologists, is described by Melody Beattie as follows:

> Many of us have suffered, and are still suffering to some degree, from a relationship with a dysfunctional person. Sometimes that person appeared in our childhoods, sometimes in our adult lives. Usually, we've had relationships with more than one dysfunctional person; this pattern began in childhood and repeated itself as we grew older (1989, p. 7).

In other words, in a situation where a victim (usually a woman) is oppressed by a "dysfunctional person" or a person who is morally and/or criminally reprehensible (usually a man), it is she, the victim, who is sick or diseased, and it is *she* who must embark on a "recovery" programme.

Referring to the huge industry that has developed around the concept of codependency, Wendy Kaminer, in her controversial, skeptical, witty critique, *I'm Dysfunctional, You're Dysfunctional*, says:

> Codependency is advertised as a national epidemic, partly because every conceivable form of arguably compulsive behavior is classified as an addiction. We are a nation of sexaholics, rageholics, shopaholics, and rushaholics. What were once billed as bad habits and dilemmas . . . are now considered addictions too, or reactions to the addictions of others, or both (1992, p. 10).

Codependency experts assert that anyone can suffer from this "disease" and, in fact, that almost everyone does! Kaminer comments that such a claim "makes this disease look more like a marketing device" (p. 10).

The many books written by codependence experts have a monotonous sameness about them, but such monotony does not seem to deter those intent on "recovery". The most popular, in terms of sales, seem to be: Melody Beattie's *Codependent No More* (1987); *Beyond Codependency, And Getting Better All the Time* (1989); Anne Wilson Schaef's books, *Women's Reality: An Emerging Female System in a White Male Society* (1981) and *Co-dependence: Misunderstood—Mistreated* (1986); and Janet Woitetz's *Adult Children of Alcoholics* (1983).

Support groups for codependents also became very popular and continue to have a large following. Those "suffering" from the "disease" of codependency can go along to a group called "Co-Dependents Anonymous" and talk with others *ad nauseam* about their own shortcomings and failures. One brochure from the approved literature of the "Co-Dependents Anonymous Service Queensland, Inc." (1993) sets out lists of traits that "need attention and transformation", under the headings: Denial Patterns, Low Self-Esteem Patterns, Control Patterns, and Compliance Patterns. As in all literature from the popular psychology movement, the victim is encouraged to blame herself.

Before she can be helped by the programme of recovery, called "the twelve-steps of co-dependents anonymous", she must acknowledge her patterns of denial, of low self-esteem, of control, and of compliance. Once the victim accepts the blame, recovery can begin—and the perpetrator, who is accorded no blame, is free to continue his destructive behaviour.

From the perspective of feminist therapy, the fact that the New Age and popular psychology movements have such appeal to women is a serious concern, because they encourage women to blame themselves for everything in their lives that causes them distress. Instead of helping women, who are the victims of male arrogance and oppression, to understand the real cause of their distress, New Age and popular psychologies encourage them to view themselves as sick and as needing to embark on a programme of recovery. Women are required to admit that they create their own problems and to realise that the desire to blame someone else is just a symptom of their own disease. Understanding and forgiveness is said to be the beginning of recovery.

In line with all therapies that have a humanist orientation, the two modern therapeutic movements discussed above blame the victim by focusing on the individual and claiming that every individual has the power to be whoever she wants to be, if only she tries hard enough. While the next chapter will deal with what appears to be a completely different kind of therapy, namely lesbian sex therapy, it will be seen that it, too, is based in a humanist philosophy and, as such, continues the tradition of blaming the victim.

8

LESBIAN SEX THERAPY

Imitating the libertarian themes of the heterosexual sexual revolution referred to in Chapter Six, lesbian sex therapy is fast becoming a booming business. In the United States, in particular, more and more lesbians are finding it fashionable to seek sex therapy, and to read the many books being produced for the purpose of encouraging lesbians to have more sex and also more varied sex. From the perspective of feminist therapy, this trend presents special areas of concern.

All sex therapies and sex advice books emanating from the humanist movement are based on similar assumptions about sexual desire, sexual behaviour, sexual ethics, and the role of the therapist. Lesbian sex therapy is no exception. The usual assumptions are as follows: there ought to be more sex in the world; those who say they are satisfied having sex occasionally, rarely, or never, are not *really* satisfied; all adults should want to expand their sexual repertoire; sexual expression is entirely personal and the only issues that matter are personal issues, such as choice, preference and consent; no one has the right to judge another person's chosen sexual behaviour; and sex therapists are the experts who can help people increase their sexual desire, learn new and better techniques, and expand their sexual repertoire.

Feminist therapists, concerned about the pressures placed on women by the sex therapy industry, find such assumptions highly questionable and the source of much oppression for women, both heterosexual and lesbian.

The focus in this chapter will be on lesbian sex therapy and, in particular, on the work of one self-confessed lesbian sex therapist, JoAnn Loulan. An examination of her writing, particularly *Lesbian Sex* (1984) and *The Lesbian Erotic Dance* (1990), reveals themes common to most of the work being produced today in the name of lesbian sex therapy, and also illustrates the victim-blaming inherent in the movement.

Before discussing Loulan's work, however, it seems important to spend some time enquiring into what it is that lesbians (and other women) are actually looking for when they speak to a therapist about sexual issues. The sex therapy industry would have us believe that women in great numbers are wanting to increase their sexual desire and their opportunities for sexual expression. Anyone who has worked as a therapist for any length of time, however, will attest to the fact that while most women who seek the help of a therapist in relation to sexual concerns do come to talk about their lack of sexual desire, the overwhelming majority do not indicate a personal wish to change their level of desire or their behaviour.

From a liberal humanist perspective, a woman who identifies as a problem the fact that she is not interested in sex, or that she has a lower sexual desire than that of her partner, is actually expressing a desire for more sex. The only real problem, libertarian sex therapists say, is that she is not yet aware of her hidden desires. This, they believe, is confirmation of the fact that women who say sex is not the central issue, or even a marginally important issue, in their lives are mistaken. The way to proceed, therefore, is to introduce such women to the kinds of new ideas and possibilities that will "turn them on".

Alternatively, feminist therapists, who are aware of the pressures on women in the area of sex and who value the pursuit of honesty in therapy, emphasise the need to help a woman talk about the circumstances in her life that led her to conclude that her lack of sexual desire was a problem. The conversation usually begins like this:

WOMAN: I need some help in the area of sex. I never seem to want it any more.

THERAPIST: [*After encouraging her to talk more about her concern and also about the relationship she has with her partner*] Would you like to have sex more often?

WOMAN: No. I'm quite happy the way things are—except that I feel guilty sometimes.

THERAPIST: Guilty about . . . .?

WOMAN: Knowing that my partner wants it, but rarely gets it.

It is at this point that the therapist's own beliefs about the place of sex in a relationship have a great effect on the way therapy proceeds. Those who believe that sex must be given priority, that there ought to be more sex in the world, that sex is liberating for women, that the feminist revolution is about sexual freedom, will point a woman in the direction of external aids to help increase her desire. Such external aids include vibrators, dildos, erotic and pornographic literature, X-rated videos, information about sex games, and sadomasochism.

Those therapists, on the other hand, who do not believe that lack of sexual desire is, inherently, a bad thing and who do believe that sex is a normal and natural, though not necessarily a dominant, part of a loving relationship, will move in the direction of talking about differences in sexual desire. When a woman realises, through the attitude of the therapist, that wanting sex only occasionally is just as legitimate and healthy as wanting it often, she usually feels free to talk about her *real* reasons for seeking therapeutic help. Not surprisingly, the reasons usually reflect her partner's needs and desires rather than her own. Commonly, a woman will give one of two reasons: either "My partner wants sex more frequently than I do"; or "My partner wants to experiment with new techniques, and I don't."

Regarding the issue of frequency, by the time a woman seeks the help of a therapist to deal with the fact that her partner wants sex more often than she does, the relationship has usually reached a critical point. Sex has become the central cause of conflict and its significance to the relationship has grown out of all proportion. While one partner spends much of the day, every day, thinking, "I wonder if she'll feel like sex tonight? How can I get her to want it? What can I do to get her turned on?", the other spends much of the day, every day, thinking, "I hope she doesn't want sex tonight. What can I do to take her mind off it? How can I avoid it?"

An interesting, and somewhat disturbing, legacy of the humanist movement's emphasis on the value of sexual freedom is that it is generally accepted in Western societies that the partner who wants sex more often is simply expressing a normal, healthy need, while the partner who wants it less often is seen to be in need of help. If one could continue to read the minds of the two women above, one would see this belief reflected in the thoughts of both of them. The first partner would follow up her original thoughts with: "I can't go on like this. There must be something wrong with her. She'll have to get help." The other partner would follow up her original thoughts with: "I feel so guilty refusing sex all the time. I don't know what's wrong with me. I'll have to get help."

When she eventually arrives at a therapist's office and begins talking about wanting to increase her level of sexual desire, if the therapist does her job properly and gets her to talk more about her situation, it usually becomes clear very quickly that she wants to increase her sexual desire because she thinks she *ought* to want sex more than she does. Also, she wants to please her partner; she wants to stop feeling guilty; she wants to stop hurting her partner by rejecting her all the time; she is afraid of losing her partner; her partner has threatened to leave or have an affair.

When someone is so willing to take on the blame, it is easy for a therapist to allow the blame to rest with that person and to proceed by focusing attention on finding a remedy for *her* problem, instead of working with her toward an honest evaluation of her situation. From the perspective of feminist therapy, a woman blaming herself for not wanting sex, combined with a libertarian therapist who believes sexual freedom is what women need, is a recipe for therapeutic disaster, a recipe for psychoppression.

Regarding the issue of experimentation, a very important rule about sexual behaviour is that no one should ever be forced or cajoled or seduced into doing something she does not want to do. No matter how important it is to a person to experiment with different kinds of sexual behaviour—oral sex, anal sex, bondage, sex games—if that person's partner does not want such involvement, then it is imperative for the long-term viability of the relationship that it not occur.

When such a situation arises and a therapist is consulted, a libertarian sex therapist would most likely label what is occurring between the couple as a *sex* problem, while a feminist therapist would see it as a *relationship* problem. The difference in labelling is crucial because the diagnosis determines the direction in which the therapy proceeds. As a sex problem, the one who is reluctant to experiment will be encouraged to "try out" different things in order to find something new that she enjoys—for the purpose of saving the relationship. As a relationship problem, on the other hand, the couple would be encouraged to acknowledge the impasse they have come to and work together to find ways to resolve it. It may be that the relationship will end because of it, but such a result is seen to be preferable to a situation where one partner feels she is continually compromising her integrity for the sake of the sexual needs of the other.

Honesty requires that a therapist make it perfectly clear to couples in therapy that any attempt to increase sexual desire by artificial and, in many cases, degrading means will not result in a loving relationship where sex is but one aspect of the whole. Rather, it will result in a situation where sex and the pursuit of sex become the central focus of the relationship.

Any therapist who considers working to help a woman increase her sexual desire for the purpose of "saving" her relationship needs to be aware that this strategy very rarely works. Furthermore, such a therapist is in danger of colluding in the woman's oppression, for the following reasons:

- it is usually the woman's partner who benefits from the increased sexual activity or experimentation, and not the woman herself; and
- it turns sex as an expression of love and passion into sex as a power game where one partner is sure to lose.

JoAnn Loulan

JoAnn Loulan's work is situated, unmistakably, in the liberal humanist tradition and, as such, must be viewed with caution by feminist and lesbian feminist therapists. Sheila Jeffreys warns:

> The new libertarian lesbian sex therapists are involved in constructing lesbian sex to resemble the heterosexual version as nearly as possible. They are recycling the old shibboleths of male supremacist ideology to lesbians. They are telling lesbians that they are sexually deficient, that they are erotophobic, heterophobic and generally just not very good at sex (1993, p. 47).

They are involved, she says, in "the reconstruction of lesbian sex by teaching lesbians how to develop . . . 'heterosexual' desire, that is desire which eroticises inequality". While the lesbian sex therapists see themselves as ushering in a lesbian sexual revolution, Jeffreys insists that

> this lesbian "sexual revolution" is no more positively linked with freedom for lesbians than the heterosexual revolution was with freedom for heterosexual women . . . [It] is not coming from the separate space that lesbian feminists have . . . tried to create. It is permeated with old-fashioned patriarchal woman-hating values (p. 47).

The following is a critique, from a feminist perspective, of some of the major themes running throughout Loulan's work.

Sex is an entirely personal issue

JoAnn Loulan makes it clear that her choice to write "for individuals" (1984, p. xii) is based on her belief that sex is an entirely personal matter. She quotes Amber Hollibaugh, who asks: "Who defines the terms of anybody else's erotic system? Who gets to say what's real or bad with anybody else's sexuality?" (Loulan, 1990, p. 26). Loulan's concern is to help individual lesbians accept themselves as they are and, in particular, to accept the way they like to have sex (1984, p. 9). "As we each accept ourselves and our sexuality," she says, "we will break through our sexual blocks and create a body of knowledge about what women's sexuality is truly all about" (p. 15).

She is highly critical of "members of the lesbian community" who try to "politicize sex". She accuses them of "[fostering] homophobia by trying to establish 'politically correct' ways in which lesbians may express their sexuality" (p. 23). In direct response, it seems, to the work of feminists like Sheila Jeffreys, Loulan insists that no one has the right to tell others what is acceptable sexual activity. No one has the right to judge lesbians whose views and sexual practices differ from their own. She expresses it like this:

> The majority culture engages in more than enough legislating around sexual behavior, and we lesbians do not need to also dictate what is or is not acceptable lesbian sex. Sex should dwell within the privacy of our own lives. If we do not like a particular sexual act, we do not have to engage in it. Sex between two consenting women means that what they do and how they do it is between them (1984, pp. 23–4).

Such a statement of blatant libertarian philosophy reveals a serious lack of understanding of the relationship between the personal and the political. To suggest that what individuals or couples do in the "privacy" of their own lives can actually be confined to the private arena is naive in the extreme. The truth is that the ways in which individual lesbians choose to behave do have an effect on the general culture of the lesbian community. Consequently, it is important that such behaviour be open to political analysis.

Jeffreys suggests that feminists "should surely be suspicious of the argument that any area of 'private' life should be immune from political criticism" (1993, p. 58). Those who want to "privatise sex and exclude feminist insights", she says, are working to "protect the heteropatriarchal construction of sexuality". The other option, the preferred option, is "to understand that sexuality is fundamental to the oppression of women and to direct the courage and vision of lesbian feminist political analysis to what lesbians do in bed" (p. 58).

There must be total acceptance of all sexual "rhythms"

Closely connected to the theme of sex as an entirely personal issue is the theme that calls for open-mindedness and acceptance of all sexual rhythms and styles. No matter what individual lesbians choose to do, there is an expectation of total acceptance. Loulan is so positive in her attitude that she calls for a language to describe the variety of lesbian sexual styles that are possible. With just a little thought, she came up with twenty-five styles, and they all have to do with "fun", she says. "They're to be played with, tried on, hung out to dry" (1990, p. 140). She confesses that her favourite in the "fun" category is the style called "Lesbian Vampire", inspired by the ancient vampire myths.

Lesbian vampire

A lesbian vampire, so the myth goes, "sucked the blood of another woman, creating an extremely sexualized, erotic experience for both". Sounds like fun! Referring to a paper by Sue-Ellen Case, Loulan says "the early use of lesbian vampire imagery was of a powerful female seducing another woman who was thrilled at being taken" (pp. 164–5).

Loulan then translated this somewhat questionable image into what she calls "the modern day 'lesbian vampires'", namely those lesbians who are "practiced in the art of seducing heterosexual women". The lesbian vampire preys on heterosexual women and the thrill is in the success of the chase.

> Bringing these women into the ranks of her own kind is the excitement . . . It's the thrill of finding a woman who, like a diamond in the rough, is just waiting to experience her true sexual energy. The lesbian vampire is thrilled by the swoon of the woman who has been unconsciously waiting to join her sisters (p. 165).

What then? Nothing, because the lesbian vampire has had her thrills and simply moves on to the next unsuspecting heterosexual victim.

Is it too much to ask for some kind of ethical or political analysis of such behaviour? In the opinion of lesbian sex therapists, any attempt at such analysis would be called "politicising sex", which is forbidden. Any and every sexual style chosen by individuals or couples is to be accepted by the lesbian community without question.

While it is not necessary, here, to discuss all twenty-five of Loulan's "rhythms" or "styles", it is important to examine a few of them to see the kinds of behaviours the lesbian community is being encouraged to accept.

Butch and femme role-playing

Loulan applauds the return of the 1950s scenario of lesbians imitating the roles they observed in heterosexual relationships. Instead of simply acknowledging butch and femme role-playing as part of lesbian history, Loulan calls them "two of our primary sexual archetypes" (1990, p. 24), and is highly critical of lesbian feminists who insist that such role-playing is nothing more than the eroticising of unequal power relations. She says:

> There was tremendous pressure with the advent of feminism to deny and even debase the concept. Yet despite all the efforts at silencing, butch/femme remains an erotic archetype that has become an almost universal symbol to lesbians (p. 24).

In an attempt to counter the feminist argument (though it seems to do more to *support* the feminist argument than counter it), she quotes a butch lesbian explaining that there is nothing unequal, no imbalance of power, in her relationships with femmes. She says:

If the woman can be submissive and surrenders and receives, I feel she is in control, not me. I'm not looking to her to satisfy me. I'm looking more to satisfy her and to be satisfied. If she is receptive, I can be aggressive. There is absolutely no way I can express this part of me and get this part of me fulfilled if she wasn't receiving, if she was closed to it, if she felt oppressed. It's really different for me than traditional male stuff (p. 51).

The question that automatically springs to mind is: How? When the expectation is that one partner will be "aggressive" and the other "submissive", "surrendering" and "receptive", how is it any different from the inequality and oppressiveness of heterosexual relationships?

Undeterred, Loulan maintains that it is the "denial of . . . [these] core sexual images" that has deprived the lesbian community of "a language of eroticism" (p. 26) and it is for that reason that she argues for their resurrection and total acceptance.

Sadomasochism

While deliberately ignoring the political ramifications of sadomasochism (S/M) by declaring that she does not intend to discuss "the politics of whether or not S/M is correct or incorrect", Loulan tells readers they just have to "admit that S/M is definitely another sexual rhythm out there". Since "it's not going to go away just because some people wish it would", she says, we may as well acknowledge it, accept it, and "try to create a loving and safe dialogue" about it (pp. 144–5). As for Loulan herself, in true humanistic, non-judgmental, open-minded, tolerant fashion, she expresses a sincere interest in those involved in sadomasochism. "What makes the S/M lesbian sexual energy different from other types of lesbian sexual rhythms?" she wonders, and then adds: "I'm interested in the dance that these women create with one another" (p. 145).

In contrast to this totally permissive attitude that lesbian sex therapists boast of, feminist therapists wholeheartedly reject the call for acceptance and tolerance, and point instead to the need for serious ethical analysis together with personal and professional integrity. In this respect, the stand taken by feminist therapists is informed by the work of feminists like Sheila Jeffreys, who refers to the acceptance and support of sadomasochism by lesbian sex therapists as promoting "eroticised inequality" (1993, pp. 50–3).

Jeffreys draws attention to the words of one lesbian sex therapist who not only supports, but actively promotes, S/M. Margaret Nicholls states: "it is critical that as therapists we play a role helping gay women renew and revive flagging sexuality" (Jeffreys, 1993, p. 51). Nicholls refers to herself as "a sexual enhancer" who, according to Jeffreys, "teaches sadomasochism to revive sexual activity in long-term relationships" (p. 51). In addition to promoting sadomasochism, Nicholls also recommends butch and femme role-playing, fighting in relationships, tension, taboo, and power discrepancy, because all of these activities, she maintains, are good for sex (pp. 51–2).

Those therapists who accept sadomasochism and promote it as an interesting and daring form of lesbian sexual behaviour do no favours for the lesbian community. Instead of encouraging lesbians in the development of new patterns of intimacy, patterns that are not dependent on the heterosexual model of dominance and submission, Loulan and others are encouraging lesbians "to reintroduce the power differences of hetero-sexuality into their relationships" (Jeffreys, 1993, p. 52). Such eroticising of inequality results in sexual oppression.

Taking charge

Other sexual rhythms discussed by Loulan continue to eroticise inequality. Comment-ing on the one she calls "taking charge", she speaks of the "thrill of letting yourself really get into the desire for momentary mastery over someone else" (1990, p. 149).

Surrender, lesbian style

Contrasted with "taking charge" is the sexual style called "surrender". Loulan says "there are lesbians who revel in the emotional and sexual art of surrender. There is a freedom in giving in" (p. 150).

Macho sluts

Another sexual style Loulan suggests we accept and not criticise is that which Pat Califia called the macho slut. Califia saw the macho slut as directly related to S/M practices, but Loulan believes "women who celebrate being sluts" appear in every sexual style. Describing this particular style of sexual expression, Loulan says:

> The macho slut loves sex. She loves sex with her partner . . . with different women . . . with men . . . with herself. Sex by any other name is sex . . . She wants to flaunt it, try everything.

Then, in what appears to be a congratulatory tone, Loulan reports: "The macho slut has finally reclaimed this behavior as powerful, fun, and filled with surprises" (1990, p. 152).

In a previous work, Loulan wrote about sexual addiction. It seems that she makes a distinction between a sexual addict whom she sees as sick and needing "professional counseling help" (1984, pp. 105–12), and a macho slut whom she congratulates for her courage in reclaiming her right to have fun, but the distinction between the two is not exactly clear.

While there are many more sexual rhythms discussed by Loulan, those already mentioned are sufficient to show the variety of sexual behaviours involved in the call for total acceptance of all sexual rhythms.

Lesbians must celebrate lesbian differences

This third theme is closely related to the second. Instead of criticising the sexual prac-tices of each other, lesbians are called upon to welcome and celebrate the differences between them. Otherwise, Loulan suggests, they are participating in "horizontal hatred" (1990, p. 38). Proclaiming the right of every individual to express her sexuality as she wishes, Loulan makes use of the popular concepts of the heterosexual sexual revolution, namely, choice, consent and freedom.

Catharine MacKinnon, in an article called "Liberalism and the Death of Feminism", gives a brief critique of some of these "sacred concepts" from the perspective of the feminist movement of the 1960s and 1970s (Leidholdt and Raymond, 1990, p. 3). Regarding *choice*, she says, the movement knew that "when material conditions preclude 99 percent of your options, it is not meaningful to call the remaining 1 percent . . . your choice". Also, she says, the movement was not fooled by a concept like *consent*.

> It knew that when force is a normalized part of sex, when no is taken to mean yes, when fear and despair produce acquiescence and acquiescence is taken to mean consent, consent is not a meaningful concept (p. 4).

The feminist movement also criticised the concept of *freedom*, as MacKinnon explains:

> It also criticized the ruling concept of freedom, especially sexual freedom, unpacked and unmasked it as a cover for the freedom to abuse. When people with power defended their oppression of women as freedom, this movement knew it was the thrill of their power they were defending. This was a movement that was critical of the freedom to oppress, not one that thought women would be free when we had more of it (p. 4).

In proclaiming the right of every lesbian to express her sexuality as she wishes, and calling upon all lesbians to celebrate the differences that exist between them, Loulan has chosen concepts that feminism judges to be radically flawed. When lesbian sex includes the eroticising of inequality, when it encourages power plays, when there is a situation of dominance and submission, then the concepts of choice, consent and freedom are devoid of meaning.

"You can if you try"

This fourth theme represents the catchcry of all libertarian lesbian sex therapists. When a lesbian goes to talk to a therapist about her lack of interest in sex or her reluctance to experiment as her partner wants her to, a feminist therapist begins with the assumption "you don't have to, if you don't want to", whereas a libertarian sex therapist begins with the assumption "you can if you try".

JoAnn Loulan's commitment to this assumption is demonstrated clearly in the introduction to her earlier work, *Lesbian Sex* (1984). Expressing what she calls her "very strong views about sexuality", she says: "I believe that sexual practice . . . can be changed with willingness and consciousness." Again, "We can take responsibility for our sexual lives." And again, "We don't have to accept our sex lives as they are" (1984, p. xi). Then, with all the confidence of a New Age guru, and all the positivity required to sell the wares of the sex therapy industry, she says:

> I am here to tell you that our powerlessness and passivity in regards to our sexuality is unnecessary. We have the means within ourselves to create the kind of sex lives that we want. I have seen lesbians change. I know it's possible, and I've written this book to share with you what I know about how to do it (p. xi).

If "we have the means within ourselves to create the kind of sex lives that we want" and if our lack of sexual desire continues, it must mean that "we" have not tried hard enough.

Loulan has developed "a new model of the Female Sexual Response Cycle" which she calls the "JoAnn Loulan model" (p. xiii). First, there was the Masters and Johnson model which described four stages through which female sexual response moved: excitement, plateau, orgasm and resolution (Loulan, 1984, pp. 40–1). Then, there was the Helen Singer Kaplan model which described three stages: desire, excitement and orgasm (pp. 41–2). Now, there is the JoAnn Loulan model which describes six stages of female sexual response: willingness, desire, excitement, engorgement, orgasm and pleasure (pp. 42–5).

While Loulan's decision to begin her model with "willingness" appears, at first, to be a positive addition to the previous models, her discussion of this first stage reveals her intent. She says: "You do not even have to *want* to have sex. You may just be willing to have sex . . . You may also move to this stage because you think you ought to be having more sex" (p. 42). In other words, "you can if you try", and if you do not increase your sexual activity, it is because you have not been "willing" to try.

In addition to these statements, she also has advice for those lesbians who are reluctant to try new and daring sexual behaviour:

> If you feel very resistant, investigate the reasons why. If there's fear behind your resistance, set up boundaries and rules to make the situation safe. Then see if you'd be willing to try something that seemed too scary and wild before. You may be fearful of not having control in the situation, of losing control or of being out of control. Sometimes we are as afraid of losing control and experiencing ecstasy as we are of not losing control and being bored (1984, p. 102).

Loulan presents sex as an activity that lesbians *ought* to be doing. In her discussion of "willingness", she paints a curious picture of "two women who do not experience desire, but are willing to have sex together" (p. 42). One wonders why it is necessary for two women who do not particularly desire sex to pressure themselves to a point where they are willing to "try". Is a loving, equal, enjoyable relationship, which includes lovemaking when both partners desire it, not a legitimate lesbian relationship in the opinion of lesbian sex therapists like Loulan? Is it necessary, for the sake of having more sex in the world, that lesbians "try harder" to make their relationships more sexual?

Feminist therapists emphasise the fact that sex is not, and does not have to be, the beginning and end of a lesbian's existence. They advise: "If you don't want to do it, then don't. If you don't want to experiment with new sexual behaviours, then don't be pressured by the opinion of sex therapists and others who say you ought to try."

Feminism has it wrong

Finally, JoAnn Loulan's work is clearly anti-feminist. She talks about her early involvement in the women's movement but then, as if to justify her own coming out as a "femme" (1990, p. ix), she became highly critical of what she calls the movement's "androgynous imperative" (pp. 61–78). She says:

Androgyny became the norm of the lesbian nation. Flannel shirts, blue jeans, no makeup, no jewelry and short hair were all requirements of the club. Effectively, we became desexualized in our dress codes. It was not clear who was sleeping with whom. No one stood out by her attire (1990, p. 27).

A little further on she repeats, in a more caustic tone, her criticism about dress. "Politically correct lesbians wore a particular outfit", she says. "I thought perhaps there were 'movement issue' clothes given at the border of politically correct cities" (p. 41).

The feminist movement's insistence on the elimination of the dominance/submission model in sexual relationships comes in for particular criticism. In accusing feminists of encouraging "the denial of our sexual differences", she says:

Each partner had to initiate sex, each had to make love to the other, each had to go down on the other, each had to like the same things. We were to have no dildos, no S/M, no porn, no sex with men. Each woman in a couple had to dress and look alike.
    What was strictly forbidden was the concept of butch/femme. This was "old culture", mimicking heterosexual roles (p. 41).

What Loulan does is argue for the acceptance of butch and femme role-playing by pouring scorn on the feminist call for equality of power in relationships.

Sheila Jeffreys' assessment of Loulan and other lesbian sex therapists is that they

are committed to the promotion of conventional, heterosexist notions of what is attractive and sexy. They find it difficult to recognise or imagine any erotic attraction in the absence of roleplaying or "femininity" in some form (1993, pp. 57–8).

What they have done, she says, is joined Havelock Ellis and others "in the sexological task of deriding and burying feminist insight into the politics of sexuality" (p. 58).

Loulan's arguments and illustrations in support of her anti-feminist stance are remarkably similar to media stereotypes about feminists and lesbian feminists. One suspects that she has simply chosen to imitate the media backlash myths and is pleased to recount them as if they were fact, in order to add weight to her own belief that feminism has got it wrong.

The themes identified above in the work of JoAnn Loulan are indicative of the themes and attitudes of all libertarian lesbian sex therapists: the focus on sex as an entirely personal and individual matter; the call for total acceptance of all lesbian sexual practices, including those that intimidate and oppress; the emphasis on the need to affirm and celebrate lesbian differences ("you do your thing and I'll do mine"); the pressure on lesbians to have more sex and to "try" new sexual practices; and also the criticism of feminists who dare to raise political and ethical questions about some forms of sexual behaviour.

The victim-blaming inherent in the work of Loulan and her colleagues is similar to that already identified in other humanistic therapies, a fact which is not surprising given that lesbian sex therapy is firmly grounded in a liberal humanist philosophy.

While the tone of Loulan's work is positive and celebratory, the reality is that her message is harsh and oppressive for most lesbians. The majority of lesbians (like most heterosexual women) see sex as just one part of a total relationship. Loulan's insistence that lesbians should try harder to have more sex and more variety in their sexual behaviour creates a pressure on lesbians to place sex at the centre of their lives.

The presumptions running through all of Loulan's work are that lesbians want more sex, that they want to have more dialogue with other lesbians about sex, and that they want to try out new and daring sexual practices. While that is not the case with the overwhelming majority of lesbians, such presumptions have an impact. Those who do not want more sex feel that they must be somehow lacking; those who have no inclination to get together in groups and talk about what they consider to be a very personal and private part of their lives feel somehow inferior; and those who have no desire to try out new sexual styles, such as sadomasochism and butch and femme role-playing, feel somehow inhibited and unadventurous. In Jeffreys' words, quoted earlier, Loulan is "telling lesbians that they are sexually deficient, that they are . . . generally just not very good at sex" (1993, p. 47).

Victim-blaming also occurs when lesbians, concerned about some aspect of their relationship, go to talk things over with a lesbian sex therapist, and are given the "positive" messages alluded to earlier in this chapter: "I believe that sexual practice . . . can be changed with willingness and consciousness" (1984, p. xi); "We have the means within ourselves to create the kind of sex lives that we want" (p. xi); and "You can have what you want out of sex" (p. xiv). Such positivity ignores the fact that one in four women are victims/survivors of sexual abuse in childhood, and the result for many of these women is that they do *not* "have the means within" themselves to create the kind of sex lives Loulan thinks they ought to have. But the message to all lesbians is that if they are not enjoying sex as much as they would like, or as much as others seem to be, it is definitely their own fault. All lesbians can "take responsibility for [their] own sexual lives" (p. xi), if they want to.

Loulan's discussion of her "willingness model" of sexual response, in which she makes it clear that lesbians *ought* to be having sex whether they want to or not, is another example of victim-blaming. "You do not even have to *want* to have sex", she says, you just have to be "willing to have sex" (1984, p. 42). The message is: If you do not increase your sexual activity, it is because you are not "willing" to "try". In other words, it is your fault. Also, if you "feel very resistant", analyse your reasons and, then, "see if you'd be willing to try something that seemed too scary and wild before" (p. 102). In other words, ignore your instincts. Put aside your own judgment about what is acceptable sexual behaviour. Just try. And remember, if you do not try, then the problems in the relationship are your fault.

Another example of Loulan's victim-blaming occurs in her attempts to connect self-esteem and self-acceptance to lesbian sexual desire. She says: "Our lack of tolerance and acceptance for our own sexuality is something which keeps us from learning and changing our bodily responses" (1984, p. xiii). Similarly, in her desire to encourage lesbians to be less inhibited and more sexually free, she expresses the opinion that the problem for lesbians is that they are afraid of their own sexuality. Then, she follows up by actually accusing them of being homophobic and misogynist. "The fear of our own sexuality," she says, "which I believe is generated not just from the majority oppression, but also by our own internalized homophobia and misogyny, is the obstacle that keeps us from exploring what *is* lesbian eroticism" (1990, p. 41).

Loulan makes no analysis of what she calls "the majority oppression", that is, the oppression perpetrated against all lesbians by the upholders of mainstream, hetero-patriarchal society, and does not discuss the need for lesbians to be angry and to name and blame their oppressors; instead, she proceeds to focus attention and blame on individual lesbians. Regardless of how society treats you, she says, you can and must take responsibility for your own homophobia and misogyny. You can stop hating yourself and start accepting yourself, if you want to. She even refers to this process as "healing", as if to say lesbians suffering the effects of society's oppression are "sick" and in need of healing (1984, p. 15).

To reiterate, lesbian sex therapy, in line with all humanist therapies, places the blame entirely on the shoulders of the victims. All lesbians can increase their self-esteem and self-acceptance, they say. All lesbians can be "healed". All lesbians can and ought to improve their sex lives. All lesbians can and ought to want to explore "lesbian eroticism". All lesbians can and ought to be open to experiencing new sexual rhythms. Those who do not achieve all of these, for whatever reasons, are judged to be at fault.

The one thing all of the therapies discussed in Part Three have in common is that they blame the victim herself for the distress she is experiencing. Psychoanalysis, humanist therapies, New Age therapies, popular psychology and lesbian sex therapy, all focus attention on the individual and seek to analyse the inner dynamics of that particular, individual woman rather than to focus on the oppressive and destructive context in which she lives. The task as these therapies interpret it, then, is to help each individual woman see where she has gone wrong, take responsibility for her own pain, forgive and forget, seek her own personal empowerment, think positively, and develop a better and more satisfying life for herself in the future.

Feminist therapy, on the other hand, points out that emotional and psychological health cannot be attained, in any lasting way, when justice does not prevail. Justice demands that blame be directed at those who are blameworthy. Those therapists who, because of convenience, focus the blame on the victims instead of on the agents of their oppression are participating in acts of injustice and destroying women's hopes of long-term peace and resolution of their pain, for the sake of short-term "success". Letting go of one's pain and distress can only occur after anger has been expressed and after the appropriate naming and blaming has been done. In other words, one cannot be a "survivor" until one acknowledges one's status as a "victim".

The task of a therapist, therefore, is to promote honesty and a sense of justice by ensuring that the blame is placed on the one who is blameworthy, and not on the victim. Only then will lasting emotional and psychological health be possible.

PART FOUR

PRACTICAL APPLICATION
OF A FEMINIST THERAPY

9

ELEMENTS OF A FEMINIST THERAPY

Therapies that blame the victim, that begin with the premise that women are deficient and therefore the cause of their own problems, that encourage women to deal endlessly with their feelings so that the pursuit of "healing" becomes a lifelong preoccupation, are clearly not acceptable to feminists because of the fact that they add to the oppression of women and work to keep women de-pressed and re-pressed.

As discussed in Part Two, a feminist alternative to blame-the-victim therapies begins with a radical political analysis of the oppression of women and acknowledges that the emotional and psychological problems experienced by individual women have their root in women's collective and individual oppression. The aim of such therapy is to help individual women recognise the oppression/s that has kept them feeling inadequate, be angry about the deception that has kept them mystified for so long, name and blame the agents of their oppression, and find the courage to be who they truly and passionately are.

In addition to knowing where a feminist alternative begins and what its aims are, it is important that we discuss "place". Where will this therapy be situated in relation to the feminist revolution? There is no doubt in my mind that it must be viewed as an activity of the feminist movement and, therefore, must be accepted as an integral part of our ongoing quest for social justice for all.

To Australian feminists who have not yet witnessed in our society anything like the insanity of the proliferation of modern-day therapies in the United States, such a suggestion will seem reasonable. Most Australian feminists are still able to acknowledge the potential for good inherent in a therapy that is not oppressive because, here, therapy has not yet become a multimillion-dollar industry that encourages people to submit to therapy for therapy's sake.

The warning signs are evident, however, and must not be ignored. The so-called self-help books for women, such as the ones discussed earlier, *You Can Heal Your Life*, and *Women Who Love Too Much*, are becoming very popular amongst Australian women. There are codependency groups emerging all over the country. More and more self-made dispensers of personal happiness are advertising and trying to convince people of their need for personal growth experiences to give "meaning" to their otherwise "meaningless" lives. While it does appear that some Australian feminists are already caught up in this relatively new trend, there is an impression that the majority would be much more interested in a therapy that responds to the *real* problems of women's lives. They would welcome the suggestion that a therapy based on feminist principles and concerned with helping women rise above the effects of their oppression be accepted as an integral part of feminism.

American feminists, however, are probably no longer able to think about therapy as anything other than an activity that exploits the vulnerable by encouraging them into a dependence on therapists, twelve-step programs, self-help groups, etc. For them, the suggestion that therapy be located as an activity of the feminist movement will sound like sacrilege and their impulse will be to reject the idea out of hand.

The feminist alternative proposed here rejects the idea of a therapy industry and the deliberate exploitation that has women focusing endlessly inward, never able to move beyond their problems because preoccupation with their own healing has become an end in itself.

It may be that we need to forsake the word "therapy", as Mary Daly suggests, to give it over to those who misuse it and exploit it for their own purposes, and find an entirely different word to describe the activity referred to in these pages. Such a move at this time would, I think, be premature, but it certainly must not be discounted as a possibility in the future. At the moment, it seems important to attempt to reclaim it.

According to *The New Shorter Oxford English Dictionary*, the word "therapy" derives from the Greek *therapeia*, meaning "healing", and the word "therapeutic" from *therapeuein*, meaning "minister to". The Therapeutae (*therapeutai*) were "members of a Jewish mystical and ascetic sect, close to the Essenes, living in Egypt in the 1st Century A.D.", and they were "servants, attendants, (spiritual) healers". Given its historical association with such important functions as healing, ministering, serving and attending, it does seem appropriate at this point in time that we attempt to reclaim the word "therapy" and give it a place in the forefront of our feminist activity.

This call for a radicalised feminist therapy to be located within the bounds of the feminist movement comes from my understanding of the implications for women of living in a war zone. We do live in a war zone and there are daily casualties. Our feminist analysis of society leads us to say often enough that the numbers of attacks, woundings, murders of women by men, the daily harassment, intimidation, exploitation of women by men, are all clear evidence that women live in "occupied territory". Men are at war with women, and women and their offspring are the victims. For those women who are victims of multiple oppressions, including racism, ableism, classism and heterosexism, the devastating effects of the war are magnified even further.

Since the 1960s, when Second Wave feminism began, the war men wage against women and the effects of that war on its victims have been constant themes in feminist literature. In more recent times, Susan Faludi in *Backlash: The Undeclared War against*

Women (1991), and Marilyn French in *The War against Women* (1992), have highlighted the magnitude and horror of this war.

Naming the war and rebelling against it are basic to feminism. So, too, I would argue, is the need to recognise that war brings casualties and that it is incumbent upon us as a movement to respond with some urgency to the pain and distress of individual women, both feminists and non-feminists.

The claims by feminists that any sort of therapeutic help is, without question, oppressive and that women ought to be able to get all the support they need from friends, sisters and lovers, seems somehow insufficient when one considers the deep pain and alienation some women live with. This is not to say that such a view should be ignored, but rather that it must be seen simply as one side of a very important and timely debate.

The argument for the total rejection of therapy is put passionately and, in many ways, convincingly by Celia Kitzinger and Rachel Perkins in *Changing our Minds: Lesbian Feminism and Psychology*. While I disagree with the book's central thesis, I nevertheless recommend it as compulsory reading for all feminists and lesbian feminists who are therapists, counsellors or women's centre workers. It is crucial that those of us who insist on the need for therapy as an ongoing activity of the feminist movement do so with our eyes wide open to the potential for oppression inherent in its practice.

As I said earlier, the argument for the development of a feminist therapy begins with the recognition that there are daily casualties in the war against women and that many of those casualties, namely women and children, are left by the wayside without support and with no safe place to go. Some who are escaping physical and sexual violence go to women's refuges where they do receive support and the kind of caring they need at that time.[1] Others are battered and bruised emotionally and are often desperate for help. In their desperation, many find themselves going to their doctor and then to a therapist or psychiatrist recommended by their doctor. It is at that point in their search for some relief from their oppression, that women can be in danger of suffering further oppression—psychoppression—in the name of "healing".

For that reason, it is a matter of urgency that the feminist movement take seriously the need to provide support for all women and ensure it is available whenever it is needed. In the past, support was haphazard, "you're lucky if you have friends who care about you"; it is no longer enough to hope that friends care. We need a feminist therapy that acknowledges the existence of the war, understands its lethal intent, and has the resources to respond competently and with caring to the needs of those who suffer beyond their own endurance.

Some feminists who work with victims/survivors of incest, rape and domestic violence are already doing that and are to be commended. Women's refuges, women's centres, rape crisis services, indeed all such services that operate under a deliberate feminist philosophy, begin with an awareness that they are not simply responding to

---

1. The situation of victims having to leave their homes because of the violent actions of perpetrators raises questions of justice which refuge workers are constantly addressing.

women in need. Rather, they are responding to women who are casualties of a war that is integral to the "successful" functioning of patriarchal societies.

Because the war is against *all* women, the support offered by a politically aware feminist therapy must also be for all women. It must be available equally to those women who do not claim to be feminists and who have given little or no thought to the root cause/s of their emotional pain and suffering, and also to those who do claim to be feminists and who have a real awareness that the suffering they are experiencing is a direct result of the courageous stand they take every day in the front line of the battle.

As we move now into a discussion of the practical application of a feminist therapy, it will be seen that there is a deliberate emphasis on simplicity and honesty. What is being suggested is not an elaborate, complicated, oppressive system where all but the academically qualified elite are excluded from its practice, nor a trendy, superficial, "positive" focus where everyone who has learned the jargon is involved in either doing or receiving therapy. Rather, the suggestion here is that the feminist movement provide a simple and honest interaction in a caring and safe environment where women not only get relief from their immediate distress, but also are encouraged to allow the scales to fall from their eyes so that they can see clearly the cause of their distress and begin to insist on change.

In the practice of a feminist therapy that is radical and political, there are two main elements: support and demystification.

Support

In a situation where a woman seeks help either from a particular feminist therapist or from a women's crisis centre, the support that is required is almost always emotional, sometimes financial (as in emergency relief), sometimes physical (as in the protection offered by refuges or by accompanying a woman to court), sometimes in terms of advocacy.

With particular reference to emotional support, it must be said that while emotional support is a feature of the *entire* interaction, there are three identifiable stages where such support by the therapist is crucial. The first is when a woman begins to open up: when she talks about her confusion, her fear, her inability to cope; when she expresses self-loathing, self-blame, sadness, despair; when she shares with the therapist her deep sense of hopelessness and helplessness; when she talks about her experience of failure. It is important to remember that because most women usually seek the help of a therapist only after they have exhausted their own ideas and used up their own resources in relation to the problems they are experiencing, they are often emotionally exhausted, vulnerable and fragile when they come. Support in terms of listening, genuine interest, gentleness, affirmation and empathy is imperative at this initial stage.

The next stage where solid support is required is when a woman goes through the painful experience of opening her eyes and allowing herself to see the ways in which she has been deceived. This can be a devastating, shattering, humiliating experience, and many women understandably choose not to put themselves through it. For many, it would involve calling into question life as they have known it since early childhood. For some, it would mean questioning the basis on which their entire marriage has been built, and dismantling years of explanations, justifications and excuses they have made to themselves for their husband's withdrawn, uninterested behaviour. For others, it would mean deliberately and consciously setting about to unravel the mystery that has constituted their marriage for the past few years and allowing themselves at last to see the true meaning of their partner's self-centred, dismissive manner toward them. The role of therapy in helping individual women unravel the mysteries of their past will be discussed more fully in the section dealing with demystification.

The other stage where support is required is actually the final stage of any therapeutic relationship based on a feminist philosophy. After a woman allows herself to see that the emotional distress that has been robbing her of energy and passion is not her own fault but is, in fact, the result of her oppression, she will respond in one of two ways. Either she will sink deeper into depression, identifying herself as "ill" and in need of medication and, in a manner that speaks of surrender, continue to focus blame for her condition on her own inability to adjust to the circumstances of her life; or she will become angry, confront the agent/s of her oppression, and deliberately work to change the circumstances that caused her emotional distress.

Those who respond by becoming more depressed will not want to continue with a therapy that urges women to insist on change, and will usually cease contact. All the therapist can do is encourage such women to seek out assertiveness training or courses in self-esteem, and also leave the door open for them to come back and talk whenever they feel the need. Those who respond with anger and a determination to work for change, on the other hand, will emerge from their ordeal with new energy, new enthusiasm for life, and a new vision for the future. During this final stage of the therapeutic relationship, they will still need the support of the therapist for a brief time, but the support of other women who have had similar experiences is much more beneficial. Ensuring that there are appropriate support groups available so that women may join as they wish is an important task of any feminist therapist.[2]

Continuing the focus on support as a major element of feminist therapy, the following discussion highlights the skills required by anyone wanting to offer support that is neither patronising nor condescending. They are: being there, being real, listening, and empathy.

---

2. Women's Centres which operate according to a feminist philosophy usually organise such groups as part of their ongoing service to women. An example is described by Coralie McLean (1994), "Townsville Women's Centre", in Wendy Weeks (ed.), *Women Working Together: Lessons from Feminist Women's Services*, p. 235.

   It is important that a feminist therapist maintain an awareness of the kinds of support groups available in her community at any given time, so that such information can be passed on to women who express an interest. If no such groups are readily available, then it is incumbent upon a feminist therapist to set them up as required.

Being there

One of the most difficult tasks feminist therapists face in the 1990s is that of distancing themselves from what we now know to be the worst features of the liberal humanist era. The skill of "being there" is given priority in this list of skills not only because, chronologically, it is the first thing that must happen in a therapeutic encounter of any kind, but also because it is the skill that has suffered most in terms of the harsh libertarian emphasis on individualism.

The belief that "everyone is responsible for themselves" did not give high priority, for example, to simple needs: greeting women when they arrived, making sure they were comfortable, making sure they felt welcome, talking with them, offering them a cup of tea or coffee. The result was that frightened and vulnerable women who had ventured out in search of kindred spirits, affirmation and support experienced a situation where, yet again, no one was there for them.

The trend toward leaderless groups was also a result of the belief that, in order for women to become "empowered", they had to take responsibility for dealing with their own pain. It was often the case, however, that women who responded to publicity regarding the setting up of a group (for adult survivors of childhood sexual abuse, for example) found themselves in a situation where nobody knew anything about group process and where everybody seemed to be competing for air-time. The result was that the verbally confident were heard and those who were shy and nervous about speaking were ignored. Again, this philosophy of "throw them in at the deep end and let them learn to stay afloat" caused women to drop out of groups because, if they were to feel totally alone and unsupported, they preferred to have that experience at home by themselves rather than in the company of others.

Feminist therapists must not only increase our awareness of the ways in which our practice of therapy has been influenced by the philosophies of liberal humanism, but we must also look at the influence of radical therapy. One of the beliefs of the Radical movement was that the therapeutic relationship ought to be a relationship of equal power, and therapists were encouraged to proceed as if they and the person who had come for help actually had equal power, when in fact they did not. Acting as if the therapeutic relationship is a relationship of equality does not make it so. Acting as if a particular woman's oppression is similar to one's own does not make it so. The belief in the need to make therapy into an occasion of equal power often resulted in a situation of "you tell me your problems and I'll tell you mine". What occurs in such a situation, of course, is that instead of the therapist being there for a woman who has come for help, she in fact trivialises the woman's pain by turning the situation into an opportunity for sharing.

In a programme on ABC Radio National, a few years ago, a therapist who had been accused of having sex with her female patient defended her behaviour by saying she operated out of a radical philosophy and, conveniently, did not accept that there was an unequal power relationship in therapy. Consequently, her argument went, the patient was equally responsible for the sexual encounters that occurred between them. When a therapist rejects the idea that she needs to be there for those who seek her help, on the grounds that such a notion is patronising or encourages dependence, the end result is often that she uses the therapy situation to "be there" for herself.

The skill of being there involves a kind of humility that enables one to put aside one's own needs for the time being in favour of focusing on the needs of someone else. Also, it requires an acknowledgement of the power imbalance inherent in any therapeutic or helping relationship rather than a pretence that it does not exist. The importance of opening one's eyes to the truth about power lies in the fact that one can then be sensitive to the situation as it is, and be careful never to exploit one's position of greater power.[3]

Being real

It seems strange to speak of "being real" as a therapeutic skill when being oneself ought to be the most natural thing anyone does. The fact is, however, that many therapists are caught in the trap of role-playing. They take on the role of therapist or helper and, in so doing, who they really are is lost for the duration. When a real live woman is trying to relate to a person who appears as nothing more than the role she is playing, the situation is impersonal and alienating. When a feminist therapist can put aside the idea of the exalted role of her profession and see therapy as it really is—one woman talking to another woman about problems she is having[4]—she then opens the way for herself (and the interaction) to be real.

Being real, as a therapeutic skill, involves being real to oneself and also to those who seek one's help. If the support a therapist offers is to be effective, there is an absolute requirement that she be honest with herself about the power the situation gives her, about the values she holds, about her own biases and philosophies. No therapist comes to any therapeutic encounter devoid of power, values, biases or philosophies, and should not pretend that she does.

This is not to say, however, that one ought to make it a rule to discuss one's own values and beliefs with women when they first come. Apart from the fact that that would

---

3. In Carter Heyward's personal account of eighteen months in therapy, *When Boundaries Betray Us: Beyond Illusions of What is Ethical in Therapy and in Life* (1993), the role of the therapist is puzzling. While the pseudonymous Dr Elizabeth Farro was aware of the potential for abuse of power inherent in the therapeutic relationship and refused Heyward's advances, she nevertheless seems to have had some ambivalence around the issue of power.

    She said clearly enough what she would *not* do (that is, she would not misuse her power by having a sexual relationship with Heyward or by making any promises about a future friendship), but was not able or willing to exercise the power that was hers to bring about an honest confrontation of the issue, and insist that it not be a continuing theme in their therapeutic relationship. A therapist has the power to terminate therapy and, indeed, must terminate it if it becomes unworkable.

    As I see it, Heyward's book presents an interesting study of the misuse of power by both therapist and recipient of therapy. Heyward, a lesbian feminist, does not seem to have learned one of the basic tenets of feminism, that "No means No", while Farro, in not being willing to exercise the power that was hers to terminate therapy and refer Heyward to someone else, allowed a dishonest situation (that is, game-playing dressed up as therapy) to continue.

4. Given the power imbalance and the fact that, in many cases, a woman pays the therapist for her services, I do not intend to imply that therapy is *only* "one woman talking to another woman about problems she is having". It is that, but it is also more than that.

be a gross intrusion, most women are, frankly, not interested at that stage, and would prefer to move immediately into talking about the events in their lives that have prompted them to seek help. Being real about one's values or biases simply means being prepared to talk about them when asked or when the occasion seems appropriate. Incidentally, no matter how careful feminist-based women's centres and individual feminist therapists might be to share their values and philosophy with women only when it seems appropriate, we are often faced with unfair criticism. The main accusation, at least in the community where I live, is that feminism is being pushed on to unsuspecting women when they come in a state of weakness and vulnerability.[5] This criticism, of course, does not take into account the fact that, when a woman chooses to go to a therapist whose reputation is clearly that of a feminist or to a centre that is open about its feminist philosophy, she does so precisely because that is the bias she wants. If she wanted a Christian bias, she would go to a church for help. Realness and honesty require that a therapist or a helping agency be as open as possible about their values and biases.

Listening

The skill of listening has had a prominent place in most mainstream therapies since the late nineteenth century when Freud's patient, Anna O, discovered the value of what she called "the talking cure". While listening has been regarded as an important therapeutic skill since those early days, it has clearly been less important in psychoanalysis than the spoken word of the therapist. It is the analysis done by the "expert" and the words that come out of his or her mouth that are of utmost importance.

Carl Rogers, with his emphasis in the 1960s on the need for therapy to be client-centred rather than therapist-centred, succeeded in focusing attention on listening as the primary skill of therapy and, since that time, therapists trained in any of the humanist therapies have been taught to take seriously the need to listen.

Many of us who were trained in liberal humanist techniques learned that the skill of listening involves listening to feelings as well as to words. Feminist therapy, while agreeing with the emphasis on listening to women's words and feelings, takes it much further. For feminist therapists, the skill of listening is not just a skill that must be learned alongside many others; it is, in fact, an attitude. In relation to a woman who has come for help, a therapist must have an attitude of listening, openness, respect and receptivity at all times. The theory is that if our listening is genuine, wholehearted and skilful, women will find their own voices, their passion, their courage, and will speak themselves into existence.

Dale Spender's research for *Man Made Language* (1980) revealed that, in all the work done in the area of communication, very little attention had been given to listening. She said that, although any event of communication always involved a talker and a

---

5. An example, from my own experience, is that of a doctor who, for a time, referred women to me because of my expertise in a certain area. Two of the women he referred confided in me that he had warned them to "be careful she doesn't brainwash you into becoming a feminist".

listener, "the almost exclusive emphasis in research has been on talking" (p. 121). She asks why listening as a skill of communication has been so devalued, and suggests that it is probably because listening is what women do and talking is what men do.

Is it coincidence that listening is something which women do more than men, something which is less "visible", and which has therefore (mistakenly) been associated with passivity? Is it coincidence that women are often considered to be the "better" listeners, providing the understanding and sympathetic ear, being more inclined to "hear someone out"?

Is there any connection between the devaluation of women and the devaluation of listening? I suspect that there might be. I suspect that women may be more familiar with and more appreciative of the "art of listening" . . . It would seem reasonable to assume that, from the perspective of the dominant group, listening may well be a skill which can be overlooked (p. 121).

In feminist therapy, listening is central. Most women who live or work with men are accustomed to not being listened to or, at best, to not being listened to fully or accurately. A common experience of women is that of being urged by their partner or colleague to speak, to talk about what is troubling them, only to be interrupted in mid-sentence and offered advice, or a judgment, or a justification, or a "solution". These various forms of non-listening are often accompanied by an impatient, dismissive manner, a barrage of words, verbal abuse and/or anger. The result of men's unwillingness to listen fully and accurately to women is that there has developed a general belief among women that women are not worth listening to: that they have nothing of interest to say, and that whatever they do say makes little sense and is of even less consequence.

Consequently, when a woman finds the confidence to speak to a therapist about her pain, her loneliness, her alienation, her feelings of worthlessness, it may well be the first occasion in a very long time, or perhaps in her entire life, that she has been really listened to. Given that this is the experience of so many women, it would be impossible to overstate the importance of listening as a skill for feminist therapists.

No discussion of listening, in this context, would be complete without reference to the work of American feminist theologian Nelle Morton, who spoke of listening as a "more divine act" than speaking. It was in 1973, when asked to deliver a lecture on the topic "Preaching the Word", that Nelle Morton introduced her now famous phrase: "hearing to speech". In her lecture, she challenged the institution of theology to examine its emphasis on the Word, the *Logos*, and suggested that such imagery was derived from "*a patriarchal way of perceiving and experiencing the universe*" (1985, p. 54). She argued that the church's emphasis on Logos "reduces communication to a one-way relationship—that of *speak*-ing—and bypasses the far more radical divine aspect of *hearing*" (p. 54). The more divine act, she says, is "*hearing to speech*" rather than speaking in order to be heard (pp. 54–5).

Emphasising the value of women's listening to each other, she says:

Every liberation movement rises out of its bondage with a new speech on its lips. This has been so with women coming together, seeking to get in touch with our own stories and

141

experiences which we have discovered welling up from within, from underneath, from out of our past, from out of our traditions rather than down from above . . . Women are literally hearing one another to speech. But the speech is our speech. It may come on stumblingly or boldly. But it is authentically our own (p. 55).

Just as "hearing to speech" was an important aspect of the consciousness-raising groups of the 1970s, so it continues to be an important and necessary activity of the feminist movement today, and feminist therapy is one arena in which women ought to be assured of such a "hearing".

Listening, as a skilful activity, consists of receptivity to the whole person, active listening, and reflective and responsive listening.

Being receptive to the whole person involves, as humanist therapies have emphasised, developing the ability to listen accurately to words, to non-verbal cues, and to feelings. Feminist therapy agrees with this emphasis, but issues a warning about the way certain techniques have been misused over the past twenty years. Courtesy of the liberal humanist therapies, some people have actually made a living out of writing and lecturing on such gimmickry as "body language" and "non-verbal communication".

While there is no doubt that non-verbal gestures can be indicators of emotions and unconscious intentions, far too much has been made of the "meaning" of certain body movements and the need to "read" body language. If a woman folds her arms or crosses her legs, it may very well be that she simply feels comfortable that way. If she raises or lowers her eyes, it could be for any number of reasons, including that she is simply avoiding the glare from the window behind the head of the person she is speaking to.

Giving prominence to the meaning of non-verbal gestures has caused many therapists to ignore or disregard or diminish the importance of the words coming from a person's mouth. If a woman in therapy cannot depend on a therapist to believe her words, then the whole activity, from beginning to end, is pointless. Sometimes a therapist may suspect the existence of a different reality from that which the words reveal, but it serves no purpose (except, perhaps, to massage the therapist's ego) to attempt to expose discrepancies in the woman's story. As she experiences the therapist's careful and patient listening, she will share the real story of her pain and distress when she is ready.

It is important to realise that most of us are encouraged to speak, or not, through the quality of another person's listening. If a person looks uninterested or bored, there is no encouragement for us to speak; but when someone is actively involved in listening to what we are saying, we feel encouraged and are much more likely to continue revealing our story. Some who call themselves therapists seem to have misunderstood the meaning of "client-centred" therapy and, instead of listening, actually do nothing. A woman goes to them seeking help in sorting out a problem and, taking their role as listener to the extreme, they actually say nothing for the duration of the session. They are mute, passive and totally uncommunicative. Their uninterested, lazy, sleepy appearance places a huge question mark over whether they have listened at all.

Our listening must be active, responsive, reflective, so that women will be encouraged to speak, to express their feelings, to examine their own story with courage and determination, to question how they might change their situation so that it will no longer have the power to oppress and inhibit and diminish them.

Before moving on to look at empathy as another of the supportive skills in feminist therapy, it is important to remind readers that it is not the intention of this book to enter into a discussion of "how to" in relation to the skills mentioned. There are many books devoted to step-by-step instructions in regard to the skills of communication, human relationships and counselling. For anyone not familiar with these practical guides, Barbara F. Okun's *Effective Helping: Interviewing and Counselling Techniques*, 3rd edition (1987), is a good place to start.

Empathy

Empathy is, in fact, another form of listening but, because of its importance as a therapeutic skill, it is given special mention here.

Empathy is usually described as "feeling with" another person or, the ability to see the world from the other person's "frame of reference". In other words, when a woman seeks help from a therapist, an empathic attitude begins with the recognition that the story she is recounting is *her* story, her journey, her struggle. She *owns* it, and it is not the therapist's prerogative to take it away from her by judging or reinterpreting it. The therapist's only task, at this stage, is to get inside the other woman's struggle and feel it with her. The steps that must be taken in order to achieve this are as follows.

First, the therapist must have a genuine desire to find out from the woman what her struggle actually is, to encourage her to describe her pain and frustration as carefully as possible so that, as she talks, her situation becomes clearer to *her* while also becoming clear to the therapist. The importance of the woman's own expression, exploration and discovery cannot be over-estimated: it is through that sometimes painful exercise that women most often achieve the understanding and insight that enable them to confront their situation honestly, and make the changes necessary to restore their emotional and mental health. Such expression, exploration and discovery begins during the first session of therapy and continues for as long as the therapy lasts.

Another step that assists empathy is to ask what the woman has done in the past to attempt to alleviate the pain. This will reveal information about doctors and therapists she has seen, friends and relatives she has spoken to, books and articles she has read, drugs she has taken, whether she has tried yoga, relaxation, exercise, and whether she has experimented with different diets.

In such a discussion, it is not the information itself that is important but rather, the fact that the therapist is enabled to meet the woman where she is in her struggle to deal with her own problem, and move on with her from there. It is an acknowledgement that her decision to visit this particular therapist is not a decision taken in isolation but is, in fact, one of several attempts on her part to put things right for herself. She owns the problem; as therapists, our task is to get involved at whatever stage she invites us in, and to work at seeing the circumstances of her life from her perspective.

One other step a therapist must take if empathy is to be real is to ask the woman what her theories are about the cause/s of her distress, when she thinks it all started, at what point it began to get worse, etc. The belief on the part of a therapist that she is the "expert" and that her theories are, therefore, more credible than the woman's own theories about her situation, is an example of considerable arrogance. A woman who has lived with depression or anxiety or addictive behaviour for months or years will, in most cases, have much more accurate theories about her condition than a therapist who has only just come on to the scene. It must be said of any therapist who refuses to engage in a joint venture of analysis and discovery with the one who has come for help, that she is more interested in the importance of her own role than in the other woman's liberation from that which oppresses her. Not only does the woman own the *problem*, but the *solution* also belongs to her, and if she is prevented from finding her solution by the efforts of a therapist who has lost sight of the real meaning of empathy, then she becomes a victim of psychoppression.

In practical terms, then, empathy requires that the therapist let go of her own impulse to talk, to give advice, to be the expert, to make things better. It involves an ability and a readiness to put one's own problems and concerns aside for a time. It requires an understanding and an acceptance of the fact that life is made up of all kinds of emotions, that sadness and grief and despair are just as much a part of life as are joy and peace and happiness. A therapist who is comfortable with the full range of emotions will be able to empathise with a woman in the depth of her despair as well as at the height of her joy. Empathy requires a kind of self-emptying. It involves humility. It is other-centred. One would think, therefore, that empathy would be easy for women because, as girls and women, we learn and never doubt that one of our most important roles in life is that of caring for others and not for ourselves, having empathy with others and not with ourselves. The fact is, however, that real empathy with others is not possible unless we first develop the ability to empathise with ourselves. For that reason, empathy can be much more difficult than it seems.

Self-emptying, humility and other-centredness in one who has not also learned the value of caring about oneself are usually expressed as: giving oneself away to others, making a martyr of oneself, sacrificing oneself, denying oneself, giving, giving, giving, and feeling eternally guilty about not being able to give more. These experiences, coupled with the resentment, the emptiness, the despair that are always involved when one gives oneself away, make empathy with others extremely difficult, if not impossible.

The woman who does care about herself, on the other hand, finds empathy with others much easier and much more satisfying. For her, self-emptying never results in actual emptiness because she remains "full of herself". Humility is never self-deprecating because it is accompanied by a sense of pride and dignity. Other-centredness is never a matter of losing herself for the sake of another because it is actually made possible, and constantly supported, by a healthy self-centredness.

Support, then, is the first of two major elements in feminist therapy. While it has been said that the skills a therapist requires in order that adequate support can be offered are being there, being real, listening and empathy, it must be acknowledged that these are not the only support skills a therapist needs. Other skills, such as problem-solving, decision-making and advocacy, also have a place in the practice of feminist therapy, and readers needing assistance in these areas are directed to other texts on counselling skills such as Barbara Okun's work mentioned earlier.

The fact that some mainstream therapies place so much importance on practical, "how to" skills means that feminist therapists ought to regard them with suspicion or, at least, caution. While refusing to help a woman confront the real problems of her life and work to change them, blame-the-victim therapies emphasise the need to help her "solve" her problems by adjusting her own needs to fit in with the circumstances around her. Problem-solving, in those terms, comes to mean adjustment rather than courageously confronting the cause of one's problems and insisting on change.

Such problem-solving therapy is epitomised in the title of one of the many American self-help books for women that have emerged during the liberal humanist era: *How to Love a Difficult Man*. It seems that the real problem, namely that the man is "difficult", is ignored and thereby allowed to remain undisturbed. His difficult behaviour is treated as a given, around which the woman must work. She is encouraged to see herself as the one with the problem and to compromise herself by learning to adjust to his unacceptable, difficult behaviour. Surely a more appropriate title for a book addressing this all-too-common situation women find themselves in would be *How to Leave a Difficult Man*, or *Fifty Ways to Get Rid of a Difficult Man*, or simply, *Why Bother?*

One more thing that must be said about practical, problem-solving skills is that too much focus on them gives the impression that those who seek the help of a therapist are not capable of solving their own problems or making their own decisions. Feminist therapy believes that when a woman receives the emotional support that she needs through *real* interaction with a therapist who actually listens to her in her distress, two things happen. The first is, she feels free to express her emotions and, in a reasonably short time, experiences herself beginning to get rid of some of the sadness, resentment, disillusionment, anger that has been clogged up inside her, restricting her ability to think clearly and rationally. The second result follows from the first. Once she has begun to free herself from that which was preventing her from thinking clearly, she is on the way to making her own decisions and solving her own problems.

Demystification

The other major element in the practice of feminist therapy is demystification. If one accepts the premise, as outlined in Chapter Two, that it is oppression that causes most of the problems women go to see therapists about, it follows that a very important task of feminist therapy is that of helping women see and acknowledge their oppression, past and present, collective and individual, so that they can begin to rise above it. This "seeing and acknowledging" is called demystification.

Mystification is a very effective form of oppression: when a woman does not have access to all the facts because they have been hidden from her, she is naturally confused and uncertain about how to respond in particular situations. She feels powerless. Added to this, she lacks confidence and feels incompetent due to her confusion, uncertainty and powerlessness, and blames herself for not being able to cope. Consequently, the strength required to begin questioning the reality she is experiencing is difficult to find as a lone woman living in the midst of her oppression.

In an attempt to define mystification, one might say it is a form of oppression still used effectively against women in Western countries despite all the efforts of the feminist movement over the last thirty years. It is the deliberate use of mystery, deceit, lies and half-truths for the purpose of presenting a false reality. While it is acknowledged that mystification can occur as a result of either protectionist or sinister motives, it must be stressed that mystification is always oppressive, regardless of motive.

Those who use mystification with the aim of protecting someone else obviously have no idea of the serious emotional and psychological effects that such a situation can have on a person who generally senses she is not being told everything there is to know. The belief that what a person does not know will not hurt her is fundamentally wrong. It is usually what a person does not know, an event from the past that is shrouded in mystery or a situation in the present that nobody is permitted to talk about, that causes serious problems, such as anxiety, depression and insomnia.

It is common for therapists to see women who are troubled, haunted or obsessed by mysterious events in their childhood. All a woman might know, for example, is that her mother mysteriously disappeared out of her life when she was five years old. She knew her mother had been ill. She still has vivid memories of relatives crying, friends coming to the house looking very serious, people hugging her or patting her on the head in a caring way, but nobody ever told her what was going on. Whenever she asked about her mother in the months that followed, someone would tell her not to worry and quickly change the subject. She soon learned that speaking about her mother was taboo.

As an adult, she has no idea how long it took her to realise her mother had, in fact, died and was not coming back, but what she does know is that nobody ever actually told her. To this day, the mystery surrounding her mother's illness and death remains and, at different times throughout her life, she has been obsessed with the need to know.

Similar situations in which children are left mystified "for their own good" are those involving the separation or divorce of parents. One day a child has two parents, the next day one parent is no longer there, no longer part of her day-to-day experience. Because nobody ever talked to her about it, she grew up with the mystery and is still, from time to time, tormented by the need to know what happened. So-called protectionist motives for keeping a child mystified do not make the mystification any less destructive.

Women, too, are supposedly "protected" from the truth by husbands, adult children, doctors and other professionals conspiring against them "for their own good". It is quite common for a woman not to be told all the facts, for example, about her own or her partner's illness, even when she expresses a desire to know. Another situation in which a woman is commonly not told all the details is when her spouse or child commits suicide. In this most disturbing of all situations, when the need to know is extremely intense, a woman is often kept in a shroud of ignorance by those who think they have the right to judge what is best for her.

Common examples of mystification prompted by more sinister motives include a man's determination to hide the truth from his partner about his extra-marital affairs or his squandering of their joint money. Most women in these situations live with a sense of their own mystification, a sense that they are being lied to, that there is something they are not being told, but all their attempts to find out are met with accusations that they have an "over-active imagination", that they are "paranoid", that they "lack trust" or that they are "going mad".

In lesbian relationships, too, the same kind of mystification sometimes occurs, where one partner goes to great lengths to keep hidden from the other the fact of her affairs. The result often is that the one from whom the truth is hidden lives every day with a sense of being betrayed, but can find no way to confirm or relieve her suspicions. Her partner's determination to continue the mystification means that she is denied the right to confront the issue honestly, to find relief from the trauma she is suffering, and to make choices about her own future.

Some women admit to a feeling of ambivalence in these situations. They desperately want to know the truth that is being hidden from them, but are at the same time afraid of what they may find out. In terms of a woman's emotional and psychological health, however, the truth is always preferable. Of course, the truth may cause sadness, grief, anger and depression in the short term, but these are emotions that can be faced and eventually moved beyond. The sense that there is a different reality to the one being presented causes a woman much more serious and long-term psychological problems.

At the base of all these individual experiences is the collective mystification of women. It comes as a shock to most women to learn that the reality we have been given in our socialisation is a reality constructed deliberately for the benefit of men and that, even in the 1990s, the place given to women in the whole scheme of things is still that of assisting and servicing men.

As girls, we are born into a reality that we automatically accept. We do not necessarily *like* everything that is presented as reality, but the powerlessness that constitutes childhood ensures that the reality given to children by parents and other adults perceived to have authority over them is almost always accepted. The mystification is so effective that most girls do not even notice when their brothers consistently receive more attention than they, or when the attention they receive from teachers in the classroom amounts to being thrown the scraps after the boys have had their fill, or when they are allowed access to facilities such as computers and sports equipment only after the boys have finished with them.

When a girl does notice the double standard and rebels against it, the disapproval from peers, parents, teachers and others usually ensures that, in future, she will keep her anger and resentment to herself. Instead of expressing it, she will bury it inside and blame herself for wanting more than she is going to get.

As girls grow into women, we are deceived into believing that there are certain things we cannot do simply because we are female; there are certain roles we must perform, certain loyalties we must uphold regardless of the number of times we ourselves are betrayed. And it does not stop there. Not only are we deceived into believing our role in life is what others say it must be, but we are also deceived into believing that such mystification has no ill-effects on us. We are expected to believe that any ill-effects, any feelings of discontent and unhappiness, any sense of hopelessness and despair, are of our own making.

It is in this state of confusion and despair, de-pressed by multiple layers of mystification which prevent a woman from seeing the truth about her situation, that she often seeks the help of a therapist. Mainstream therapies focus narrowly on the inner dynamics of the one who seeks help and blame her for the problems she is experiencing; they serve only to compound the mystification. Feminist therapy, on the other hand, emphasises the fact that a large part of a therapist's task must be that of helping a woman uncover the mystery and confront the facts of her oppression.

Demystification, then, can be defined as: taking away the mystery; revealing what is hidden; the *real*-ising of that which is hidden; seeing and acknowledging one's oppression as a first step toward rising above it.

In the 1960s and 1970s, a central activity of the Women's Liberation Movement was the demystification of women, commonly called consciousness-raising (CR). Women met together in groups, usually in each other's homes, and talked about their lives and, as they talked, they began to see a different reality. CR groups were radically political because, as women shared their experiences with each other, they enabled one another to see that which patriarchal society had forbidden them to see.

It is important here to spend a moment discussing the difference between CR and psychotherapy, because one of the problems for feminist therapy in the past has been the attempts by some to claim CR as therapy. It must be stated here categorically that, while the political act of consciousness-raising did prove to be therapeutic for many of the women involved in the early groups, consciousness-raising is *not* therapy. Any attempt to reduce it to the status of therapy robs it of its function as a powerful political force and turns it into nothing more than a personal growth group.

Feminists who are therapists must always be clear on this one point—that feminism, with CR as one of its central mechanisms of change, is not simply a way for individual women to feel better. It is a political revolution aimed at nothing less than changing a corrupt and inequitable patriarchal system. While demystification is a very important task of feminist therapy, it is imperative that feminist therapists not attempt to reduce the political agenda of the feminist revolution to a therapeutic endeavour.

That is what appears to have happened when one looks back at the history of the relationship between CR and therapy. In the early days, CR was, without a doubt, a radical political activity, but as soon as the therapeutic effects of women's meeting and talking together in this way became apparent, there were those who proceeded to turn

CR groups into therapy groups or self-help groups.[6] It was as though the political agenda became too difficult and the resultant anger too "negative". Changing the focus to the personal, however, served to take the political power out of CR: women were once again encouraged to look to themselves for the cause of their unhappiness.

Among those who resisted the therapeutising of CR groups was Marilyn Zweig, who explained the difference between a Women's Liberation Group and a therapy group in this way:

> our primary goal [in CR groups] is not to attempt to help individual women find individual solutions for the problems each has in her life as a woman. We have the fundamental conviction that only a change in the life conditions of *all* women can help bring about a solution for the troubles of individual women (Zweig in Agel, 1970, p. 161).

In more recent times, the term "consciousness-raising" to denote group therapy experiences has, fortunately, been replaced by more appropriate terms, such as self-help groups, support groups, etc., allowing the CR group to be restored to its rightful place in the history of the feminist movement as a powerful political vehicle for change.

Demystification, or the raising of women's consciousness to the ways in which they are oppressed, is a continuing activity of the feminist movement and is, therefore, an important element in feminist therapy. Miriam Greenspan speaks of the need to demystify "the woman's problem, the therapist's 'magical power', and the process of therapy itself" (p. 235).

In an attempt to demystify the problems that individual women come to talk about, therapists need to incorporate into their repertoire of skills one which might be called educating for reconceptualisation, or educating for demystification.

While the main role of the therapist will always be that of listening, empathising, supporting, there will also be times when it will be appropriate for a therapist to introduce material for educative purposes. Indeed, there will be times when it will be *imperative* for a therapist to comment or ask questions for the purpose of educating. A feminist therapist, for example, cannot simply sit there listening, without comment, when a woman speaks of her own or her children's abuse. To do so would be to appear to condone the abuse and give the impression that she is unmoved by such behaviour.

Of course, it would not be appropriate for the therapist to fly into a fit of rage about male violence, causing the woman to feel bewildered and, perhaps, ashamed that she has taught herself to accept his behaviour over the years in order to survive. Rather, a therapist must learn the art of asking questions or making comments in such a way as to encourage a woman to begin questioning her partner's right to treat her the way he does. For example, "Was that OK with you when he did that?", while technically a

---

6. For a detailed discussion of the relationship between CR and therapy groups, see Diane Kravetz, "Consciousness-Raising and Self-Help", in A. M. Brodsky and R. Hare-Mustin (eds) (1980), *Women and Psychotherapy*, pp. 267–83.

closed-ended question (requiring only a "yes" or "no" answer), is a simple, but often effective, question to get a woman started. A comment, instead of a question, might be something like: "Lots of men seem to think they have the right to treat their partners like that." Such questions and comments are designed, of course, to lead somewhere, but when a woman chooses not to respond to the lead, her wishes must be respected. For a therapist to push her own agenda when it has clearly been rejected or ignored would be to add to the woman's oppression.

When a woman begins to ask herself the right questions about her own situation, she is much more likely also to look beyond herself and do her own analysis of what it is like for women in general. Demystification of the problems that a woman experiences, both as an individual and collectively with other women, enables her to stop blaming herself and begin placing the blame where it belongs.

In addition to the above, there must also be a readiness to demystify the therapy process. Some therapists make it a rule to discuss the aim and process of therapy during the first session, but such a practice seems to me to make therapy more clinical and more organised than it needs to be and takes the focus off what the woman has come to talk about. To many women, any discussion about process or the role of the therapist would seem inappropriate and a waste of time. If explanations about the therapy process happen, they ought to happen naturally and not because they are part of the therapist's agenda. For example, on occasions a woman begins by giving the therapist a thumb-nail sketch of the problem she is experiencing and then sits back and waits for the "expert" to produce a diagnosis and suggestions as to what she ought to do. In such cases, it is important that the therapist say something like: "I'd like you to tell me a bit more about what actually happens between you and your daughter when . . . My job, you see, is to help you explore what's happening, to help you discover for yourself what's going on . . .". This kind of comment allows demystification of the therapy process to be a natural part of the interaction between the two women.

The two major elements of a feminist therapy discussed above are support and demystification. It is important that the support available to women in therapy be of the highest quality possible because the amount of support and nurturing most women are accustomed to receiving in male-focused societies is virtually nil. The practice of feminist therapy is based on the belief that most women will discover their own answers to their own problems if demystification occurs and if they are given the kind of support they need to enable them to find the courage to explore the truth about their lives.

10

FEMINIST THERAPY IN PRACTICE

In order that the practice of feminist therapy be a radical and political activity, it must be informed by the theoretical considerations discussed in previous chapters dealing with oppression, access, honesty, passion and justice. Having asserted in Chapter Nine that the two major elements in the practice of feminist therapy are support and demystification, it remains now to show how therapy can proceed in those terms.

Contributions to feminist therapy

It might be helpful, first, to take a moment to focus attention on the strengths and weaknesses of work produced in recent years by other proponents of feminist therapy. While this is not intended as an endorsement of everything they have said, serious students and practitioners of feminist therapy are, nevertheless, urged to read them.

Lucia Albino Gilbert's article on "Feminist Therapy" in Annette M. Brodsky and Rachel Hare-Mustin, *Women and Psychotherapy* (1980), is a good place to start. Gilbert's aim is clearly not to attempt to develop a feminist therapy but, rather, to describe its process and goals and to suggest appropriate directions for further research into its practices and results. She describes feminist therapy as follows:

> This approach, now called feminist therapy, not only incorporates an awareness of the effects of ideology and social structure on the behavior of women but also contains several principles considered essential to the development of autonomous self-actualized women and to the eventual establishment of a social structure consistent with the feminist ideology of egalitarianism (p. 247).

In a section headed: "What Happens in Feminist Therapy?", she suggests that the practice of feminist therapy is based on two core principles. The first, "the personal is political", gives rise to the following practices:

> *Separating the Internal from the External* . . . [Through a process of demystification] therapists encourage clients to evaluate the influence of social roles and norms on their personal experience and to see the relationship between sociological and psychological factors.

> *Validation of the Female Experience* . . . [One of the results of demystification is that the woman] learns that she is not crazy.
>
> *Exploration of Values and Attitudes by Therapists* . . . Therapists constantly explore their own values and attitudes towards women and confront tendencies within themselves toward maintaining things as they are.
>
> *An Emphasis on Change Rather than "Adjustment"* . . . Given the way that women have been socialized and their present status and role in society, societal changes are necessary for significant improvement to occur in women's lives (1980, pp. 248–9).

The second principle on which feminist therapy is based, according to Gilbert, is: "the therapist–client relationship is viewed as egalitarian". This second principle is expressed in the following practices:

> *Shopping Around for a Therapist.* The client is encouraged to take a consumer attitude . . . This attitude keeps her informed and "demystifies" the therapist as a person of unique power and knowledge.
>
> *Enhancement of a Sense of Personal Power.* Throughout therapy, the client is encouraged to experience greater self-confidence and to be more self-directed and autonomous . . .
>
> *Encouraging of Self-Nurturance.* Rather than always nurturing others first, women are made aware that they, too, have rights and can nurture themselves . . .
>
> *Modeling by the Therapist.* [This] is thought to help the client validate her experience as well as to widen her options and goals.
>
> *Expression of Anger* . . . Wherever she looks, she will be aware of how she has been oppressed . . . When this occurs, . . . she will experience a great deal of anger about expected societal roles . . . This anger, and working through it, are part of the feminist therapy (p. 249).[1]

Miriam Greenspan's *A New Approach to Women and Therapy* is by far the most important work on theory and application to come out of the 1980s. Indeed, the development of my own "feminist alternative therapy" owes much to her analysis and insights. In addition to a thorough examination and critique of psychoanalysis and the humanistic therapies, Greenspan includes an important discussion of the development of feminist therapy, which is what she calls "A New Approach to Women and Therapy" (1983, pp. 161–335). In Chapter Ten, "Changing Women's Stories/Feminist Therapy in Action", she discusses her own attitude toward, and practice of, therapy.

First of all, she stresses the importance of the relationship between therapist and client by saying, "it is crucial not to lose sight of the fundamental fact that whatever else it may be, *therapy is always a relationship between persons*". Without discounting the value of therapeutic tools and techniques, she goes on to say: "*The therapist's most essential tool is herself as a person.* It is the creative use of oneself to further the interests of another that constitutes the therapist's work" (p. 234). She insists that:

---

1. Gilbert returns to a discussion of these core principles later in the chapter; see pp. 256–9.

A genuinely new, women-oriented approach to therapy must enhance rather than shun the connection between people in the therapeutic relationship. It must say good-by to the Expert–Patient model of therapy in favor of a more equalized relationship between women working together. It must stress caring cooperation, rather than rigid, hierarchical distance (p. 234).

Continuing her discussion of therapy as a relationship, she says: "It is my firm conviction that no therapy can be really successful without a basic, real relationship of mutual respect, caring, and trust between therapist and client" (p. 238).

After firmly establishing the importance of the relationship between therapist and client and stating that the most essential tool of a therapist is herself as a person, she then makes it clear that being fully aware and developed as a person is not generally all that is required of a therapist. Skills are also important. She says:

good therapy for women does require a great deal of therapeutic skill. In my own experience, the major skills of the therapist in this new style of therapy relationship are an ability to listen to, intuit, empathize with and understand another person's experience—and to communicate that understanding to her; an ability to use one's own feelings toward the client as a tool of help; and an ability to educate the client toward a greater understanding of the social roots of her personal pain (p. 239).

Greenspan's treatment of issues such as listening, empathy, power, anger, self-disclosure and demystification (pp. 232–52) is required reading for all feminists who are also therapists. Indeed, her entire book, written from a socialist feminist perspective, ought to be studied in detail by anyone working on developing her own practice of feminist therapy.

Much more conservative in approach is Jocelyn Chaplin's *Feminist Counselling in Action*. She sees feminist therapy/counselling as having been influenced by: "(1) The ancient roots of 'feminine wisdom'; (2) modern feminism; (3) psychoanalysis; (4) humanistic psychology" (1988, p. 10). The insights integrated into feminist counselling from the "ancient roots of feminine wisdom" include an understanding of "the great cycles and rhythms of nature, involving a sense of the interconnection of all things" (p. 10). Some of the ancient religious symbols and goddess imagery, she says, "can be useful to us today in our own psychological cycles, to help us understand ourselves better and to grow and change" (pp. 10–11).

Chaplin describes the relationship between feminist counselling and "modern feminism" in terms of feminist counselling having grown out of "consciousness-raising or active groups". When women met together and began to realise "how society's structures, attitudes and actions have depowered them", many were led into "one-to-one counselling" because of a desire "to explore more deeply the effects of society on their psyches" (p. 13).

In her discussion of psychoanalysis and humanistic psychology, Chaplin is careful not to reject them and encourages feminists not to "ignore the useful insights" contained in them (pp. 13–15). She is also careful not to exclude men from her discussion. In her introduction, she describes feminist counselling as "training people, men as well as women, for a society that does not yet exist; a society in which so-called 'feminine' values and ways of thinking are valued as much as so-called 'masculine' ones" (p. 2).

Her emphasis throughout the book on balance, rhythm, the opposites, empowerment and equality, together with the absence of discussion of therapy as a political activity, places her work squarely on the liberal humanist side of feminism.

Looking at other examples, some of the best work in feminist therapy has been done by feminists working with women in particular areas of women's oppression. One example is that by Mary MacLeod and Esther Saraga in their article on feminist theory and practice in relation to victims/survivors of child sexual abuse. In "Challenging the Orthodoxy: Towards a Feminist Theory and Practice", they give a feminist critique of three influential orthodox approaches to child sexual abuse—the libertarian, the psycho-analytic and the family dysfunction theories (1988, pp. 24–39)—and then present what they call "the feminist challenge" (pp. 39f).

The feminist approach, as they discuss it, clearly includes the need for honesty, justice, anger and blaming. Right at the beginning of that section, they invite readers to listen to the voices of women survivors of childhood sexual abuse, who are saying in "an overwhelmingly convincing" way:

> don't tell us we like it, we want it, we need it or we agree to it. Don't tell us you're freeing us from sexual repression, educating us for a more fulfilling adult life. Don't tell us you do this because nobody loves you. Don't tell us we are dirty. Don't tell us we are worthless. And don't tell us we can't recover. You may have fucked our bodies, but you're not going to fuck our minds (p. 39).

Acknowledging that there are strengths and weaknesses inherent in all forms of therapy available to victims/survivors of child sexual abuse, they conclude:

> Disclosing, talking, telling is important in challenging the power of the secret, of shame, in facing and confronting the pain, and in reaching catharsis, but it is not everything and it may not be enough. There have to be a range of resources for self-help, therapy, and for women who need to "breakdown" within a safe environment (pp. 49–50).

From Germany, Ute Winkler and Traute Schönenberg, in their article "Options for Involuntarily Childless Women", discuss the important work being done by feminist therapists and counsellors at the Feminist Health Centre in Frankfurt with women who are victims of abuse in relation to genetic and reproductive technologies. The work of the centre began, they explain, with "the recognition that involuntarily childless women have no voice in the discussion of genetic and reproductive technologies and that their thoughts in the matter are trivialized or ignored" (Winkler and Schönenberg, in Klein, 1989c, p. 208). The counselling service is offered for the purpose of helping women "to clarify their conflicts and arguments concerning human fertility/infertility by pro-viding them with time and space to reflect" (p. 208). Describing the work of the centre further, they say:

Counseling is available for all women whose wish for a child cannot be fulfilled . . . We make space for emotions arising from an unfulfilled desire for a child, the disappointed hopes and wishes, the grieving and inner mourning as it affects the women (p. 208).

With regard to therapeutic practice, they speak of discussions taking place "on a one-to-one basis, or in groups, just as the women prefer. The counselling is designed to air problems, to put them in words and make them public" (p. 208). The counselling proceeds in the following way:

The woman is at the centre of the discussion and determines what course it will take. The counsellor's job is to support her in the formulation of her own thoughts, to assist her in seeing connections and to point out areas which have been consciously or unconsciously omitted in the discussion (p. 209).

It is clear that the creation of "a place where women have a chance to express their own thoughts about the complex of problems and to help them develop these thoughts further" is not simply a therapeutic endeavour. Winkler and Schönenberg describe it also as a "politically important" act (p. 209).

Bonnie Burstow, in *Radical Feminist Therapy: Working in the Context of Violence*, describes her book as an attempt "to radicalize feminist therapy further and to offer detailed and grounded guidance" (1992, p. xiv). Written from the perspectives of radical feminism, radical therapy and the anti-psychiatry movement, Burstow has developed her theory and practice of feminist therapy in a remarkably thorough and comprehensive way. She deals with various areas of violence against women (childhood sexual abuse, rape, battery, etc.) and discusses the variety of psychological responses women have to such violence (depression, self-mutilation, troubled eating, problem drinking, etc.). She also stresses the need for feminist therapists to come to terms with women of difference and includes an important emphasis throughout the book on groups such as lesbians, indigenous women, Jewish women, immigrant women, women with disabilities, and prostitutes.

While there is no doubt that Burstow's work makes an extremely important contribution, it nevertheless gives rise to two concerns that need to be mentioned. The first is that two out of the three movements in which her radical feminist therapy is grounded are movements established and dominated by men. One, the anti-psychiatry movement, noted for its courageous work in the 1960s and 1970s in exposing the oppressive nature of psychiatry and other forms of therapy, was the work of men like Ronald Laing and Thomas Szasz. The other, the radical therapy movement, is generally identified with Claude Steiner, Eric Berne and others who, as Burstow rightly points out, were also deeply involved in Transactional Analysis (TA). The close relationship between radical therapy and TA has always been a curious one, since radical therapy claimed to be based in a radical socio-political philosophy while TA, clearly a favourite with the liberal humanists, was notably mainstream.

While there is no suggestion here that radical therapy and anti-psychiatry would have nothing at all to offer the development of a feminist therapy, there is, nevertheless, a serious concern about developing a feminist therapy from the basis of predominantly male input. Given that feminist therapy begins with the premises that the distress individual women experience is almost always caused by oppression and that the agents of women's oppression are almost always men, the grounding of a radical feminist therapy in philosophies developed by men leaves a lot to be desired.[2]

Another concern about Burstow's theory is that, in her attempt to show that "All women are subject to extreme violence at some time or live with the threat of extreme violence" (p. xv), there is the danger of understating the violence done to those who really are victims of actual violence. The use of continuums to show that childhood sexual abuse, rape and battery are "our common plight as women" (p. 113) always presents a difficulty because, although it does make the important point that all women are surrounded by and vulnerable to violence in male-dominated societies, it also promotes the "everything is relative" philosophy that robs victims of actual abuse of the special attention and anger that their situations deserve.

Even with these significant concerns, Burstow's work must still be regarded as a major contribution to the development of feminist therapy.

Stages of therapy

The practice of feminist therapy, where emotional distress is involved, proceeds through four identifiable stages, and it is the role of the therapist to ensure that the tasks of each stage are dealt with adequately. It is important to mention that, as with many stage theories,[3] the stages of therapy suggested below are not neatly defined in the sense that they are clearly distinguishable from each other. Each stage does not have an identifiable beginning and end. As a matter of fact, it is common in therapy for two or even three stages to occur at the same time. Nevertheless, it is an important task of the therapist to be able to identify each stage amongst all that is happening—not in order to draw attention to it at that moment, but simply to be aware of it—because it is the therapist's responsibility to ensure that each stage is given adequate attention.

If one stage is not dealt with adequately, therapy is blocked and progress toward total resolution of the problem is not possible. When such blocking occurs, there is a need to go back over the stages in search of words and emotions that need to find expression. This process can be started simply by saying something like: "Tell me again about . . ."

The following are the stages through which a feminist therapy must proceed, together with a discussion of the tasks to be carried out, at each stage, by the therapist and also by the woman who has sought help.

---

2. To avoid any misunderstanding, let me say clearly that I am not expressing a biologically determinist view about men's role in oppressing women. Rather, I am arguing from a social constructionist position.

3. See Erik Erikson (1959), *Identity and the Life Cycle*; Elisabeth Kübler-Ross (1969), *On Death and Dying*; Elizabeth (Betty) McLellan (1977), "Lesbian Identity" (unpublished doctoral dissertation).

Stage one: Telling the story

The first thing that must happen in any therapeutic encounter is the telling of the story. The woman who has come to the therapist for help must be prepared to tell her story, and the therapist's task is to listen.

While it is true that the telling and retelling of the story will go on throughout the entire period of the therapy, the first session is always crucial. Sadly, there is a widespread tendency on the part of therapists to waste time during this most valuable of all sessions. There is a mistaken belief that a therapist's main task during an initial session is to ensure that the woman feels comfortable and relaxed; as a result, many therapists chatter inanely about the weather and other equally rivetting topics, wasting a unique opportunity that can never be repeated.

The fact is that a woman's motivation is almost always high at the initial session because of the lead-up to that moment. If she is like most women, she has thought about her situation for months, trying to decide whether or not she really "needs" to seek the help of a therapist. Then, having decided, she summons all her courage and actually makes the appointment. Anticipating the first session with a fair degree of nervousness, she psyches herself up for the moment when she can begin telling her story. She has already decided how she should start and how much of her story she will tell.

On arrival, if she likes the therapist and senses she can be trusted, she will want to begin talking immediately. Even if she finds it difficult to talk, she nevertheless wants to, and will be disappointed and disillusioned if the therapist insists on chatting about superficial things to "break the ice". Similarly, those therapists who like to use part of the first session to discuss and demystify the therapy process, or to take particulars for their own records, or to make a "contract" with the woman regarding number of sessions, etc., actually take the focus away from the woman's needs at a crucial moment.

In other words, if a woman who is all geared up to tell her story is prevented from doing so because of the therapist's own needs and requirements, she may never do so. She may never be as motivated at any subsequent session as she is during that first one. The message is, therefore, that when a woman is geared up to talk, as she almost always is at the beginning of the first session, the therapist must be geared up to listen, or a unique opportunity will be lost.

The woman's initial task, then, is to tell her story, to tell it as clearly and in as much detail as possible, so that she herself can see it more clearly than she ever has before. The importance of detail in the telling of the story cannot be over-emphasised, as the following explanation will illustrate.

When a woman reaches a stage where she feels unable to cope, it is often the case that her confusion, helplessness, powerlessness began with a reasonably simple event. Both the actual event and her immediate emotional response to it were easy for her to understand at that time. The event, for example, may have occurred like this: One day, early in her marriage, she found a range of pornographic magazines in her husband's desk drawer. Her immediate response was clear. She was outraged. She spoke to her husband about it, expressing her anger and disapproval, only to be told that what he chose to read was his business and that she had no right "snooping" in his desk. As far as he was concerned, the subject was closed but, for her, there was never an end to it. She was devastated. Her whole world was shattered.

Over the ensuing days and weeks (in some instances, years), her anger turned to helplessness, disillusionment, betrayal, numbness. It was not just the knowledge of his involvement with pornography that devastated her, but also his absolute refusal to engage with her on the issue, to open up the issue for discussion and compromise. Her opinions, her feelings, the extent of her revulsion to pornography, were of no consequence to him.

What could she do? Talking it through was not an option: he had made that clear. The only options open to her were: to leave him immediately; to issue an ultimatum and then leave if he refused to comply; or to try to see things his way, be more understanding, love him unconditionally, lower her expectations.

It was at that moment—when she decided to lower her expectations and be more understanding of him and his "needs"—that she began the process that would lead to her own confusion and alienation. To accept the unacceptable is never possible, yet so many women try to do it in the name of "love". With every betrayal, small or large, a woman who is intent on accepting what she finds unacceptable finds more and more explanations with which to fool herself, until who she is and what she wants is totally lost. By the time she seeks the help of a therapist, her anxiety or depression or insomnia or eating problem seems not to have a cause outside herself. It is accepted by everyone, including herself, that *she* has a problem. If she were to seek help from a mainstream therapist, she would probably be encouraged to look within herself, to try to get rid of those hidden resentments, to try to forgive, to think more positively, and also to congratulate herself for the work she has done in keeping the marriage together and supporting her husband as he climbed the ladder of success.

From the perspective of feminist therapy, however, it is obvious that any therapy that does not get to the root of the problem will, in fact, compound the problem. Any woman's depression, insomnia, eating problem, etc., had to start somewhere, and the only chance for recovery lies in her finding, admitting and coming to terms with the truth about her situation.

It is for this reason that stage one is such a crucial part of therapy. The telling of the story, *in detail*, is the main task of the woman during this first stage, and the telling of the story must continue for as long as there is more to be told. The tasks of the therapist, at this important stage, include being there, being real, listening, empathising, reflecting, gently probing, in an attempt to help the woman achieve clarity and detail. As the emerging picture uncovers the truth, the way in which the woman's present problems developed makes more and more sense to her.

Stage two: Expression of sadness and helplessness

In therapy with women, stage two sometimes begins before stage one. In other words, some women are so distressed by the time they decide to seek the help of a therapist that the tears come pouring out as soon as they attempt to speak. Some are so emotionally distressed that they cannot speak at all until some time into the first session. Such a situation is never a problem for a feminist therapist who experiences the free expression of emotions as one of the rewarding things about working with women. So long as the therapist's caring support is obvious to the woman, she will begin to speak when she is ready.

More commonly, however, stage two begins sometime during stage one. As a woman talks about why she has come and begins to tell her story, there will often be moments of intense emotion. It does not mean, of course, that every woman who comes to talk about an emotional problem will cry, or even ought to cry. What it does mean is that some parts of every woman's story will be more emotionally charged than others. One of the important tasks of the therapist, in stage two, is to notice when those moments occur and to probe a little at those points. If the woman prefers not to focus on something and simply goes on with the telling of her story, a good therapist will file that point away in the back of her mind and seek an opportunity to focus attention on it again before the session ends.

Some women, in psyching themselves up for their first appointment, make a firm resolve that they will tell the therapist the whole story—without crying. It seems to be incredibly important to them that the therapist hear the story clearly and rationally. Any inability on their part to "control" their emotions will, they believe, only get in the way. In these situations, when emotions are deliberately put aside in the interest of logic and clarity, a therapist needs to be particularly skilful in sensing the emotional moments of the story and encouraging the woman to explore those moments further. The expression of one's sadness, frustration, helplessness and despair is integral to the telling of one's story, and a therapist must listen, reflect, empathise, probe in such a way that the whole story (words and emotions) eventually comes out.

Feminist therapists need to be aware that the influence of the liberal humanist era, and also of the feminist movement to date, makes this much more difficult to achieve now than it would have been thirty years ago. The message from liberal humanist and New Age philosophies is that women are now supposed to think positively and believe that we are empowered, and that any problem we have must be of our own making. This influences women to try very hard not to acknowledge their "weaker" feelings, not to "give in" to their feelings of helplessness and despair. Such women attempt, in therapy, to jump from stage one to stage four. First, they tell their story. Then, they want the therapist to help them to be logical and rational about finding a solution so that they can get on with their lives. The simple fact is, it does not work.

Feminism, too, has influenced women in relation to the expression of emotions, but in a different way. Feminism, particularly radical feminism, has rightly emphasised the need for women to acknowledge and express our anger so that we are not constantly incapacitated by self-pity and self-blame. "Don't break down; break *out*" has been one of the important and empowering slogans of the feminist movement. Some women, however, particularly feminists, have been so influenced by the emphasis on the need to express anger that, whenever they confront a problem in their lives, they "break out" but never "break down". In other words, the first and last emotion they allow themselves to have is anger. Any sign of sadness, fear, helplessness, etc. is seen as weakness and defeat. In therapy, these women attempt to jump from stage one to stage three. They tell their story and express their rage, and what they want the therapist to do is help them find the peace that eludes them without having to acknowledge and explore their "weaker" feelings. Again, it does not work. In psychological terms, breaking out only works after one has first broken down.

The important task to be achieved, at this stage, by the woman who has sought therapy is to allow her emotions to flow. Stage two involves: giving in to one's sadness when one is sad, admitting to defeat when one is defeated, allowing oneself to be depressed when one is depressed, accepting one's anxiety when one is overwhelmed by it, expressing one's fear, confusion, disappointment, indeed, all past and present emotions that surface during the telling of one's story. The role of the therapist, here, is similar to that required during stage one with, perhaps, an even greater emphasis on the reflecting of feelings and on empathy.

Stage three: Acknowledgement of oppression, expression of anger

When a woman tells her story fully and expresses her deepest despair, confusion, fear, sadness and self-hatred, it usually has the effect of enabling her to explore her situation in such a way that she sees the truth about her life much more clearly than before. If a therapist is skilful in the art of demystification, of helping a woman uncover the truth about the source/s of her emotional and psychological distress so that she stops blaming herself, the woman will find anger welling up inside her.

Regarding demystification, since the acknowledgement of one's oppression is so crucial for one's emotional and mental health, and since it is the process of demystification that enables the acknowledgement of oppression and the subsequent expression of anger, it is important that we give special attention here to the skills required by a therapist for this task.

The art of facilitating demystification occurs at two levels: one relates to *the therapist's own thought processes*, and the other to *the words spoken by the therapist* in the context of the therapeutic interaction. First, when a therapist is aware of the need for demystification, as every feminist therapist must be, she is very conscious of the importance of her own thought processes. She listens in a particularly urgent way. Her mind is alert and her hearing accurate. As a woman talks about her personal circumstances, the therapist listens for the political reality inherent in what she is saying. In the mind of the therapist, there is a constant filtering, a constant processing of what is being said; the therapist continually links the words to the political reality, and evaluates the woman's readiness to hear and consider an alternative interpretation of her situation.

For many women, a feminist perspective provides a totally new way of looking at the circumstances of their lives; as such, it may be accepted or rejected. The therapist must make decisions all along the way about what to say to encourage a woman to broaden her understanding of her problem, how to say what she wants to say, and when.

If the therapist's attempts at demystification are ignored, decisions must then be made about whether or not to try again and, if so, how and when.

The thoughts, the filtering, the processing, the evaluating, play a crucial role in determining what the therapist will actually say, and that brings us to the second point. When a feminist therapist speaks for the purpose of demystifying, her words and tone are chosen carefully. The political necessity, and that which makes feminist therapy different from other therapies, is educating for demystification. When education occurs, however, it must be as a natural part of the therapeutic interaction.

My own experimenting with different methods of demystification in the context of therapy has revealed the effectiveness of at least three ways of proceeding. The following discussion of each method, including practical examples, is offered as a guide.

Leading questions

The first method of demystification is the use of leading questions or comments. Take the example of a woman who comes to therapy to talk about the relationship she has with her male partner. She may begin by talking about his "good points" but then moves on to talk about the distress she experiences, as a daily fact of life, due to his attitude and behaviour towards her. Often a woman will recount incidents of brutal verbal, physical or sexual humiliation as if such incidents were a normal part of women's lives, to be expected and accepted and, therefore, of no concern. When this happens, a very effective question for the therapist to ask is the one mentioned in the previous chapter: "Was that OK with you when he threatened you in front of your friends?" Or, "Is that OK with you that he 'knocks you around' when he gets angry?"

The initial response to such questions is usually something like: "Oh well, you get used to it", to which a feminist therapist must reply: "But is it OK with you?" The therapist's reason for asking such a question is to raise the ethical issue of justice. Does the woman judge it to be acceptable behaviour? Whether or not one gets "used to it" is beside the point. The therapist's persistence in pursuing the ethical issue will have one of two results: either the woman expresses her unwillingness to enter into discussion about it, in which case the therapist must accede to her wishes; or the woman opens herself up to the process of exploring an alternative interpretation of her situation. When the latter occurs, demystification will begin and liberation from her oppression will become a possibility.

Regarding the wording of questions, humanist therapists would, no doubt, criticise the closed-ended nature of the questioning I suggest above. They would argue that an open-ended question (that is, one that requires more than a "yes" or "no" answer) would be more effective, such as: "How did you feel when your husband threatened you in front of your friends?" It must be said, however, that the wording of questions depends upon the goal the therapist wants to achieve. If I want to help a woman explore her feelings about something, I will ask: "How did you feel when . . . ?" But if my goal is demystification, if my goal is to encourage her to begin to ask the kinds of ethical and political questions that will lead to a real resolution of her pain and distress, then I will begin by asking: "Was that OK with you when . . .?"

Other examples of questions and comments I often make for the purpose of demystification occur in a situation where a woman is blaming herself for not being able to cope, or where she is talking about the criticism that is directed at her from all sides. Sometimes I will simply say: "Society is really hard on women." Or "I think men often blame women as a way of avoiding the blame themselves." Or "Isn't it strange how *women* are always the ones to be blamed? Whenever anything goes wrong, it's always the woman's fault, the mother's fault? Have you noticed that?"

In a situation where a slightly more sophisticated or analytical comment is called for, I might say to a woman who is suffering under the weight of what she considers to be unfair criticism from her children: "I think children find it much more satisfying to heap blame on their mother because they know they'll get a reaction out of her. They know she'll care. They know she'll be hurt by what they say. Any attempts at blaming their father in the past have got them nowhere. He just doesn't respond. That's probably why kids blame their mothers. But it doesn't make it right."

When a woman is emotionally exhausted, worn out, highly stressed, not coping very well, and is feeling badly about herself because she "ought" to be able to cope, the kind of comment which often helps her see the unfairness of "normal" family dynamics is: "Everyone always expects a woman to be there for them. A husband expects his wife to be there when he wants to talk about something. Children expect their mother to be there when they need her to do something for them. But nobody ever thinks about being there for *her*. It's as if she's just taken for granted."

A different kind of situation involves a woman who, after mentioning quite incidentally that she is a lesbian, then goes on to talk about her inability to cope at work with a boss who is constantly giving her a "hard time". She has worked with difficult people before, she says, and has always managed to cope, but this time is different. An important leading comment here would be: "I wonder how much of the hard time you're getting from your boss can be attributed to the fact that you're a lesbian."

These examples of the kinds of remarks that can be used for the purpose of demystification show that they are, in fact, *leading* questions and comments. They are designed to lead somewhere, but the decision to respond to the lead, or ignore it, rests with the woman concerned.

Giving information

Another method of demystification I have found effective is that of giving information about feminist therapeutic principles as the therapy proceeds. The information given, of course, must be pertinent to the woman's story as she is telling it, otherwise it would be experienced as an unnecessary intrusion and would serve to hinder, rather than help, the work of demystification.

One example of this method is that which I often find helpful early in the first session. Most women seeking therapy are firmly convinced that the problems they are experiencing are entirely their own fault and that all they need to do is get some help to discover where they are going wrong, so that they can make the necessary changes and put everything right. As a woman talks about her situation and the therapist becomes aware that she is taking the whole burden of responsibility on her own shoulders, it is important to say something like: "You know, what I find is that a person's unhappiness or inability to cope is often caused by what's going on around her." Depending on her response, this can then be followed by a more focused statement, like: "When things go wrong in our lives, it's not always our own fault." Then, "Tell me about your relationship with your partner . . ."

Let us look at another example of giving information about the principles of feminist therapy for the purpose of demystification. With regard to the principle of honesty: "One of my tasks as a therapist is to help you explore what's been going on in your life, so that you discover the truth. From what you tell me, several well-meaning people have told you 'it's this' or 'it's that', but you and I have to ask: What is it about your past or your present that is *really* to blame for your depression?"

Take the example of a woman confined to a wheelchair who comes to talk about her depression and her thoughts of suicide. It is of primary importance that this woman be given the space to be honest with herself. A therapist encourages honesty by making leading comments such as: "It must be hard, sometimes, being confined to that wheelchair and always having to put on a brave face." If the woman talks about feelings of powerlessness and helplessness, the therapist must then look for an opportunity to give information about the role that oppression plays in emotional health and happiness: "When society discriminates against people who are 'different', when people like yourself are treated as second-class citizens, it affects your self-esteem and undermines your self-confidence." Taking care to avoid the temptation to give too much information all at once, a therapist should wait and see how such a comment is taken up. If the woman is receptive, the therapist should go on to say something like: "It seems the only acceptable way to be in our society is male, white, middle-class, heterosexual, able-bodied, Christian, and so on. Anyone who is different from that 'standard' is usually given a clear message that she (or he) is inferior, lacking something, not as good as members of the dominant group."

Input about the woman's own oppression and its effect on her is relevant here. "As we delve into the depths of your depression and attempt to understand it, it's important not to ignore the fact that you are oppressed on, not one, but two, counts: one, because you are a woman and two, because you are disabled. When one is doubly oppressed, the potential for emotional and psychological distress is also doubled. In other words, with every oppression, one's potential for distress is magnified".[4]

---

4. It must be remembered that the giving of this kind of information is appropriate only where women do not already have an awareness of the effects of oppression in all its forms, and then only when they appear to be open to receiving such information. It is quite a different situation, for example, when the woman in the wheelchair contemplating suicide, or the lesbian suffering unconsolable grief because her lover has left her, is a feminist. It might be important to remind such women that their pain and distress is probably worsened because of their multiple oppressions but, as feminists, they would not need anything more than a reminder.

Educating about oppression as a feminist therapeutic principle would, in these instances, be inappropriate. Rather, the focus of therapy should be on helping these women express the depth of their sadness, agony, despair, and enabling them, when they are ready, to begin to allow their anger to surface.

One of the feminist therapeutic principles that raises its head continually in therapy with women is anger. The kinds of informative comments a therapist can make are: "The expression of anger plays a very important role in getting rid of depression." Or "To be angry at someone who has deliberately hurt you is a very healthy response." Or "Most women find it hard to be angry because, right from when we were little girls, we were told it wasn't 'nice' for girls to be angry. No one will like us if we are angry, we were told. So, as we grew up, we taught ourselves to keep our anger hidden even from ourselves."

With regard to forgiveness, we can say: "It isn't always appropriate to forgive, you know." Or, "We've always been taught that we must forgive everyone, but when someone doesn't even acknowledge the hurt they've inflicted on us, or does acknowledge it but isn't sorry, then to forgive that person is wrong. When we try to forgive in those circumstances, it causes us a lot of conflict."

Regarding justice: "Justice plays a very important part in our mental and emotional health. If justice hasn't been done in relation to something that happened to you, then that issue will remain unresolved for you until you can find a way to bring it to a conclusion that satisfies you.[5] That's one of the things we can do in therapy."

These are just a few examples of the kinds of liberating information that can be imparted to women in the context of therapy. Readers who are therapists are urged to trust their own impulses and give information by making such comments where it seems appropriate.

Referring to feminist theory

The third method of demystification I have experimented with and found effective is that of making reference to feminist theory and writing. Most women find such input interesting, some find it satisfying because it confirms what they have already figured out for themselves, and others find it exciting and challenging. As with the first two methods of demystification discussed above, it is necessary with this one, also, that any input by the therapist be concise and relevant. It must be remembered that such information is not introduced for the purpose of starting a long and involved discussion of feminist theory but, rather, for the purpose of presenting an idea that will facilitate demystification.

A simple example of this third method is one that is based on the early work of Jessie Bernard in *The Future of Marriage* (1972). When a woman is talking about problems related to being married, the therapist can say: "Marriage is made for men, of course." This can be followed with: "A study about marriage done by a woman in the 1970s

---

5. To reach a conclusion or "closure" that satisfies is not to say justice has been achieved. The achieving of justice is often dependent on the actions of someone else and is, therefore, out of the control of the one who has sought the therapist's help. In such situations a therapist's task is to help a woman do all that she can do in terms of expressing her despair and anger, either face-to-face with the perpetrator or "as if" she were talking to the perpetrator. She can only do what she *can* do, and while the result may not be as satisfying as it would be if justice were achieved, it is often enough (and the aim of therapy is that it be enough) to allow the woman to let it go and leave it behind her.

showed that the most contented group of people in society were single women, the second were married men, the third group were married women, and the least contented were single men." Or the therapist can refer to more recent studies done in Australia with regard to women and work, by saying: "I read recently that as soon as a woman begins living with a man, her workload around the home increases something like 60%."[6]

Another reference that women have found helpful, particularly in understanding the dynamics that take place in their relationships with men, is the work of Simone de Beauvoir in *The Second Sex*. A therapist can say: "You know, Simone de Beauvoir wrote in the 1950s describing the way men relate to women. She said men see themselves as 'subject' and women as 'other'. While men relate to other men as subjects, they relate to women as 'others' whose purpose in life is simply to revolve around them." More can be said about de Beauvoir's thesis but not initially. After the therapist's opening reference, it is important to see if and how the woman takes it up and relates it to her own situation. The emphasis must always be on the woman's working through of her own issues and not on the therapist's need to talk about her favourite feminist theories.

It is not always necessary to mention the name of the feminist writer whose ideas you are referring to. Sometimes it seems appropriate, but at other times it is clear that such information, at least in the initial statement, would complicate the interaction.

Other examples of references I often use are: "Dale Spender conducted a very interesting study in the 1980s dealing with communication between women and men. She discovered that men dominated conversations in social situations. Men talk more, interrupt more, get more attention, and so on."[7]

Again, "Shere Hite, in a recent study, asked women about the emotional support they get from their male partners, and 96 per cent of the women said they don't get back from their partners anywhere near the emotional support that they, themselves, give. They felt they were always giving out, but getting very little back."[8]

On a different note, when a woman who has chosen to live her life in a way that is different from mainstream expectations—a feminist, a lesbian, an Aboriginal activist for example—comes to talk about the devastating effects of society's hostility toward her, I have found Mary Daly's concept of living "on the boundary" to be very helpful. I say: "Mary Daly, in one of her earlier books, talked about the concept of living on the boundary. She said, in effect, that people like you and me, who choose to live outside mainstream society, should never be surprised when society rejects us or tries to destroy us. We have chosen a different life—life on the boundary—and the male-stream hate us for it."[9]

---

6. Office of the Status of Women, Department of the Prime Minister and Cabinet (1991), *Selected Findings from Juggling Time: How Australian Families Use Time*, p. 15. This booklet presents a selection of findings from the study *Juggling Time* in which Michael Bittman "analyses the results of a Pilot Survey of Time Use conducted in 1987 by the Australian Bureau of Statistics" (p. v).

7. Dale Spender (1980), *Man Made Language*, pp. 41–51.

8. Shere Hite (1987), *Women and Love. A Cultural Revolution in Progress*, pp. 77–9.

9. Mary Daly (1973), *Beyond God the Father: Toward a Philosophy of Women's Liberation*, pp. 40–3.

The purpose of this input is not to explain or justify the oppressive behaviour of those who have caused this woman's pain and distress, but to remind her of the fact that patriarchal society punishes those women who make their own choices in life. The effect of this kind of input in the context of therapy has been to strengthen the woman's resolve to continue defying an unjust and oppressive society, and to seek more support from her sisters on the boundary.

There are many more examples of references to feminist theory which I make in the context of therapy, but those recounted above are sufficient to illustrate the way such references can be used for the purpose of demystification.

Whatever method of demystification a therapist chooses at any one time, demystification enables the acknowledgement of oppression which, in turn, prompts the expression of anger. Whenever a woman's anger begins to surface in therapy, it is the therapist's task to help her express the anger she feels. The pace at which this occurs, the level of its intensity and the method of its expression must be in accordance with what feels right and appropriate to the woman herself. While there are techniques that can be suggested by the therapist to assist her in getting in touch with her anger, it must be stressed that the dramatic acting-out encouraged by some humanist therapies (like encouraging a person to beat a cushion with a tennis racquet or baseball bat) is not recommended.

A not-to-be-sent letter

An example of a more gentle approach—which, incidentally, is much more effective— is the widely used technique of letter-writing. The therapist asks the woman to find some time during the coming week, when no one else is around, to sit down and write a letter to one of the people she has mentioned as she has explored the cause of her present distress. The person to whom the letter is to be written is discussed and agreed upon by the woman and the therapist. It should be explained to the woman that she will not be asked to send the letter, and that she therefore should see it as an opportunity to say whatever she has always wished she could say to that person.

The directions from the therapist are that, in the letter, she should: recall for the person all the events as she remembers them; write about her emotions as they come to the surface; allow herself the freedom to blame him or her; and express that blame in as angry a way as she can. It should also be explained that the letter is then to be brought to the next therapy session and read to the therapist. Many women find the writing of the letter so painful that they shrink from the thought of reading it aloud. They come to the next session and hand the letter to the therapist to read for herself but, of course, it is very important that the therapist not read it. The point of the exercise is not to make sure the therapist knows all the details. What the therapist knows, or does not know, is of no consequence. Rather, the point of the exercise is to encourage and enable the woman to express emotions that she has found too painful to face in the past, emotions that have intimidated her, perhaps for years. The only way she is going to be released from the hold those repressed emotions have on her is to express them, to talk, to cry, to be angry, to keep on talking and expressing the emotions as they surface, until they no longer have the power to intimidate her. The effectiveness of letter-writing as a therapeutic exercise lies partly in the fact that it allows two opportunities for the expression of emotions—first as the letter is being written, and then as it is being read to the therapist.

The desire to take back anger

While such techniques are often effective in helping women turn blame and anger away from themselves and toward those who are truly blameworthy, it would be quite wrong to give the impression that the process is easy. As a matter of fact, it is one of the most difficult things to achieve in therapy with women: first, because women's conditioning is such that many believe anger to be inappropriate; and second, because, if a woman does express anger, she will more than likely feel guilty and want to take it back. So, therapy often proceeds as follows.

A therapist who is mindful of the high level of motivation usually present in the first session will encourage the expression of sadness and other such emotions so that the stage is set, by the end of the first session, for the woman to explore her emotions further through some form of "homework" suggested by the therapist. If the writing of a letter is suggested and agreed upon, it is usually the case that the expression of anger, precipitated by the writing of the letter, will be central to the therapeutic work done in the second session. What often follows, however, either at the end of the second or during the third session, is a desperate attempt on the part of the woman to take her anger back. Many women feel overwhelmed with guilt after criticising someone they love, or feel they "ought" to love. They feel that they have been disloyal, that they had no right to judge their father or their husband in the way they did. After all, "He had a very hard childhood himself", or "He has a good side to him too." It is at this point that a woman who has dared to criticise someone close to her, particularly if it is a man, can become inordinately protective of him.

While this turn of events can be frustrating to a therapist, it is important that we not try too hard to stop a woman taking back what she has said. The free expression of blame and anger can cause a rush of fairly severe anxiety, and a woman must do whatever she needs to do to relieve her anxiety. She may simply not be ready, at that time, to accept the consequences of naming her oppressors, but at least she has experienced the beginnings of a new consciousness. As feminist therapists, we must view such a situation as a large step forward and only a small step backward. A degree of demystification *has* taken place in this woman's consciousness even if, for the time being, she is making the choice to deny it.

An even more difficult situation, from the perspective of the therapist, arises when a woman not only denies what she has discovered, for example, about her husband's contemptuous attitude toward her, but also ceases therapy and makes up her mind to devote her energies to being a better wife! It is important, in such circumstances, for a therapist to remember that therapy is part of a process. It cannot solve all of any woman's problems no matter how long she stays in therapy, and any therapist who aims for such an unrealistic goal is setting herself up for a career of disappointment and failure. We must learn to be satisfied with whatever degree of demystification occurs, and see it as part of a larger process.

Stage three, then, consists of the expression of anger, naming, confronting and blaming one's oppressors, either face-to-face or in the context of therapy. Also, at this time, there is a growing awareness of solidarity with other women and a feeling of urgency about the need to demand justice and to work for change.

To recapitulate, the tasks of the woman who has sought therapy are: to allow her anger to surface, to acknowledge it, to feel it, and to express it by naming and blaming her oppressor/s. The tasks of the therapist are: to listen and respond; to ask questions and make comments with the aim of educating for demystification; to feel comfortable with the expression of anger; and to encourage complete honesty even when the uncovering of the truth causes pain in the short term.

Stage four: Working for change

One of the life-enhancing results of demystification is, as mentioned above, "a growing awareness of solidarity with other women and a feeling of urgency about the need to demand justice and to work for change". Consequently, the best outcome of therapy occurs when a woman who has progressed through the first three stages makes up her mind to work for change both in her own life and in the structures of society. This is the fourth and final stage of therapy.

The decision to make changes in one's own situation can be a very frightening proposition and, while it is the woman herself who must make her own decisions, it is most important that the therapist's support and encouragement at that time be unwavering. As well as looking to the therapist for support, most women intent on making changes in their lives find involvement with other women beneficial in terms of the strong support they receive. Many have their own group of women friends or relatives who support them unconditionally, but those who do not should be encouraged to find a group of women to relate to. To this end, one of the tasks of feminist therapists is to make sure different group opportunities are available—support groups, educational groups, seminars, courses, reading groups—so that women can be encouraged to link up with such groups as they wish.

To avoid the unhelpful situation which sometimes occurs, where a woman consistently uses a group to work through emotions that she has not been able to resolve, it is advisable that individual therapy be continued until such time as a woman is ready to move beyond the emotions that are blocking her progress. It is for this reason that group involvement is recommended *after* a woman has progressed through the first three stages and is moving into stage four.[10]

---

10. While feminist therapy values women's involvement in groups very highly, it must be remembered that there may be times in any woman's life when she is not an appropriate candidate for group work. For a group to work successfully, it has to work for every member of the group, and anyone who has not resolved her own emotions adequately is in danger of dominating a group with her own concerns.

In this fourth stage of therapy, the decision to work for change to the structures of society is, of course, far less common than the decision to work for change in one's own life. The anger that rises up in a woman during therapy is usually for herself and her own situation, and her decision to work for change usually means working to change her own situation. The development of a sense of collective anger, however, and a determination to work together with other women to bring about changes in society, are also very important for the woman's own ongoing journey through life. When she is able to see herself as part of a collective whole, she will never again have to experience herself as an isolated individual, alone and vulnerable in a society that disapproves of, and is hostile toward, women.

While the encouraging of a greater understanding of the collective oppression of women is an important part of a therapist's role, there are some dangers we need to be aware of. One is that, in coming to such an awareness, it is possible for an individual woman to convince herself that her particular oppression, together with the devastating effect her oppression is having on her, is not significant when viewed from a global perspective. Another danger is related to the tendency in women to look for ways to excuse or justify bad behaviour, especially that of men. Some women may be tempted to use the knowledge of collective oppression—for example, that male violence against women is common in Western societies—to excuse the violence perpetrated against them by the particular male/s in their lives.

Both of these responses are unhelpful because they result in further mystification, further moving away from the bitter truth. All a therapist can do in the face of these possibilities, however, is be aware of such dangers and attempt to discourage any moves toward them.

The tasks of the woman at this final stage of therapy are: to allow the process of demystification and honesty and anger to continue; to acknowledge the greater degree of power and freedom she is beginning to feel; to decide to make some changes in her life instead of continuing to adjust her life to fit in with those around her. Typical changes are: leaving her partner or her job; drawing herself back emotionally from someone who continually hurts her; confronting the one who sexually abused her in childhood; breaking the silence and naming the perpetrator of her abuse. Other stage four tasks to be achieved are: to seek contact with other women and experience a feeling of solidarity; to find opportunities for group discussion and consciousness-raising; and to begin to work with other women to bring about real changes in society.

The tasks of the therapist are: to continue support and encouragement; to educate for a better understanding of the global oppression of women; to ensure that there are opportunities available for a variety of group experiences; to encourage the woman to anticipate the future and celebrate her new consciousness; and to see that therapy is brought to a close.

These four stages of therapy give a clear indication of the important emphases in feminist therapy. Other therapies, as a result of their preoccupation with a woman's "illness" or "helplessness" or "inability to cope", choose to emphasise one or more of the following: the need for drugs; transference; the therapist as expert; helping a woman think positively and take responsibility for her own problems; or helping her adjust to and cope with a bad situation rather than leaving or changing it.

The practice of feminist therapy begins, not with a set of preconceived ideas in the mind of the therapist, but with the telling of the woman's story. Together with the careful and detailed telling of her story comes the expression of pain, sadness, helplessness and despair. Then, through the therapist's unwavering support, and also because of the redefining that occurs through demystification, she is able to reach an understanding and an acknowledgement of her oppression which, in turn, gives rise to the expression of anger. Motivated by her anger, the woman then makes a conscious decision to work for change in her own personal situation and on behalf of women collectively.

While the best possible long-term result, from the perspective of feminist therapy, occurs when a woman proceeds to stage four, the reality is that many women cease therapy after the second or third stages, for the simple reason that the problem they came to talk about has been resolved and they feel better. Remembering that feminist therapy exists to respond to women's perceived needs, it is important that therapists do not try to prolong therapy in an attempt to get women to proceed through all four stages. The four stages are presented not with the intention of urging feminist therapists to go into their work with a set agenda, manipulating women into dealing with all four stages, but rather as an example of an ideal situation of feminist therapy in practice.

Having analysed the actual therapeutic encounter and the relationship that takes place between the therapist and the one who seeks her help, and having identified four stages through which therapy proceeds in an ideal situation, the following discussion of the important characteristics of feminist therapy will address some of the practical issues involved. Attention by the therapist to the practical details set out below will serve to strengthen a woman's confidence in the process and facilitate her progress in uncovering the truth about her life and making decisions for her own future.

Characteristics of feminist therapy

It occurs in both individual and group settings

There are those who insist that a therapy grounded in a radical socio-political philosophy, and that begins with the fact of the collective oppression of women, ought to be available only as a group experience. Individual therapy, they say, encourages the splitting off of women from each other, placing them in a vulnerable position vis-à-vis the therapist and encouraging a self-indulgent, inward-looking, individual focus.

It cannot be denied that such dangers do exist in relation to individual therapy, but the fact is that the overwhelming majority of women in Western societies shy away from the idea of talking about personal pain and distress in group settings. Women are much more likely to seek the help of another woman, in a private setting, when they want to talk through a problem they have not been able to resolve themselves. First, they will speak to a friend or neighbour or relative and, if the problem persists, they will then consider seeking the help of a therapist. Once they have spoken in a one-to-one setting and experienced the support of the therapist, they are more likely to consider the suggestion of involvement in a group.

For those who choose not to air the private details of their lives in public, individual therapy offers total privacy and confidentiality. It also offers the opportunity of focusing on and working through one's pain without delay, thereby enabling one to make any necessary changes and to get on with one's life much more quickly.

Group experiences, such as support groups and educational groups, also have a very important role to play in feminist therapy. As I mentioned in the discussion of stage four of the therapeutic process, feminist therapists must see to it that a variety of group experiences are available, and encourage women in individual therapy to avail themselves of the opportunity of taking part in a group that has some relevance to their own experience.

Just as extended involvement in individual therapy is discouraged, so is extended involvement in any group designed for the purpose of focusing on a particular problem. Such groups must be organised for short-term support only, in order to prevent the possibility that the women will become dependent on their group and use it to give false meaning to their lives. The kinds of experiences that are helpful on a longer-term basis are reading groups, educational groups and political action groups.

Oppression is seen to be the root cause of women's distress

Feminist therapy names oppression as the cause of most emotional and psychological problems for which women seek the help of a therapist. It is recognised, also, that when a woman suffers more than one oppression (from racism, classism, anti-Semitism, ableism, heterosexism, etc.), there can be, and almost always is, a magnifying effect in terms of her potential for emotional distress.

An Aboriginal woman living in poverty, for example, experiences powerlessness on three counts: because she is female, Aboriginal, and economically disadvantaged. On each count of oppression, she is vulnerable to humiliation, low self-esteem and lack of confidence, which can lead to more serious problems, such as depression, anxiety, substance abuse and self-mutilation.

The aim of therapy is change, not adjustment

While mainstream therapies endeavour to help women discover ways to adjust their own needs and desires and standards so that they can cope with difficult and unjust circumstances, feminist therapy insists that emotional health and happiness is possible only when justice is done. If a circumstance is unjust, if a person's behaviour is oppressive, then that circumstance and that person's behaviour must change. When the circumstance does not change, or when the other person refuses to change his or her behaviour, then feminist therapy encourages a woman to make her own changes and choose a different future for herself.

The purpose of therapy is to help a woman through a "rough patch"

It is often the case that women choose to go to a therapist when they are "stuck", when they are in a rough patch and are having difficulty getting through it. They have tried everything they could think of to resolve a particular problem—to encourage better communication in their relationship, to rise above their depression, to calm their anxiety—but without success. Most women, when they decide to seek the help of a therapist, do so with the aim of getting "unstuck", of getting over this particular rough patch and moving on. From the perspective of feminist therapy, such an attitude is healthy: both the therapist and the woman who is seeking help view therapy as an intervention, when needed.

Those who go to a therapist in search of "healing", whatever that may mean to them, are likely to be disappointed with the final outcome, because total healing can never be achieved. The more healing one experiences, the more need there seems to be for further healing, and the search never ends.

The purpose of therapy, then, is not to get all of one's problems sorted out at once, because that would necessitate most of us being in therapy for the rest of our lives. Rather, the purpose of therapy is to help a woman through a difficult time so that she is then able to continue on her journey unaided.

Individual therapy is a relationship between two people

Feminist therapists are encouraged to see therapy as something that takes place in the context of a relationship. It is a relationship between two women who have come together for a clearly defined purpose and, when that purpose has been fulfilled, the relationship, as such, will be over. The roles are clear. The difference in power is clear, though not an issue. There is no need for game-playing, no need for transference or countertransference, no need for labelling or manipulating or other such power plays. It is a situation where one woman seeks the professional help of another woman, and the relationship proceeds in a normal way.

Feminist therapy is for feminists and non-feminists

Any woman can seek help from a feminist therapist. It is not necessary that a woman be a feminist or understand feminist philosophy in order to benefit from the therapy offered. Some women will choose not to seek help from a therapist who is known to be a feminist for fear that she has an "agenda", or is "biased". She *is* biased, of course. She is biased against the oppression of women and against the agents of that oppression. And she does have an agenda. Her agenda is to help women uncover the truth and to work to make changes in their lives, so that mental health will become a reality.

Feminists who feel the need to discuss a problem with somebody outside their immediate group of friends are strongly advised not to consider any therapist who is not herself a feminist, for the simple reason that society is not kind to feminists. Nobody but another feminist understands the particular brutality meted out to women who dare to be different, who dare to have a feminist analysis of society and its institutions, and who dare to speak out against structural and individual oppression of women. There is a desire in society to punish feminists, to "tame" those women who will not be tamed. Therefore, at times when we are feeling vulnerable, defeated and in need of support, it is not wise to place ourselves in the hands of those who would subdue us.

Most therapy is short-term

If the purpose of therapy is to help a woman get herself through a particularly difficult time, a time when she feels "stuck", then it follows that most therapy ought to be short-term.

Mainstream therapists, particularly in the liberal humanist era, invested a huge amount of energy into the push to have therapy accepted as an everyday activity in society, as a way of life, as something everyone would benefit from and, therefore, something everyone ought to consider. It came to be seen as an activity or a process one goes "into" and commits oneself to for as long as it takes to get oneself "sorted out". This perception must be changed through the efforts of feminist therapists.

The purpose of life is to live it, not to reflect on it obsessively. Those who spend months or years in therapy are in danger of developing a life-long habit of achieving satisfaction from perpetually analysing what they are doing and feeling, instead of simply getting on with their lives.

In an ideal situation, therapy is a short-term intervention measure, with sessions once a week for three or four weeks. Sometimes this needs to be extended to six weeks and, on very rare occasions, to eight, but four weeks seems to be an acceptable average. One option women often choose is to work with a therapist for a few weeks, then take a break for a couple of months to see how they manage with the changes they have already put in place, and then come back for one or two sessions, if required.

Naturally, there is no suggestion here that duration of therapy ought to be legislated, but rather that the perception of therapy ought to be changed to that of short-term intervention, when needed. If a therapist is careful to make the most of the initial session, when a woman's motivation is high, then much more work will be done in a much shorter time.

Certain situations call for long-term therapy

Having argued for a new perception of therapy as a short-term intervention, a pause along the way, a "moment" of reflection that enables new decisions to be made and new directions to be taken, it is important to add that there are, nevertheless, some situations where the availability of long-term therapy is crucial. Victims/survivors of childhood sexual abuse, for example, often need time with a safe person in a safe place to sort through the debris of their childhood. Sexual abuse robs its victim of a normal childhood. Consequently, after a woman has told the story of her childhood as it was, and explored and expressed her pain and disillusionment, her resentment and anger, it is often helpful for her to be able to talk about childhood as it could have been for her under different circumstances. For a woman who is herself a mother, it is often helpful for her to talk about what she has done to ensure that her own children had very different childhoods from her own. All of this takes time.

Whenever a woman seeks the help of a therapist to deal with problems resulting from a confusing and oppressive childhood, where there was sexual abuse, physical abuse, emotional abuse, where one or both parents were alcoholics or had a mental illness, etc., long-term therapy in a supportive and safe environment is often what is needed. Long-term therapy can also be appropriate in situations where women have been through deeply traumatic experiences of loss, for example, when murder is involved, or the suicide of a loved one, or the death of a child or a partner.

"Homework" is an important part of the therapeutic process

In order that the problems about which a woman has sought the help of a therapist be explored as quickly as possible, it is necessary that the therapeutic work being done by the woman is not confined to one hour a week in the therapist's office. To this end, it is helpful to make use of the concept of "homework".

Letter-writing, as described earlier, is an effective technique to use as homework. Other assignments include: writing the story of one's childhood, either in the first person ("I") or the third person ("she"); writing a poem; writing a play. Any written homework will have two aims: to tell one's story in detail, and to express one's emotions.

Many people find writing very helpful, but it must be remembered that some do not. Other forms of homework include: drawing, listening to certain kinds of music, looking through old photographs, talking on to a tape, and practising new behaviours. The kind of homework chosen must first be discussed and agreed upon by the therapist and the woman who will do it. The purpose of the homework must be clear. Then, it is important that the homework, whether it was actually completed or not, be used as the starting point for the following therapy session. This ensures that each session begins where the woman is and not where the therapist thinks she ought to be.

Even though homework ought not be something that is given religiously at the end of every therapy session it, nevertheless, ought to be seen as a very important part of the therapeutic process.

Taking notes is unnecessary

In true medical-model style, many mainstream therapists feel compelled to take notes, either during a therapy session or immediately afterwards. If notes must be taken, it is far preferable, of course, to do so after the session has ended than while the person is pouring out the story of her pain and distress but, either way, it is an unnecessary preoccupation. The practice, no doubt, comes out of the psychoanalytic belief that the therapist is the expert and, as such, must remember everything a woman says in therapy in order to be able to analyse the material and come up with a solution.

Some therapists take notes of personal details, such as name, address, marital status, family history, even though the relevance of such a practice is not readily apparent. As mentioned previously, a good therapeutic outcome does not depend on what the therapist knows from reading her notes, what the therapist gleans from family history, what the therapist remembers from previous sessions, or what theories the therapist is able to come up with.

Again, it must be stated that it is not my intention here to suggest a hard and fast rule about note-taking. I realise that feminist therapists often work in agencies where note-taking is required as part of a system of accountability to other members of the team, and while keeping notes is not necessary, accountability is very necessary. Other therapists may have different and equally acceptable reasons for jotting down a few notes after a therapy session. The point being made here is simply that taking notes is not a necessary part of working as a therapist and can, in fact, amount to an invasion of privacy. I recommend that feminist therapists who do take notes re-examine their reasons for doing so, with the aim of minimising the practice or ceasing it altogether.

Keeping files is unacceptable

Another practice that has developed out of the belief that the therapist is the expert, the all-knowing one, is that of keeping a file on every person who comes for therapy. The idea is that a therapist writes a brief report after each therapy session and that report is placed into a folder or file especially prepared for that particular person. The result is that the filing cabinets of therapists all around the world are full of the personal details of people's lives, and those details remain there years after the period of therapy has ceased.

Regardless of the care taken by most therapists to see that confidentiality is maintained, in terms of privacy and of the potential for invasion of privacy, such a situation is unacceptable.

One of the serious dangers of keeping files full of people's personal, confidential stories is that posed whenever a political party for whom civil rights is not a priority issue is in government either at state or federal level. A few years ago in the state of Queensland, the government of the day obtained a court order that enabled the police to raid abortion clinics throughout the state and confiscate thousands of patient/client files, thereby having access to details about the private lives of all of those people—women who had had abortions and men who had had vasectomies.

Keeping files on people does seem a legitimate practice when the prescribing of medication is involved. Doctors need to know with certainty what drugs they or other doctors have prescribed, and there is no better way than keeping such information in a file or on a computer. To keep files containing personal stories and private details of people's lives, however, is both unnecessary and unacceptable.[11]

---

11. On those rare occasions when a therapist is asked by a woman she has seen in therapy to testify in court on her behalf, the therapist must rely solely on her memory. Similarly, if the therapist were ever charged with an offence in relation to her work, the absence of files might prove to be a disadvantage, but that is a chance that a feminist therapist would probably be prepared to take in the interest of the privacy of all who have come to her for help over the years.

On those more common occasions when a therapist is faced with a possible subpoena to testify *against* a woman she has seen in therapy, the absence of files and notes works to her advantage. It is much less likely that she would be placed in a situation of having to defy the court and refuse to break confidentiality, if there is no written information to be had.

A therapist ought to receive payment for her skills

An awkwardness seems to have developed in the feminist movement over the years around the issue of payment for services. When a feminist sister decides to open a therapy practice, a bookshop, a coffee shop, a restaurant, an icecream shop, or other business venture, her decision is usually met with much joy and encouragement and congratulations. As the business proceeds, however, that initial support often turns to criticism when friends realise they are expected to pay full price for the service being offered.

In the case of therapy, such criticism probably springs from the erroneous belief that help in times of trouble ought to be freely available to everybody—especially to one's friends. A more reasonable attitude, surely, would be that help in times of trouble ought to be available to everybody at a price each can afford.

In a society where people expect to pay for services rendered, most women seeking help from a therapist prefer to pay some money so that they are not left with a feeling of obligation or with a sense of being beholden to the therapist. If it is a clear business arrangement, the woman is able to feel some degree of power and dignity as the buyer of services.

It is important, then, that feminist therapists not be embarrassed or defensive about charging for our time and skills, provided our charges are reasonable and that there is some provision for those who cannot afford what we do charge. Some therapists use a sliding scale and charge according to a person's income or economic situation, while others prefer to make a decision on an individual basis each time they are approached by someone who requests special financial consideration.

Many of the above characteristics of feminist therapy demonstrate its uniqueness in relation to mainstream therapies. The socio-political philosophy in which it is grounded ensures that the attitude and skills of a feminist therapist are such that justice and truth and liberation are always the aims of therapy. It remains, now, for us to ask the question: what qualities and attitudes and skills must a woman have in order to qualify to be called a feminist therapist?

Profile of a feminist therapist

The term "feminist therapist" as used throughout this book includes feminists who work as therapists, counsellors, health workers, workers in women's centres, refuges, rape crisis centres, incest survivor programmes and other services concerned with the emotional and mental health of women.

The following profile of a feminist therapist, in many respects, is a summing up of all that has been said in previous chapters. It is presented here with a view to enabling those who work with women in the depth of their pain and distress to see at a glance what is required of us if we are serious about actually changing the situation of women. Our task is not simply that of helping individual women to change their individual situations, or to learn new strategies for coping with life, or to work at empowering themselves. It is much broader than that. Our task includes working in such a way as to confront and expose the structural and individual oppression of women so that the woman-hating structures of patriarchal societies will be rendered impotent, and women, individually and collectively, will be free.

A feminist therapist:

- has a philosophy of life that is radically and unapologetically feminist;
- has a genuine concern for the well-being of women, feminists and non-feminists;
- has a feminist analysis of the oppression of women;
- sees oppression as the root cause of most of the emotional and psychological problems of women;
- has a clear understanding of the cause-and-effect relationship between the structural oppression of women generally, and an individual woman's inability to cope;
- has a feminist analysis of the oppressive nature of racism, heterosexism, ableism, etc. and is aware of the magnifying effect of more than one oppression;
- is a feminist activist, and sees such activism as an opportunity to demonstrate against the oppression of women, and to name the agents of that oppression;
- values honesty, passion and justice, and incorporates them into her own philosophy of therapy;
- grapples with the issue of access to therapy for those who have been denied access for so long, and opens herself up to dialogue with members of society's disempowered groups;
- values realness and gives high priority to being herself in every situation;
- has no need to complicate therapy in order to appear clever or important;
- has highly developed therapeutic skills and is careful to work at improving her core skills of listening, reflecting, empathising, encouraging, and educating for demystification;
- feels comfortable with, and knows the value of, the expression of anger;
- directs her work towards change, not adjustment;
- is not easily discouraged by those who are opposed to her own feminist system of values regarding therapy; and
- acknowledges the need for her own personal support and nurturing and devotes energy to developing and sustaining a network of women for mutual support.

Any attempt at profiling a feminist therapist is a difficult undertaking, in that it would never be possible to list all the qualities, attributes and skills required. While this list is reasonably comprehensive it is not, in any way, intended to be exhaustive. Rather, it is intended as a guide: as a quick reference for those who are already involved, or who are contemplating being involved, in working with women from the perspective of feminist therapy.

Conclusion

Now is the time for the feminist movement as a whole to say a loud "no" to the psych-oppression that occurs in all mainstream and popular therapies, and to take seriously the task of developing a feminist therapy that is able to respond to the individual and collective needs of women. Following in the tradition of Phyllis Chesler, Naomi Weisstein, Miriam Greenspan, Bonnie Burstow and others, this book represents another step in the work of developing a feminist therapy that is radical and political.

Given the fact that men are at war with women and that women are forced, as a consequence, to live in a war zone; given the pain and distress, the humiliation, the isolation, the emotional and physical battering experienced by individual women as a daily fact of life in a woman-hating society; given the victimisation of women inherent in the Judaeo-Christian and liberal humanist philosophies that continue to dominate Western societies; and given the oppressive nature of mainstream therapies, it is no longer acceptable for the feminist movement to close its collective mind to the need for a deliberately feminist therapy.

To close our minds to the plight of individual women immobilised by prolonged and deep depression, or to women who are starving themselves to death, or to women confined to their homes because of an overwhelming fear of their next anxiety attack, is to abandon women, at the height of their vulnerability, to the victim-blaming attitudes and practices of mainstream therapists.

It is true that our collective political agenda, our determination to work together to change the patriarchy's oppressive structures, is and must be our main focus; but it cannot be our only focus. As long as individual women continue to suffer, at a personal level, from the consequences of women's oppression and victimisation, it is crucial that the feminist movement provide a system of support that is relevant to feminists and non-feminists alike. When a woman feels the need to talk to someone outside her own circle of friends, it is important that she have a safe place to go and a safe person to talk to.

In these pages, I have presented a feminist alternative therapy consisting of a system of support and a process of demystification based on the important socio-political issues of oppression, access, honesty, passion and justice.

I see a future where the practice of therapy will be incorporated as a necessary and integral part of the feminist revolution. For the present, however, let the discussion continue.

Bibliography of Works Cited

Armstrong, Louise. (1978). *Kiss Daddy Goodnight*. New York: Hawthorn Books.

———. (1987). *Kiss Daddy Goodnight: Ten Years Later*. New York: Pocket Books.

———. (1990). Making an Issue of Incest. In Dorchen Leidholdt and Janice G. Raymond (eds). *The Sexual Liberals and the Attack on Feminism*. New York: Pergamon.

———. (1994). *Rocking the Cradle of Sexual Politics*. Reading, Mass.: Addison-Wesley.

Bailey, Linda J. (1984). *How to Get Going When You Can Barely Get Out of Bed*. Englewood Cliffs, New Jersey: Prentice-Hall.

Beattie, Melody. (1987). *Codependent No More*. New York: Harper/Hazeldon.

———. (1989). *Beyond Codependency, And Getting Better All the Time*. Burwood, Vic.: Collins Dove.

Bernard, Jessie. (1972). *The Future of Marriage*. New York: Bantam.

Bernheimer, Charles, and Claire Kahane (eds). (1985). *In Dora's Case: Freud—Hysteria—Feminism*. London: Virago.

Bloom, Lynn Z., Karen Coburn and Joan Pearlman. (1975). *The New Assertive Woman*. New York: Delacorte Press.

Brodribb, Somer. (1992). *Nothing Mat(t)ers: A Feminist Critique of Postmodernism*. Melbourne: Spinifex.

Burstow, Bonnie. (1992). *Radical Feminist Therapy: Working in the Context of Violence*. Newbury Park, Ca.: SAGE.

Chaplin, Jocelyn. (1988). *Feminist Counselling in Action*. London: SAGE.

Chesler, Phyllis. (1972). *Women and Madness*. New York: Avon.

———. (1994). *Patriarchy: Notes of an Expert Witness*. Monroe, Maine: Common Courage Press.

Conran, Shirley. (1977). *Superwoman 2*. Sidgwick and Jackson. Republished (1979) as *Superwoman in Action*. New York: Penguin.

Cooke, Joanne, Charlotte Bunch-Weeks and Robin Morgan (eds). (1970). *The New Women*. Greenwich, Conn.: Fawcett.

Coote, Anna, and Beatrix Campbell. (1982). *Sweet Freedom: The Struggle for Women's Liberation*. London: Pan Books.

D'Aprano, Zelda. (1977). *Zelda: The Becoming of a Woman*. Canberra: National Advisory Committee for International Women's Year 1975. Republished (1995). Melbourne: Spinifex.

de Beauvoir, Simone. (1952). *The Second Sex*. New York: Alfred A. Knopf. (1961). New York: Bantam.

Daly, Mary. (1973). *Beyond God the Father: Toward a Philosophy of Women's Liberation*. Boston: Beacon.

——. (1978). *Gyn/Ecology: The Metaethics of Radical Feminism*. Boston: Beacon. (1979). London: The Women's Press.

——. (1984). *Pure Lust: Elemental Feminist Philosophy*. London: The Women's Press.

——. (1992). *Outercourse: The Be-Dazzling Voyage*. San Francisco: Harper. (1993). Melbourne: Spinifex.

Dworkin, Andrea. (1988). *Letters from a War Zone*. London: Secker and Warburg. (1993). Brooklyn, New York: Lawrence Hill Books.

Easteal, Patricia. (1994). *Voices of the Survivors*. Melbourne: Spinifex.

Erikson, Erik H. (1959). *Identity and the Life Cycle*. New York: International Universities Press. (1980). New York: W. W. Norton.

Faludi, Susan. (1991). *Backlash: The Undeclared War Against Women*. London: Chatto and Windus.

Faust, Beatrice. (1993). *Benzo Junkie: More Than a Case History*. Ringwood, Vic.: Penguin. New York: Viking Penguin.

Ferguson, Marilyn. (1980). *The Aquarian Conspiracy: Personal and Social Transformation in the 1980s*. Los Angeles: J. P. Tarcher. Ontario, Canada: Nelson.

Firestone, Shulamith. (1970). *The Dialectic of Sex: The Case for Feminist Revolution*. London: The Women's Press.

French, Marilyn. (1992). *The War against Women*. London: Hamish Hamilton.

Friedan, Betty. (1963). *The Feminine Mystique*. New York: Penguin.

Gilbert, Lucia Albino. (1980). Feminist Therapy. In Annette M. Brodsky and Rachel Hare-Mustin (eds). *Women and Psychotherapy*. New York: Guilford.

Gornick, Vivian, and Barbara K. Moran (eds). (1971). *Woman in Sexist Society: Studies in Power and Powerlessness*. New York: Mentor.

Greenspan, Miriam. (1983). *A New Approach to Women and Therapy*. New York: McGraw Hill.

Greer, Germaine. (1970). *The Female Eunuch*. New York: Bantam.

Grosz, Elizabeth. (1990). *Jacques Lacan: A Feminist Introduction*. Sydney: Allen & Unwin.

Hall, Marny, Celia Kitzinger, JoAnn Loulan and Rachel Perkins. (1992). The Spoken Word: Lesbian Psychology, Lesbian Politics. *Feminism and Psychology*, 2 (1), 7–25.

Hawthorne, Susan. (1994). A Case of Spiritual Voyeurism. *Feminist Bookstore News*, 17 (4), 31–3.

Hay, Louise L. (1984). *Cancer: Discovering your Healing Power* (audiotape). Santa Monica: Hay House Inc.

——. (1984, 1988). *You Can Heal Your Life*. Concord, NSW: Specialist Publications.

Heyward, Carter. (1993). *When Boundaries Betray Us: Beyond Illusions of What is Ethical in Therapy and in Life*. San Francisco: Harper.

Hite, Shere. (1987). *Women and Love. A Cultural Revolution in Progress*. London: Penguin.

James, Muriel, and Dorothy Jongeward. (1971). *Born to Win: Transactional Analysis with Gestalt Experiments*. Reading, Mass.: Addison-Wesley.

Jeffreys, Sheila. (1990). *Anti-climax: A Feminist Perspective on the Sexual Revolution*. London: The Women's Press. (1991). New York: New York University Press.

——. (1993). *The Lesbian Heresy*. Melbourne: Spinifex.

Jeffs, Sandy. (1993). *Poems from the Madhouse*. Melbourne: Spinifex.

Jongeward, Dorothy, and Dru Scott. (1976). *Women as Winners: Transactional Analysis for Personal Growth*. Reading, Mass.: Addison-Wesley.

Kaminer, Wendy. (1992). *I'm Dysfunctional, You're Dysfunctional*. Cambridge, Mass.: Addison-Wesley. (1993). New York: Vintage.

Kitzinger, Celia, and Rachel Perkins. (1993). *Changing our Minds: Lesbian Feminism and Psychology*. London: Onlywomen Press.

Klein, Renate. (1989a). *The Exploitation of a Desire: Women's Experiences with In Vitro Fertilisation*. Geelong, Vic.: Deakin University Press.

——. (1989b). Women with a Fertility Problem: An Increasing Group of Clients for Feminist Therapists. *Feminist Therapy Newsletter*, 5 (2), 11–15.

——. (ed.). (1989c). *Infertility: Women Speak Out about their Experiences of Reproductive Medicine*. London: Pandora.

——. (1994). Survival is a Privilege which Entails Obligations. *Australian Women's Book Review*, 6 (2), 34–5.

Kravetz, Diane. (1980). Consciousness-Raising and Self-Help. In Annette M. Brodsky and Rachel Hare-Mustin (eds). *Women and Psychotherapy*. New York: Guilford.

Kübler-Ross, Elisabeth. (1969). *On Death and Dying*. New York: Macmillan.

Loulan, JoAnn. (1984). *Lesbian Sex*. Minneapolis: Spinsters.

——. (1990). *The Lesbian Erotic Dance*. San Francisco: Spinsters.

MacKinnon, Catharine. (1990). Liberalism and the Death of Feminism. In Dorchen Leidholdt and Janice G. Raymond (eds). *The Sexual Liberals and the Attack on Feminism*. New York: Pergamon.

McLean, Coralie. (1994). Townsville Women's Centre. In Wendy Weeks (ed.). *Women Working Together: Lessons from Feminist Women's Services*. Melbourne: Longman Cheshire.

McLellan, Betty (Elizabeth). (1977). Lesbian Identity: A Theological and Psychological Inquiry into the Developmental Stages of Identity in a Lesbian. Unpublished doctoral dissertation, School of Theology, Claremont, Ca.

——. (1992). *Overcoming Anxiety: A Positive Approach to Dealing with Severe Anxiety in your Life*. Sydney: Allen & Unwin.

MacLeod, Mary, and Esther Saraga. (1988). Challenging the Orthodoxy: Towards a Feminist Theory and Practice. *Feminist Review*, 28, Spring, 16–55.

Mander, Anica Vesel, and Anne Kent Rush. (1974). *Feminism as Therapy*. New York: Random House.

Masson, Jeffrey. (1988). *Against Therapy*. USA: Atheneum. (1990). London: Fontana.

Millett, Kate. (1970). *Sexual Politics.* London: Jonathan Cape and New York: Doubleday. (1972). London: Abacus.

——. (1991). *The Loony Bin Trip.* London: Virago.

Mitchell, Juliet. (1974). *Psychoanalysis and Feminism: A Radical Reassessment of Freudian Psychoanalysis.* Harmondsworth, Middx: Penguin.

Mitchell, Juliet, and Jacqueline Rose (eds). (1982). *Feminine Sexuality: Jacques Lacan and the école freudienne.* London: Macmillan.

Morgan, Marlo. (1991). *Mutant Message Down Under.* New York: Harper Collins.

Morgan, Robin (ed.). (1970). *Sisterhood is Powerful: An Anthology of Writings from the Women's Liberation Movement.* New York: Vintage.

Morton, Nelle. (1985). *The Journey is Home.* Boston: Beacon.

Nairne, Kathy, and Gerrilyn Smith. (1984). *Dealing with Depression.* London: The Women's Press.

Norwood, Robin. (1985). *Women Who Love Too Much.* London: Arrow.

——. (1989). *Letters from Women Who Love Too Much.* London: Arrow.

Office of the Status of Women, Department of the Prime Minister and Cabinet. (1991). *Selected Findings from Juggling Time: How Australian Families Use Time.* Canberra: Commonwealth of Australia.

Okun, Barbara F. (1987). *Effective Helping: Interviewing and Counselling Techniques.* Pacific Grove, Ca.: Brooks/Cole.

Perls, Frederick. (1969). *In and Out the Garbage Pail.* Lafayette, Ca.: Real People Press.

Raymond, Janice. (1986). *A Passion for Friends: Toward a Philosophy of Female Affection.* Boston: Beacon. London: The Women's Press.

Rich, Adrienne. (1979). *On Lies, Secrets, and Silence: Selected Prose 1966–1978.* New York: W. W. Norton.

Rogers, Carl. (1961). *On Becoming a Person: A Therapist's View of Psychotherapy.* London: Constable.

Rowland, Robyn. (1988). *Woman Herself: A Transdisciplinary Perspective on Women's Identity.* Melbourne: Oxford University Press.

——. (1992). *Living Laboratories: Women and Reproductive Technologies.* Sydney: Pan Macmillan.

Rowley, Hazel, and Elizabeth Grosz. (1990). Psychoanalysis and Feminism. In Sneja Gunew (ed.). *Feminist Knowledge: Critique and Construct.* London: Routledge.

Ruitenbeek, Hendrik M. (ed.). (1972). *Going Crazy.* New York: Bantam.

Rush, Anne Kent. (1973). *Getting Clear: Body Work for Women.* New York: Random House.

Rush, Florence. (1980). *The Best Kept Secret: Sexual Abuse of Children.* Englewood Cliffs, New Jersey: Prentice-Hall.

Schaef, Anne Wilson. (1981). *Women's Reality: An Emerging Female System in a White Male Society.* Minneapolis: Winston Press.

——. 1986. *Co-dependence: Misunderstood—Mistreated.* Minneapolis: Winston Press.

Scott, Ann. (1988). Feminism and the Seductiveness of the "Real Event". *Feminist Review,* 28, Spring, 88–102.

Scutt, Jocelynne. (1993). Language, Law and Liability: The Case of the Credible Client. Unpublished paper.

Smallwood, Gracelyn. (1992). Cross Cultural Mental Health: A North Queensland Perspective. Unpublished paper.

Smith, Dorothy E., and Sara J. David (eds). (1975). *Women Look at Psychiatry.* Vancouver: Press Gang Publishers.

Spender, Dale. (1980). *Man Made Language.* London: Routledge and Kegan Paul.

——. (1982). *Women of Ideas (And What Men Have Done to Them).* London: Routledge and Kegan Paul.

——. (ed.). (1983a). *Feminist Theorists: Three Centuries of Women's Intellectual Traditions.* London: The Women's Press. New York: Pantheon.

——. (1983b). *There's Always Been a Women's Movement This Century.* London: Pandora.

——. (1984). *Time and Tide Wait for No Man.* London: Pandora.

Summers, Anne. (1975). *Damned Whores and God's Police: The Colonization of Women in Australia.* Ringwood, Vic.: Penguin.

Thompson, Denise. (1994). Feminism and Racism: What Is at Stake? Unpublished paper.

Ward, Elizabeth. (1984). *Father–Daughter Rape.* London: The Women's Press.

Weisstein, Naomi. (1970). "Kinder, Kuche, Kirche" as Scientific Law: Psychology Constructs the Female. In Robin Morgan (ed.). *Sisterhood is Powerful: An Anthology of Writings from the Women's Liberation Movement.* New York: Vintage.

Winkler, Ute, and Traute Schönenberg. (1989c). Options for Involuntarily Childless Women. In Renate Klein (ed.). *Infertility: Women Speak Out about Their Experiences of Reproductive Medicine.* London: Pandora.

Woitetz, Janet. (1983). *Adult Children of Alcoholics.* Pompano Beach, Florida: Health Publications, Inc.

Wolf, Naomi. (1990). *The Beauty Myth.* London: Chatto and Windus.

——. (1993). *Fire with Fire.* London: Chatto and Windus.

Zweig, Marilyn. (1970). Is Women's Liberation a Therapy Group? In Jerome Agel (ed.). *The Radical Therapist.* New York: Ballantine.

Index